WINONA *at* 100
THIRD WAVE RISING

WINONA *at* 100
THIRD WAVE RISING

The Remarkable History of Winona Lake, Indiana

by TERRY WHITE *with* STEVE GRILL

BMH Books
bmhbooks.com
P.O. Box 544
Winona Lake, IN 46590

Winona at 100: Third Wave Rising
The Remarkable History of Winona Lake, Indiana

© 2013 by Terry White

ISBN:978-0-88469-284-3 (trade paper)
ISBN: 978-0-88469-291-1 (e-book)
RELIGION/ Christianity/ History

Cover design: Terry Julien
Cover photo: Al Disbro (cover photo is the swan pond at the corner of Ninth Street and Park Avenue in Winona Lake. The statue, "The Student," was purchased in Paris and presented to the Winona Lake Christian Assembly by H. J. Heinz of Pittsburgh, Pennsylvania).

TABLE OF CONTENTS

INTRODUCTION

Winona Lake was incorporated as a town on June 2, 1913. The years surrounding the 100th anniversary of that event provide a good opportunity for an overview of what Winona Lake has been, what it is today, and what it might be in the future.

I (Terry) first came to Winona Lake in the middle 1950s when my parents and couples from my church in Pennsylvania came each summer for the Grace Brethren National Church Conference. About 1958 or so, I saw a pretty and talented young high school girl from Maryland who played piano for the Brethren Youth Conference in the old Quonset hut auditorium which is now the Town Hall. Years later, I would marry her and have a piano/organ accompanist for life.

My future father-in-law, a tool and die maker from Hagerstown, Maryland, who once had three children attending Grace College at the same time, was taken with his first visit to Winona Lake. In an article published in his denominational magazine in August of 1960, he wrote, "Winona in general seemed like another world. The complete absence of profanity, tobacco, and alcohol was in striking contrast to the outside world. Everywhere could be seen people carrying Bibles, even the teenagers on the way to and from their various meetings."

He observed that life in Winona, "seemed to center about the Eskimo Inn. If one were to be separated from his friends, he could feel confident of meeting them sooner or later at the Eskimo Inn, 'Where Friends Meet.' I wonder what the attraction is there—the good food, the air conditioning, or the pretty waitresses?"

1

About Grace College, he observed, "[The school] showed that they are abreast of the best in contemporary evangelical scholarship…deserves our support to the fullest." He later became a member of the Grace College and Seminary board of trustees, as did my own father.

My father, E. M. White of Kittanning, Pa., was one of the 12 new Grace board members (along with four from the Assembly board) who made up the combined board of directors when Grace College and Seminary took over the Christian Assembly's assets and liabilities. He and other members of the new board are pictured on page 1 of the Tuesday, October 1, 1968, *Warsaw Times-Union*.

My other memory from the 50s was seeing "Ma" Sunday, the widow of the late evangelist Billy Sunday. She was a colorful figure and still a powerful platform personality. Years later, while working on a doctoral dissertation, I would explore the love letters Billy Sunday, the White Stockings pro baseball player, wrote to her from various ballparks around the nation. Many letters contained a lock of his hair, a penny dated from the year the letter was composed, or pinches of pitcher-mound dirt from the various baseball diamonds where the White Stockings played.

I came to live in Winona Lake in 1960 as a Grace College freshman. Except for short times away for graduate study, my wife (the keyboardist) and I lived here for the next 17 years as we began our family and I was engaged in a variety of educational, civic, and business ventures. Winona as a town had declined remarkably, with much of the summer seasonal housing now ramshackle and unsightly. Along with several friends (Jim Wharton and Ron Kinley among them), we began purchasing the worst of the properties, remodeling them to higher standards, and selling them or renting them out to college and seminary student couples. But it seemed too little, too late. Winona Lake as an attraction had crumbled into sad neglect and abandonment.

Employment then called us away for 26 years, and ultimately we found ourselves planning to move back to Winona Lake in 2003. Imagine our surprise and delight at the metamorphosis the town had experienced! Park Avenue and the canal were now lined with solid, quaint shops inhabited by artists, photographers, glass blowers, potters, and woodworkers. One first-class restaurant had opened—the BoatHouse—and another, the Cerulean, was in the planning stages. The Billy Sunday Tabernacle was gone, as were McKee Courts, where I lived for two years while in college. Three buildings in particular, the Westminster Hotel, Mount Memorial (the former Free Methodist headquarters), and the Winona Hotel, had undergone spectacular restorations and were now gleaming attractions in the re-birthed little village. There had been a Park Avenue revival!

Patrick Kavanaugh, whom I had known in Virginia, moved to Winona the same month we did in 2003, to make this the permanent home of MasterWorks Festival and its parent organization, the Christian Performing Artists' Fellowship. The west wing of the Westminster, formerly Rodeheaver Hall-Mack Company, was now the Reneker Museum of Winona History. The old summer school of theology property was now a town park with play equipment, a beach, a senior center, and other attractions.

The term "third wave rising" was popularized by futurist Alvin Toffler in his 1980 book, *Third Wave*, where he observed that society was moving from the Industrial Revolution (second wave) into a third wave based on actionable knowledge as a primary resource. The broad-scope three-part framework seemed to fit, as Winona Lake's first phase included the Spring Fountain Park and Chautauqua movements, followed by the rise of Winona as the world's largest Bible conference. Now, in its third wave, which is rising, it is an artisans' colony, a center for top-flight classical music, and an educational and cultural center linking the higher education activities of Grace College and Theological Seminary with the unique opportunities afforded by orthopaedic manufacturers in neighboring Warsaw, "The Orthopaedic Capital of the World."

A word about sources. In this Internet age, a wealth of material is available through search engines, though, of course, one must always be careful about accuracy and credibility. One of the great treasures of this area is the yesteryear/Clunette website (http://yesteryear.clunette.com/). Much general history is also available, either through Wikipedia or through sites obtained via search engines. Until this writing, the definitive history of Winona Lake has been *The Story of Winona Lake: A Memory and a Vision* by Vincent H. Gaddis and Jasper A. Huffman, published in 1949 and updated in 1960. Research for this book leaned heavily on the archives of local news media, a source that is often accurate, but is always open to reporters' interpretations or to reporting mistakes made in the rush of getting an issue to press.

While living elsewhere, I missed most of the Winona Historical Society's fun times of re-enacting the Sunday/Rodeheaver days, publishing commemorative historical calendars, the "Centennial Trip with Billy Down the Sawdust Trail" in May of 1996, and much more. The then-active Historical Society was formed in 1985 to further the ideals of Winona. My collaborator Steve Grill, who has lived here continuously since his own college days at Grace, was instrumental in accumulating and re-birthing much of that history.

Now, in the years surrounding the 100th anniversary, we once again have the opportunity to share some of the delightful history of this remarkable little town. Enjoy the journey, and observe Winona Lake's third wave rising!

WELCOME TO WINONA

By Victor Hatfield

When the snow and ice have melted and you feel the breath of spring;
When the earth is bathed in sunshine, and the birds begin to sing.
When you hear the bees a-humming and the flowers are in bloom;
And the atmosphere is laden with an exquisite perfume—

It's then the time the sun is adding fervor to his rays,
Reminding you that soon will come the hot vacation days.
The question then arises, "I wonder where I'll go?"
Your mind recalls W-I-N-O-N-A, and you promptly say, "I know!"

WINONA LAKE:
A CAPSULE HISTORY

(Reproduced from the program of "Sunday! A Centennial Trip with Billy 'Down the Sawdust Trail'" on May 11, 1996, presented by the Winona Lake Historical Society and the Ma Sunday Secret Society Players at the Hillside Amphitheatre.)

THE AREA SURROUNDING EAGLE LAKE, NOW KNOWN AS WINONA Lake, was originally the home of the Potawatomi Indians. A treaty was signed with the tribe in 1834, and the first white settlers arrived soon after. In 1881, the Beyer brothers, attracted by the many natural springs on the east side of Eagle Lake, purchased the entire tract of land. There they constructed spring houses which served as cooling systems for their dairy business.

In 1890, the Beyers began the development of the farmland into a resort known as Spring Fountain Park. Prominent features included Garfield Park and the Eagle Lake Hotel, today's Winona Hotel. Soon well established as a popular vacation center, the Park was enjoyed for several years.

In 1894 Dr. Solomon Dickey, a leader of the Presbyterian Church, dreamed of building a "kind of religious Chautauqua." His search led him to Eagle Lake where he purchased Spring Fountain Park with the financial backing of his denomination. A corporation known as The Winona Assembly and Summer School Association was formed and the first Bible conference was held in the summer of 1895.

The succeeding years were a period of tremendous growth for the Assembly. It was led by a board of directors including H. J. Heinz, John Studebaker and William Jennings Bryan, and many structures were erected and improvements made on the property. A major project was the construction of a canal which transformed a low-lying peninsula into McDonald Island, named for the man who financed the endeavor. Many cottages and homes were built at this time, including Dr. Dickey's Killarney Castle, the Beyer Home and the Swiss Terrace. In slightly more than a decade, the number of seasonal visitors rose from 35 to more than 10,000.

An important aspect of Winona's early days was the remarkable educational movement that took place. Founded were the Agricultural Institute, the Technical Institute and the Winona College--a four-year liberal arts school.

By 1905 the Park was well-established and the schools were growing. The Winona Inter-Urban Railway, linking Winona to various cities, was financially profitable. Chautauqua programs held in the old auditorium brought distinguished speakers and musicians. The period of 1905-1914 was the "Golden Age" in Winona's history.

During this time, a young baseball player-turned-evangelist began to call Winona Lake home. Assisted by his song leader, Homer Rodeheaver, and pianist-composer B. D. Ackley, Billy Sunday had a dynamic ministry that reached millions across the country. The Sundays built their home, Mt. Hood, in Winona Lake in 1911. Rainbow Point was the location chosen by Rodeheaver for his "Rainbow Cottage."

The year 1920 marked the founding of the Winona Lake School of Theology while the next year saw the construction of the 7,500-seat Billy Sunday Tabernacle. During the 1920s, conferences continued to meet and the Chautauqua programs attracted crowds to see and hear famous personalities. The programs were eventually discontinued because of lack of funding and poor attendance. In 1937-38 the Winona Lake Christian Assembly, Inc. was formed with religious and evangelistic conventions as its chief focus.

More recent decades have witnessed the arrival of the Free Methodist and Grace Brethren headquarters and Grace College and Seminary, along with several businesses and an increasing population. Decline appears to have been arrested and many exciting plans are on the horizon.

THE FIRST WAVE

*Indians, Settlers,
and Chautauqua Days
(1700s to 1914)*

CHAPTER 1
Indians and Early Settlers

aya aya! teepahki iishiteehiaanki keewiihkawilotawiaanki
(Hello! We are glad you have come to visit us.)
Miami Nation of Indiana Website

THERE ARE ALWAYS INTRIGUING QUESTIONS.
What was here in the beginning?
Who came here first?
What did they find?
What was it like?

Indiana, admitted to the Union as the 19th state on December 11, 1816, was populated initially by a variety of indigenous peoples and Native Americans. Residents of the state are now called "Hoosiers," but there is no reliable information on the origin of this nickname. The leading theory, as advanced by the Indiana Historical Bureau and the Indiana Historical Society, says "Hoosier" originated from the upland South region of the U.S. as a derogatory slang term for a rough countryman, or a country bumpkin.

The name "Indiana" means "land of the Indians" or "Indian land" and dates back at least to the 1760s. It was applied to the region by the U.S. Congress when the Indiana Territory was incorporated effective July 4, 1800. It was signed into law by President John Adams, separating it from the Northwest Territory. The state's northernmost tier, which includes Winona Lake, was settled primarily by migrants from New England and New York.

The territory was first governed by William Henry Harrison, who negotiated with the native inhabitants to open up large parts of the territory to settlement. In 1810 a popularly elected government was established as the territory continued to grow in population and develop a rudimentary network of roads, government, and an education system. At the outbreak of Tecumseh's War, the territory was on the front line of battle, and Harrison led a military force in the opening hostilities at the Battle of Tippecanoe, and then in the subsequent invasion of Canada during the War of 1812. In June of 1816, a constitutional convention was held and a state government was formed. The territory was dissolved on November 7, 1816, by an act of Congress, granting statehood to Indiana.

Kosciusko County, in which Winona Lake is located, was reported in the most recent census to have a population of about 77,000. The county has more than 100 lakes and was created from Elkhart and Cass counties in 1836 by the Indiana General Assembly. Kosciusko is the fourth largest Hoosier county in area and is comprised of 17 townships. Winona Lake is in Wayne Township.

The county was formed in 1836 by John B. Chapman (not the John Chapman, known as "Johnny Appleseed," Swedenborgian missionary who is buried in Fort Wayne). Chapman was elected to the legislature in 1834 after having served as the prosecuting attorney for the Northern District of Indiana, and he was given the task of naming the county by general consent of the state legislature.

Chapman named the county Kosciusko, even though the favorite candidate name was High Plains. Chapman had been a boy in the Army during the war with Great Britain in 1812, and he had heard veterans of the Revolutionary War speaking about the noble traits of the Polish general and nobleman, Tadeusz Kosciuszko. Chapman thought the Pole had been neglected by the American people and thus named the county after him.

Kosciusko served in the American Revolutionary War and then returned to Poland. He was captured by the Russian government but was released and spent the remainder of his life in Switzerland. He revisited the United States in 1797, but there is no indication that he ever visited the Indiana county named for him. The county seat is named after Warsaw, the capital of Poland. Originally known as Red Brush, Warsaw is the larger town that adjoins Winona Lake. The current courthouse, the third to sit on the downtown square, was built between 1881 and 1884 and is considered a fine example of Second Empire architectural style. It was designed by Thomas J. Tolan and Sons of Fort Wayne, and is made from 32,000 cubic feet of Indiana limestone.

THE POTAWATOMI INDIANS

Charlotte Siegfried[1] reported that the Miami were the first Indian tribe to settle in the area (about 1750), building their villages mainly along the Tippecanoe River.

By 1760, the more numerous and stronger Potawatomi began to push the Miami from the area, taking over their village sites. The protracted final battle took place along the Tippecanoe River between what is now Leesburg and Oswego. By the time the first whites came to the area, the Potawatomi were mainly along the Tippecanoe River, and the Miami were mainly on the lakes in the northwest corner of the county. Between 1826 and 1834, the Miami chiefs ceded most of their lands to the government.

The Potawatomi Indians first lived in lower Michigan, then moved to northern Wisconsin and eventually settled into northern Indiana and central Illinois. In the early 19th century, major portions of Potawatomi lands were seized by the U.S. government. Many perished as they migrated to new lands in the west through Iowa, Kansas, and Oklahoma, following what became known as the "Trail of Death."

The Removal Period of Potawatomi history (1830-1840) began with the treaties of the late 1820s when the United States created reservations. Over the years, pressure for more land by migrating European Americans led the U.S. government to reduce the size and number of reservations.

The federal government passed the Indian Removal Act in 1830, which was intended to move the Indian population from the populated east to the remote and unpopulated lands west of the Missis-

---

[1] "Indians Settled in Kosciusko County About 1750," published in the Warsaw Sesquicentennial edition of *The Paper* on June 15, 2004

sippi. The Act specifically targeted the Five Civilized Tribes in Georgia and Tennessee, but also led to treaties being negotiated with the many other minor tribes east of the Mississippi.

Potawatomi of the Woods were those tribes living around the southern tip of Lake Michigan in Michigan and north central Indiana. In October, 1832, treaties signed at the Tippecanoe River north of Rochester, Indiana, ceded most of their remaining lands in northwestern and north central Indiana. In exchange for their lands in the east, the tribes were given lands in the west (Potawatomi County, Kansas) and annual annuities.

The Potawatomi chief whose territory included most of present-day Winona Lake, Checose (sometimes spelled Checase), was known as a shrewd land dealer with the whites. In 1826, the government had given the territory to Chief Checose and his tribe. However, the Potawatomi left the land shortly after Checose signed a treaty in 1832, giving the territory back to the government.

Before 1832, Checose's band lived on four sections of soil now occupied by residents of Winona Lake including the north, east, and south shores of Winona Lake and the land extending east, according to Gaddis and Huffman (pp. 16 & 17). They were living on land located on the banks of the Tippecanoe River northwest of Warsaw, which is now North Lake Street in Warsaw.

The lands lying within the present limits of Kosciusko County were ceded to the United States on October 27, 1832. The president of the commission, representing the United States, was ex-Governor Jonathan Jennings, and the agent for the Indians was Gen. John Tipton. The principal Indian chiefs were Flatbelly, Wawasee and his brother Musquabuck.

The treaty was ratified January 21, 1833, the county boundary was established in February of 1835, and the county was organized in April of 1836. Leesburg, the oldest town in the county, was laid out in August 1835 by Levi Lee.

Waldo Adams, writing as first vice-president of the Kosciusko County Historical Society, observed, "Most of the early settlers here hated the Indians awfully. They didn't want to hear the sound or even smell the smell of an Indian around here. So they tore down any sign of the Indians that they could. That's why there are so few Indian relics here today. About the only thing left of the Kosciusko County Indians is made of stone that couldn't be destroyed."

The *Warsaw Daily Times,* however, noted on January 21, 1932, that "Boys used to gather hundreds and hundreds of real Indian arrowheads on the Herb Robinson farm, just south of Warsaw on the Country Club road. Every boy in town had at least a cigar-box full of flint arrowheads. An Indian camp or battle had evidently been staged there at one time. Tomahawks and Indian hatchets were often found there. Many older Warsawans still have such collections gathered by themselves around Winona Lake."

THE POTAWATOMIS LEAVE

Reservation life for the Indians did not work well because the reservations were not large enough to supply game or farming space for members of the tribe. Most Indians in Kosciusko County were exiled in small groups mainly from 1837 to 1840. Some were included in the mass exodus called the "Trail of Death" in the fall of 1838, including the tribe of the well-known Potawatomi chief, Menominee.

The Treaty of Chicago, negotiated in 1833, forced removal of the Illinois Potawatomi to Nebraska and the Indiana Potawatomi to Kansas.

In 1836 the Potawatomi signed nine treaties, including the Treaty of Yellow River in Marshall County, five treaties on the Tippecanoe River north of Rochester, two treaties in Logansport, and one treaty at Turkey Creek in Kosciusko County. These treaties were called the Whiskey Treaties because whiskey was given to get the Indians to sign. In exchange for their land they were offered $1 per acre and each member of the tribe was granted a 320-acre (1.3 km) parcel of land in Kansas. In exchange, the tribe agreed to vacate their lands within two years.

The deadline for the tribe to leave was August 5, 1838. By then some Potawatomi bands had migrated peacefully to their new lands in Kansas but not the Twin Lakes village of Chief Menominee, whose village was near present-day Plymouth, Indiana. After the deadline passed and the village refused to leave, Governor David Wallace ordered General John Tipton to mobilize the state militia to remove the tribe forcibly.

On August 30, 1838, General Tipton and one hundred soldiers (actually volunteer militia) surrounded Twin Lakes and began to round up the natives, 859 in all. The Potawatomis' crops and homes were burned to discourage them from trying to return.

On September 4 the march to Kansas began. The state supplied a caravan of twenty-six wagons to help transport their goods. In the first day they traveled twenty-one miles and camped at the Tippecanoe River north of Rochester, Indiana. The second day they reached Mud Creek in Fulton County, Indiana, where the first death (a baby) occurred. By the third day they reached Logansport, Indiana. Several of the sick and elderly were left at Logansport to recover, and several of the dead were buried there.

On November 4 they reached the end of their journey, Osawatomie, Kansas, having traveled 660 miles. On arrival there were 756 Potawatomi left out of the 859 that started the journey. The difference between 859 Potawatomi who started out and the 756 who arrived in Kansas made some people think that 150 died, but many escaped. Forty-two died.

The removal of the Indiana Potawatomi was documented by Benjamin Petit, a Catholic priest, who marched with his congregation of natives on the Potawatomi Trail of Death. Petit died in St. Louis on February 10, 1839, two months after the march while returning to Indiana. He died from illness (believed to be typhoid) brought on by exhaustion. His diary was published by the Indiana Historical Society in 1941. Chief Menominee died three years later, never returning to Indiana; although many of the exiles did attempt to return. Kansas named a county after the tribe and a reservation for Prairie Band Potawatomi is at Mayetta, Kansas.

THE WHITE SETTLERS ARRIVE

The first white settler in the area, Peter Warner, came in the summer of 1834. In June, 1836, a township was established but did not see real development until later.

There was considerable swampy land around Warsaw and because outlaws and criminals were said to have lived in the swamps, few people settled in the area. There was much debate as to whether Warsaw or Leesburg should be the county seat, with Warsaw winning the title in 1837.

Most of the land that now comprises the town of Winona Lake was originally sold to William Bashford on June 30, 1837, and it consisted of 127.42 acres. After his death, the property fell into the hands of his heirs, who sold it on December 13, 1852, to Dr. Jacob Boss. On March 13, 1872, Dr. Boss deeded the property to his son, Julius Boss, after having deeded to the Pennsylvania Railroad what is known as the Gravel Pit, from which gravel had been used in the construction of the railroad.

Additional insight into early land ownership is offered by county historian George Nye (1-49).[2] In a discussion of early county finances, Nye said, "The auditor had several funds in the 1840s. Alfred Wilcox, who owned the land now comprising most of the Town of Winona Lake, was auditor." Wilcox was succeeded as county auditor by Jeremiah Burns circa 1850.

John Hamilton, who was apparently one of the first white men to love the primitive stretch of land beside Eagle Lake (later renamed Winona Lake), was crippled and taught school during his short life in Winona. Hamilton had come from Wayne County, Ohio, to Indiana in 1837 and bought 280 acres from Thomas and Jane Boydston, the original homesteaders. They had paid the usual price of $1.25 per acre to the government, and Hamilton gave them $850.

HAMILTON'S MOUND

Hamilton's purchase included the island, the area where Camp Kosciusko stood, the Indian mound, and eastward up the hill. Hamilton liked to climb the mound and sit and plan a happy future with his little son, Henry, and daughter, Maria. This knoll not only served as a gravesite when Hamilton died, but for many years it was the loca-

---

[2] The collected writings of longtime Kosciusko County (IN) historian George A. Nye (1889-1977) may be found in 37 bound volumes in the Indiana Room of the Warsaw (IN) Community Public Library. "1-49" refers to Volume 1, Page 49.

tion for an annual consecration ceremony for ministerial candidates who studied at the Winona School of Theology. A photo of one such dedication ceremony is on display in the Reneker Museum of Winona History. Hamilton died in 1839 and was reported to have been buried on top of the Indian mound, which was known thereafter as Hamilton's Mound.

Vincent Gaddis, who wrote an earlier history of Winona Lake, did not believe the Winona mound was built by the Indians, but rather was of glacial origin. Gaddis believed that Indians did not particularly favor Winona Lake as a permanent camp site because so much of its surrounding land was swampy. His research led him to conclude, also, that the real Indiana mounds were always built beside rivers, not lakes.

The mound used to be located in the southern part of Winona Lake at the foot of Chestnut Street south of Cherry Creek, approximately one-half block across the street from where the town's former disposal plant, now the street department, currently stands. According to James Y. Heaton, local residents believed the mound was built by Indians, and John Hamilton, a white man, was buried on its top in 1839. Hamilton's son crowned the mound with a monument to his father, according to authors Gaddis and Huffman.

The mound is no longer in existence. In 1944 or 1945, the mound was gradually taken down with a crane and the dirt from the mound was used to fill lowland for the development of Warsona trailer court, now extinct, but once located between the Winona Lake Dam and North Country Club Drive. The remaining dirt from the mound was used to fill holes in various places in the county. No one knows what became of the Hamilton monument.

The Warsaw newspaper noted on January 7, 1955, that human bones had been uncovered at the huge "Indian Mound," an old landmark at Winona Lake which Bruce Howe, Sr., and other workmen were leveling so the area could be converted into lots for building.

The bones were found just five feet from the foot of the grave of John M. Hamilton, who died in 1839. The newspaper reported that Howe believed the bones to be Indian.[3]

---

[3] Source: yesteryear http://yesteryear.clunette.com/indians3.html

The Hamilton land near the lake became the site of a driving park, a parade grounds, and a baseball diamond in the latter years of the 1800s.

The late Al Cuffel, the last remaining survivor who helped clear the land for Spring Fountain Park, now the town of Winona Lake, was interviewed by reporter Virginia Zuck for an article that appeared in the local newspaper on June 30, 1951. Cuffel, who was 90 at the time, recalled that when he was a boy, the local transportation system, consisting of streetcars pulled by mules, was owned by Dr. Jacob Boss and Billy Williams.

Cuffel described Boss as "a prominent physician of the town. . . one of the largest landowners in the county. He held title to much of the area that is east of Warsaw now." Cuffel also noted that when an old burial grounds on West Winona Avenue seemed unsuitable as a permanent cemetery, Dr. Boss gave the city 30 acres for a new cemetery, reserving a plot under a towering tree for his own resting place. He was the first person to be buried at Oakwood Cemetery on Pike Lake.

Cuffel recalled that the doctor willed to his son, Julius, a large section of land extending from Eagle (Winona) Lake to Road 30 and beyond. Julius Boss lived across the road and east of McDonald Hospital, which was on the northeast corner of the present-day Center and Parker Streets. In those days the steep hill was called Boss hill instead of White's hill.

About 1877, when Cuffel was 16 years old, John F. (Fred) Beyer moved to Warsaw from Goshen. According to the Beyer family history, one day Fred and his wife, Anna, were riding in a wagon along the road to Pierceton. As they came to Eagle Lake (so named, presumably, because its original outline suggested the bird with wings widespread), Papa Beyer pointed to the peaceful countryside and said, "Someday that place will be a beautiful summer resort."

In 1881 three brothers, Fred, Christian, and Edward Beyer, bought the land from Julius Boss. At one spot where a fine spring flowed they built a creamery. A handwritten diary from the Beyer brothers, provided by their granddaughter, includes this account: "In the year of 1881 we purchased a farm of Julius Boss on the eastern shore of Eagle Lake. Our first object at that time was to use the springs of cool water for the carring [curing?] of butter, having purchased a lot of butter from a farmer by name of Shipley at Wabash who had kept it in spring water from the month of June until August and finding the butter in fine condition caused us to build spring houses into which we set 20 gallon jars filled with butter and let the cool water run through it to the top of the jars, thus keeping the butter thoroughly cool and in fine condition for the summer trade."

Another entry in J. E. Beyer's handwritten diary recounted, "In the year 1890 we started the Chautauqua at Spring Fountain Park. After preparing the ground beginning in 1881, clearing the swamps, with the beautiful fish ponds with rustic bridges and beautiful flowers, we had so beautified the place that the editors of Indiana in their first meetings called it the Lincoln Park of Indiana. From the year 1884 we invited visitors."

Because they were in the creamery business, one of the first meetings held at Spring Fountain Park was a three-state convention (Indiana, Ohio, and Michigan) of the Butter and Egg Association.

On May 15, 1885, when Al Cuffel was 24 years old, he started a new job under Fred Beyer. His first assignment was to wall in a spring on the hillside overlooking Eagle Lake. Soon Cuffel's employers had decided to convert their new tract of land into a big amusement park and summer resort. Henry Deeds, who operated a restaurant and rented the rooms above it to vacationers, was bought out and preparations for the resort project got underway.

Cuffel recalls building a road along the lake, grubbing out hundreds of stumps and digging out part of the hillside to make the grounds for the new hotel which was located astride the wagon road. The new Pierceton Road was shifted to the east and became the present Kings Highway, according to Cuffel.

SPRING FOUNTAIN PARK DEVELOPS

Lumber for the new Eagle Lake Hotel was unloaded from flatcars on a railroad siding and the structure went up quite fast. When it was finished, it was named the Eagle Lake Hotel, and was proclaimed to be "one of the most elegant resort hostelries in this part of the country." It was impressively large, and was topped with an observation tower rising above the third-floor rooms. The Eagle Lake Hotel became the main section of the Winona Hotel, which was operated for many years by the Assembly.

Development of the park continued with the building of a roller coaster, a golf course, and other features. Al Cuffel recalled clearly the difficulty they encountered clearing the island for a race track. This area was originally a marshy peninsula jutting out into Eagle Lake. After the Beyer brothers established Spring Fountain Park in 1890, a drill and parade ground called Carnahan Military Park was built on the peninsula.

Touted as the "best of its kind associated with like resorts," Carnahan Park was a popular site for leisure activities such as encampments and Civil War reenactments. It was a swampy haven for muskrats and rattlesnakes and Cuffel recalled that one day they killed 22 rattlers.

With its roque courts, baseball diamond with grandstand, and harness track, the park was popular with thousands of guests who visited Winona. Many summer homes and cottages were built along its shores.

Big county fairs were held on the island for a few summers. Part of the Inn Hotel (situated approximately where the parking lot for Bake-Café now is) was the poultry and livestock exhibition building. In 1897 the building was bought by the Winona Assembly and remodeled to become a 230-room hotel. Originally called the Miniwanan Inn, this building was the largest accommodations facility in Winona Lake. The Inn was the hotel of choice for families and those on a tight budget.

There was a miniature steam railroad which ran on narrow tracks from the entrance back to Kosciusko Lodge, making a circle at a little house at the end of the line. A roundhouse for servicing the engine was located just south of the Inn Hotel.

By now many people were coming to spend their vacations at Spring Fountain Park. Some families bought land and built their own summer homes. Others camped out for a week or for the whole summer. Bringing their children and often the family dog, they lived in tents pitched in the grove near the auditorium not far from the base of the Indian mound.

The Beyers acquired several additional tracts of land during the 1880s and 1890s, including one from Mrs. Furlong, a lady doctor, and one from a couple named John and Myrtle Kelly. The largest tract was the Wilcox farm. The Beyers bought it from Aunt Rosie (Rosalie) Wilcox, a spinster who lived on the Wooster Road, now Seventh Street. The Wilcox barn and the orchard were about where the Presbyterian church now stands. Rosalie Wilcox's farm house was moved to Tenth Street and is now *The Homestead*. Rosalie's father, Alfred Wilcox, had bought the farm in about 1852 from the estate of John Hamilton, who died in 1839.

Historian George Nye (1-132) quotes a member of the Milice family: "I as a boy walked out to Eagle Lake to see the circus come in. The Beyer Brother[s] bought the old Wilcox farm to get the spring to put butter in. They were German Methodists and came from Goshen."

The Wilcox property is where the Rodeheaver Auditorium is now located. The Furlong property included Bethany Camp, which later was the Winona School of Theology and eventually the town park and Town of Winona Lake offices. The Kelly property lay south of that, and contained what is now the Chicago Boys Club property

The handwritten diary of J. E. Beyer recalls, "One of the prencable [principal] reasons that attracted them was the restrictions put upon the premises that no intoxicating liquors were allowed to be sold and that the strictest observance of the Sabbath was held. No business or excursions allowed on Sunday." The diary goes on to modestly report that "The Beyer Bros. lent a helping hand and several times donated the $5,000 payment due, when the other directors provided the rest of the deficit."

Renaming Eagle Lake

In 1894, Dr. Solomon C. Dickey was serving in the capacity of superintendent of home missions for the Presbyterian Church of Indiana. He decided the Presbyterian ministers and church workers needed a common meeting place to study the Bible and to discuss church problems. In recounting the history of Dickey's original desire to find a common meeting place for "rest, counsel, recreation and inspiration," Assembly president Thomas Kane noted in a memorial booklet that Dickey first suggested property on Bass Lake in Starke county. A plot of 160 acres was actually purchased, but plans with local authorities to build a short railroad spur from the nearest railroad to the lake fell through when the locals failed to do their part.

So Dickey sought an alternate location and, according to Kane, "A few days later Dr. Dickey met one of the firm of Beyer Brothers on the train and incidentally mentioned what he was looking for. 'Come and see Spring Fountain Park at Eagle Lake' was the prompt invitation. 'We have just what you need and we want to sell.' The invitation was accepted and within a few days the purchase was made."

Dickey arranged for the Presbyterian Church members of Indiana to buy 160 acres of land which included the northeastern shores of Eagle Lake and also the resort and social center called Spring Fountain Park, located along the eastern shore of Eagle Lake. Dickey's organization paid $100,000 for the property, even though the Beyer brothers had invested more than $125,000 to develop the park.

In 1895 the Presbyterians changed the name of Eagle Lake to Winona Lake. "Winona" was an Indian word meaning "first born" according to James Y. Heaton. Al Disbro, in his book of historical photos from Winona Lake entitled *Images of America: Winona Lake*, claims the name was imported from Winona, a small town near the Bass Lake property which Dickey first tried to purchase. Local historian Bill Darr, on the other hand, believes Dickey was going to locate on Lake Winona in Starke County, rather than Bass Lake. Darr believes Dickey had his Winona Assembly and Summer School Association stock certificates printed and then changed the name of Eagle Lake rather than reprint his stock certificates.

In a *South Bend Tribune* article dated September 7, 1996, Brent Wilcoxson, who at that time was president of the Winona town council and president of the Winona Lake Historical Society, said, "This started in 1896. They began selling lots in 1897. The assembly built the administration building in 1898 and *The Medillia*, a home on Lot No. 2, was built in 1898. *The Hillside* on Lot No. 1 in 1901. *The Swiss Terrace*—three residences with linked front porches—was built in 1902. Also that year (1902) was when the canal was dredged, creating McDonald Island, and it was the year Sol Dickey built his Killarney Castle on the island's shore."

THE MYTH OF PRINCESS WINONA

The town of Winona Lake was incorporated on June 2, 1913, and later a community symbol of an Indian princess was adopted.

The illustration was used as the symbol of Winona from almost the beginning. Miss Airy Anna Haymaker, a Winona Lake teenage girl, was dressed in a colorful Indian costume in order to secure the original princess picture. Haymaker later married P. L. Osborne of Groves, Texas.[4] A cut glass window and its mate showing the Princess Winona image were produced in the 1930s by the Warsaw Cut Glass Company and were displayed for years in the Eskimo Inn eatery (now on display in the Reneker Museum of Winona History).

There never was a Princess Winona of Kosciusko County, though her face appears on the Winona Lake Town Seal, and several Winona Lake businesses (including the now extinct Winona Dairy) used the face of a feathered miss for their logos.

Some sources trace the name Winona to Wenonah, the daughter of Nokomis and mother of Hiawatha in the 1855 epic poem, *The Song of Hiawatha,* by Henry Wadsworth Longfellow. The name Winona means "first born of a daughter" in the Sioux Indian dialect.

Tradition has it that "Winona" was the name of a favorite Indian princess of the Potawatomi Tribe, which occupied the local territory in the years before 1834. In the Indian tongue, the name was properly pronounced "Win-on-na" not "Wy-no-na."

---

[4] Jo Ann Merkle Vrabel – yesteryear.clunette.com/indians3.html

CHAPTER 2
Spring Fountain Park (1884-1895)

The day we celebrate July 4 – Spring Fountain Park.
A blaze of glory!
A day of pleasure!
A program unexcelled in the history of northern Indiana!
The Beyer Brothers

HAVING DECIDED TO CONVERT THEIR LAKESIDE PROPERTY FROM AGRI-cultural to recreational purposes, the Beyer brothers did a remarkable job of building attractions and re-ordering the entire lakeside landscape.

Spring Fountain Park, the popular Eagle Lake summer resort of Indiana, was advertised as being situated on the Pittsburg [sic], Fort Wayne and Chicago railroad, one and one-half miles from the junction of the Cincinnati, Wabash & Michigan railroad, a little more than a hundred miles from Chicago, forty miles west of Fort Wayne and less than one hundred miles from Indianapolis.

Eagle Lake, according to Spring Fountain Park publicity, had a length of about three miles and an average width of about one mile, thus having sufficient surface for sailing or rowing. It was surrounded by beautiful banks and sandy beach. Eagle Lake was so called because of the resemblance of its outline to that of the national bird. A re-markable peculiarity of this lake, brochures pointed out, is the fact that the slope from the water's edge is so gradual that at most points one can wade for a very great distance before encountering a depth of water sufficient to submerge him.

A fence was erected around the town with a turnstile entrance near the north end. There were gates at 4th, 7th, and 13th streets and everyone, even those who lived there, paid to enter the grounds. The cost was not high—$6 entitled one to all the programs for the entire six-week season. Students, ministers, and cottage owners were admitted for $3. The gates remained in use until 1930.

A curfew bell sounded late each evening, signaling to visitors and residents that quiet hours had begun. The bell, now housed in the Church of the Good Shepherd, was usually rung at 10:30 p.m. In June of 1899, the Warsaw newspaper reported that when the bell rang, "all loud talking and laughing stopped as if by magic." The newspaper added that people were quiet because they had come to Winona for a much-needed rest and were willing to do whatever it took to get that rest.

Spring Fountain Park grounds, publicity said, were especially adapted for large encampments of military and secret organizations, being provided with a large drill ground of about fifty acres, extending lake, and all necessary camping equipment. Attractions included: (1) A magnificent race track and driving park; (2) A large and commodious hotel with first-class accommodations and modern improvements; (3) A first-class restaurant, where meals can be had at all hours at reasonable rates; (4) Three new steamers, under competent and careful management; (5) Rowboats in abundance, at reasonable rates by the hour or day.

THE SWITCHBACK RAILWAY

The Switchback Coasting Railway at Winona, which early maps show was located approximately where Terrace Drive is now (the 9th Street hill street was not created until the 1950s), was advertised as "elegantly constructed, very amusing, and perfectly safe." Gaddis and Huffman describe it as "running from the entrance to the biological station," but they may have been referring to the small railway that delivered passenger luggage from the entrance to various hotels and boarding houses.

The Winona switchback was based on LaMarcus Adna Thompson's design of the original Switchback Railway at New York's Coney

Island, which was the first roller coaster designed as an amusement ride in America. For five cents, riders of the Winona train would climb a tower to board a large bench-like car which was then pushed off to coast 600 feet down the track to another tower. The car went just over 6 mph. At the top of the other tower the vehicle was switched to a return track or "switched back" (hence the name).

The park was also provided with swings, croquet grounds, roque courts, dancing halls, feed barn, electric lights, gas, a system of natural water works, springs and flowing wells, artificial lakes, flower gardens, and much more.

The 1893 published "programme" of the "Indiana State Chautauqua Assembly, Spring Fountain Park, Eagle Lake, P.O., Warsaw, Indiana" touted the medical virtues of the "magnificent springs of water" in the park. Described as "mammoth springs, bursting from the hillside everywhere," they were promoted as "having contributed to the health of thousands who have quaffed their sparkling waters."

Albert B. Prescott of the University of Michigan analyzed the waters of one spring as containing magnesium, calcium, alumenium, sodium, iron, and more. One unusual feature was the "tree spring" or "maple spring" which flowed through the trunk of a large maple tree. It was located at the foot of the hill behind the former site of the Billy Sunday Tabernacle, near tennis courts which occupied that land during Spring Fountain Park days.

Lemuel W. Royse, in his history of Kosciusko County, focuses on John Frederick Beyer whom he called "one of the vital energizers and upbuilders in the county and the City of Warsaw."

According to Royse, J. F. Beyer was born in Germany on October 17, 1850, the second of five sons. He apprenticed in the blacksmith's trade, and in 1869, at the age of 19, he came to America to visit relatives, taking 12 days to cross the Atlantic on the steamer *Donau*.

He first went to Goshen, Indiana, where his relatives were living, and he remained there seven years, working part of the time at the blacksmith's trade. But he also began on a small scale to collect and handle butter and eggs, which he gathered up from local producers and shipped to outside markets. That was the beginning of the wholesale packing business of Beyer Brothers, which eventually had three main offices in Warsaw, Kendallville, and Rochester, Indiana. The business grew rapidly and in the course of time, according to Royse, two more brothers, Christian C. and J. Edward, came to America and joined the business.

J. F. BEYER COMES TO WARSAW

J. F. Beyer came to Warsaw in February of 1877, where he conceived the idea of establishing "an educational and pleasure park at Winona Lake." He acquired extensive tracts of land along the eastern shore of the lake, and in 1888, with his brothers, founded Spring Fountain Park. When he died in 1936 at age 86, J. Fred Beyer was the largest land owner in Kosciusko County, with 1,600 acres in his name.

Modern refrigeration systems had not yet been invented, and the brothers needed a place where they could cool and store milk products. They had been attracted to this lake because of the large number of springs along the east side. Immediately, they constructed several spring houses which served as a successful and profitable cooling system.

It was not long, however, until the Beyer brothers began to recognize the possibilities their farm afforded for something better—a summer resort. Soon they began to clear out the underbrush, prepared fish ponds, built fountains, and made numerous other improvements. Because the eastern shore of the lake was so generously supplied with springs and flowing wells, it was called Spring Fountain Park.

Historian Daniel Coplen said that after the park opened in 1884, "Visitors to Spring Fountain Park usually arrived on a Pennsylvania train, which had a depot near what became the Argonne Road viaduct. From there, people walked into the park through an arched building known as the Eagle Arcade. In later years, interurban tracks ran to the Arcade and there was a gated road upon which automobiles entered the park."[5]

Boating was a significant aspect of life on the lakeshore right from the start. There were two large and commodious steamers on

---

[5] Coplen, (1995), p. 138

the lake, the *Welcome* and the *Eagle*, either of which could safely carry a hundred or more passengers. A smaller steamer, *The Rambler*, was suitable for small parties and for people desiring to go on fishing trips, to pick water lilies, or wishing to make a lively tour of the lakes.

Many rowboats were available for rent by the hour, the day, the week, or for the season, with polite and accommodating boatmen constantly in attendance to attend to the wishes of patrons and to keep the boats in good order.

The founders were determined from the beginning that the resort would be kept a clean and wholesome place. Even though it was designed primarily for amusement and recreation, the spiritual aspect was apparent from the start. The park had opened for business in the year 1884 with a Sunday school operated by the church of which the Beyer family were members. Numerous conventions, largely of businessmen, were conducted during the nine years that followed.

First Assembly Program—Summer of 1890

The Spring Fountain Park Assembly held its first gathering in July, 1890, in a hall erected for that purpose in the southern part of the grounds. It was active for three years thereafter, and the men who organized it were later among those who founded and supported the Winona Assembly.

Eagle Lake Hotel

Early promotional copy for the Eagle Lake Hotel read as follows:

> The visitor to Spring Fountain Park, having looked upon beautiful Eagle Lake, and having beheld the beauties of the Park, naturally desires to remain for a season…A splendid hotel, equipped with all modern conveniences stands at the very threshold of the park, and its inviting appearance bespeaks a welcome to all who enter the gates thereof. This is Eagle Lake Hotel and it is the finest hotel that has ever been erected at any watering place in the State of Indiana.
>
> It is located about one hundred and fifty feet from the lake beach, and some three hundred feet from the elegant new sta-

tion of the Pennsylvania Railway. Its upper floor commands a fine view of the lake and the beautiful surrounding country. This hotel is three stories high, above a basement which has ten-foot ceilings. It is crowned by a large observatory, from which the landscape for miles on every hand may be seen.

It is supplied with an abundance of light and air, and its rooms are all large and well ventilated. Wide verandas, extending along the entire length of the building on both sides, present delightful advantages for promenade and rest, while separate balconies at every room admit of a degree of seclusion that is often desired by hotel guests but rarely attained at a summer resort.

The house is supplied with gas, a perfect system of water works for fire protection, and the presence of pure spring water flowing into the houses, furnishes at all times the most healthful of all drinks—nature's perfect product. Something like fifty large and comfortable apartments are handsomely furnished, making the hotel magnificently equipped to cater to the enjoyment of visitors. Eagle Lake Hotel is under the management of Mr. Harvard Stearns, a young man of wide acquaintance and broad experience in hotel management. Transient rates, $2 per day. Special terms to families and parties remaining for a term of weeks.

The hotel opened for business in the middle of May, 1888. The massive building was designed by Washington Vanator, who was the Warsaw city treasurer; and its first proprietor was George Triplett, who had managed a hotel at Rome City. The hotel's restaurant was known for its fine food, including such tantalizing menu selections as turtle soup, trout, roast turkey, and boiled beef tongue.

CARNAHAN MILITARY PARK

Spring Fountain Park possessed one distinctive feature that placed it absolutely without peer in the U.S. In Carnahan Military Park it had the best drill and parade ground to be found in connection with any summer resort in the country.

Carnahan Park consisted of more than half a hundred acres of land, "as level as a ballroom floor, and yet having a turf so elastic that men may tramp it for hours without fatigue." Promotional material declared that, "The evolutions of a mighty army of infantry, artillery, and cavalry might be executed with greatest freedom, and as a place for the holding of encampments of any character, or for sham battles, dress parades or the execution of military maneuvers of any kind."

Adjoining this great park were immense buildings, erected at a cost of many thousands of dollars, which had been fitted up as dormitories for visiting organizations, and others where great halls had been arranged for dining. Secret societies, military organizations, or organized bodies of any kind desiring to avail themselves of the advantages of this magnificent Military Park were encouraged to write for dates to the Beyer Brothers.

James Carnahan, for whom the park was named, had been a member of the Winona Assembly grounds board of directors. He was a veteran of the Civil War, a lawyer, a judge, and the founder of a fraternal organization called the Knights of Pythias.

Carnahan was also a member of the first board of directors of the Indiana Soldiers Home at Lafayette. He died August 5, 1905, in Indianapolis at the age of 63.

GARFIELD PARK

In a shady grove in the southern portion of Spring Fountain Park, according to a publicity leaflet, "a great spring of crystal water has burst the bonds of Mother Earth, and worn for itself an outlet between overhanging banks of either side."

This magnificent spring had been placed in captivity; its waters were harnessed to a huge hydraulic ram which was capable of forcing an inexhaustible supply of pure water to the cottages along the hillside for half a mile. The hydraulic ram was from the farm of ex-president James Garfield, at Mentor, Ohio, where it was purchased by the Beyer brothers. It was touted as having real historic interest because it belonged to an assassinated president of the United States. The title "Garfield Spring" therefore, had local as well as historic force.

31

James A. Garfield, the 20th president of the United States, was shot by Charles J. Guiteau at 9:30 a.m., on July 2, 1881, less than four months into Garfield's term as president. Garfield died eleven weeks later on September 19, 1881, the same year the Beyer Brothers bought the land which was to become Spring Fountain Park.

The whole landscape surrounding the favored spot was described as "most delightful." It adjoined the picnic grounds, was within a two-minute walk of the beautiful new auditorium, and had lovely scenery, refreshing water, and delightful shade.

Literature from the time noted that in all of the artificial lakes at Spring Fountain Park, fish had been planted, and were growing well and multiplying rapidly. The carp ponds, it said, were a never-failing source of entertainment and amusement for old and young. The carp were fed on crackers and bread crumbs, and promotions noted "the avidity with which the big fellows struggle for food is always watched with great interest."

THE CYCLORAMA

A commodious circular building located between the Eagle Lake Hotel and the boathouse housed a cyclorama. A cyclorama is a panoramic painting on the inside of a cylindrical platform, designed to provide a viewer standing in the middle of the cylinder with a 360-degree view of the painting. The intended effect is to make the viewer, surrounded by the panoramic image, feel as if he or she were standing in the midst of an historic event or famous place.

The Winona cyclorama displayed a painting of the battles of Chattanooga, Missionary Ridge, and Lookout Mountain by South Bend artist Henry Kellogg, who had been a topographic engineer in Gen. Thomas' army and was at Chattanooga for the battles there. The display covered 15,000 square feet of canvas. This work of art was seen by thousands of visitors who were delighted by its realistic effects and bright coloring and felt surrounded by the flash of musket fire, the thunder of cannon, and the shouts of fighting men.

The panorama covered 10 miles and included 500 papier-mâché figures placed in front of the painting—everything from soldiers to artillery pieces and cartridge boxes. Kellogg and his aides started painting the cyclorama in 1886 and finished it for the 1888 season. By then, most of the war veterans would have been in their late 40s or early 50s.

Hundreds of men from Kosciusko County served in the Civil War and found themselves in Chattanooga. Scores of them fought in the 1863 battles that occurred near that city: Chickamauga, Lookout Mountain, and Missionary Ridge. Chickamauga was the worst for the local soldiers—many of them fought there, scores were wounded, and 15 were killed. When monuments to the Civil War were being erected many years later, it was appropriate that the one that went up in the 1880s at Spring Fountain Park memorialized the fighting that occurred in the mountains and valleys around Chattanooga.

The *Warsaw Daily Times* reported on January 21, 1932, "After the Civil War and for many years the sight of wounded and maimed Civil War veterans on the streets of Warsaw was most commonplace. Legless and armless veterans there were by the score. This county sent 2,200 soldiers to the Civil War from a sparsely settled county at that time."

Kellogg was also an art teacher, and he often gave art lessons and put on demonstrations. In one exhibition, he completed a large painting of California's Yosemite Falls in just 31 minutes. The popularity of the cyclorama and its battle scenes lasted about a dozen years.

The cyclorama was redone by Pine, an artist from New Orleans, according to sources at the time, because leaders of the Bible conferences felt that scenes of Christ were more suitable for their assemblies than scenes from a long and cruel war. This second cyclorama, the "Life of Christ" was promoted as "a work of art, a realistic representation of the principal epochs in the life of Christ. The work is complete on about 15,000 square feet of canvas, introducing about 125 figures. The artist, Prof. E. J. Pine, has secured a production that is in all its details complete."

By 1901, there were reports of the building being used as a gymnasium. The cyclorama building and its painted canvases disappeared entirely by about 1919, and the decaying building was torn down to make way for the construction of the Billy Sunday Tabernacle in 1920.

SPRING FOUNTAIN PARK

The park itself was described as a beautiful hillside, dotted with mighty forest trees, which extended for nearly a mile, like the crescent-shaped curve of a huge amphitheatre, overlooking the lake. At the base of the grass-covered hillside was a wide expanse of ground, as level as a floor, laid out with the landscape gardener's highest art and extending to the beach of Eagle Lake.

Maple fountain stood at the foot of the hill upon which the cottages are located, and near the deer park. Out of the trunk of a sturdy maple tree whose spreading branches made a shady bower overhead, flowed a never-failing stream of crystal spring water, cool, enervating, and delicious. Here visitors slaked their thirst and stopped to wonder at the strange phenomenon of a maple tree flowing pure water.

THE DRIVING TRACK

Jutting out from the picnic grounds, and extending far into Eagle Lake, was a 55-acre piece of land that was described as "level as a ballroom floor and perfectly free from shrubs or brush of any kind, and covered with a strong, thick sod, that makes it the best driving track to be found anywhere in the state." It was called a spring track because its soft turf was resilient and easy on the horses. It followed the approximate course of Auditorium and Administration boulevards, and included a grandstand. In 1902 this peninsula would be separated from the mainland by a canal, and would become known as McDonald's Island.

THE BALL GROUND

At the south side of the driving track, and in the same enclosure, was laid out "as pretty a diamond and as smooth a field as was ever played upon by the champions of New York or Chicago. The grandstand has a seating capacity of about one thousand, and there is good standing room for a million or two more."

CHAPTER 3

The Winona Assembly and
Summer School Association
(1895-1914)

"Chautauqua is the most American thing about America."
Teddy Roosevelt

SOLOMON DICKEY'S DREAM

IN 1894, SOLOMON C. DICKEY, SUPERINTENDENT OF HOME MISSIONS for the Presbyterian Church of Indiana, proposed the establishment of a "kind of religious Chautauqua where ministers and church workers would assemble for Bible study and the discussion of church problems." The Presbyterian Synod, meeting in Fort Wayne, approved.

Solomon Cravens Dickey, the central figure in the founding of the Winona Assembly and Summer School, was born in Columbus, Indiana, on June 24, 1858, into a pastor's family. He graduated from Wabash College in 1881, married Lizzie Reid of Greenville, Illinois, on June 1, 1882, and was ordained to the Presbyterian ministry in 1882. The Dickeys had one child, Lincoln Griffith Dickey, born September 16, 1884, at Auburn, Nebraska, who later became manager of the Symphony Orchestra of Cleveland, Ohio. Sol Dickey's wife, Lizzie, died at the home of her son in Cleveland on November 5, 1921, and she is buried in Warsaw, Indiana.

Dickey pastored churches in Auburn, Nebraska; Monticello, Indiana; Peru, Indiana; and then became superintendent of home missions for the Synod of Indiana in 1894, a post he served for two years. He, along with other directors, founded the Winona Assembly in 1895 and Dickey devoted the rest of his life to developing Winona properties and programming.

Dickey died suddenly at DeLand, Florida, on December 22, 1920. Funeral services were conducted at the Presbyterian Church in Warsaw and Dickey is buried in Oakwood Cemetery in Warsaw. In addition to the many well-known speakers at his memorial service, musical selections were by Homer Rodeheaver of Winona Lake, Charles Gabriel of Chicago, and Mrs. Helen Cutler Dickey of Cleveland, Ohio. Miss Katherine Carmichael played the organ.

Upon Dickey's death, Homer Rodeheaver wrote, "Just like every great man, Dr. Dickey was never fully appreciated while he lived. Now that he has gone, we get a clearer vision of his great heart as we review also the difficulties and obstacles he was struggling to overcome to bring to successful culmination these plans . . . I saw his great self-sacrificing aim, purpose and ideal for Winona Lake."

Evangelist Billy Sunday, in a tribute to Dickey, recalled,

> Twenty-five years ago I got off the train at Warsaw and got in a boat and went down the canal and crossed the lake to Winona, and Dr. Dickey and Dr. [Wilbur] Chapman and I talked of Winona. It wasn't called Winona then. It was Spring Fountain Park. There was no station there. We had to go down the canal and cross the lake. There were not the hotels and homes and boarding houses that are there today.
>
> There was no Mount Memorial, no Westminster and buildings that have arisen because of his energy and his enthusiasm. Not only that, but I believe that Dr. Dickey did more for the good and for the moral influence of Winona and Warsaw and for Kosciusko County than anybody ever did within the boundaries of the county.
>
> Sometimes our boys in the schools would come home drunk, and I remember at one time the watchman found two of our boys so drunk they could not find their way home. Afterwards, Dr. Dickey came to me and he said, 'Won't you come and help us to save our boys?' And together we fought the saloons in Warsaw until the town was made dry, and then we fought on until the county went dry, and after that the

state went dry, and after that they ratified the Eighteenth Amendment to the Constitution.

Sunday continued, "I believe Dr. Dickey was the most determined, irrepressible optimist I ever met; and his enthusiasm was as infectious as the laughter of a little child. He staggered under burdens that would have driven the ordinary man to his grave ten years before God called him, and yet, though the clouds were dark and the storms beat furiously, he did not despair."

The *Warsaw Times*, in an editorial dated December 24, 1920, said, "It has been through his personal efforts and activities that Winona, the greatest Middle-West Chautauqua, has grown to its present size and has now become nationwide in its importance." The paper further noted, "Without question it can be said that Dr. Dickey has been a man of real worth, and has done more for the community— and with Winona one must include Warsaw and Kosciusko County— than any other man living here during the period of his activities."

Assembly president Thomas Kane recorded,

As Winona grew and became known to the outside world the need of better transportation facilities suggested itself and Dr. Dickey conceived the idea of building an interurban line. He interested H. J. Heinz of Pittsburgh, J. M. Studebaker of South Bend, and other men of money in the project, and the result was the construction of the Goshen division of the Winona Interurban Railway Company.

This was followed by the construction of the Peru division, connecting Warsaw and Peru, and completing the link between the north and central parts of the state. The interurban line was completed in 1907 [ed. note: This recollection is faulty—the Warsaw to Peru segment was completed in February, 1910]. The Winona and Warsaw Railway connecting Warsaw and Winona, another project fathered by Dr. Dickey, was placed in service in the summer of 1903.

Dr. Dickey's vision also suggested the possibility of making Winona a great educational as well as religious and recreational center and it was through his influence and guidance that the Winona College and Winona College of Agriculture were founded. He also had a vision of extending the scope of Winona's educational influence by founding the Winona Technical Institute at Indianapolis, an institution which did not prove a financial success.

Kane noted also that, "Activity on the part of Dr. Dickey was responsible for the erection of many of the fine buildings at Winona and his influence made Winona Lake the annual meeting place for many organizations." (from the Memorial Book in honor of Dr. Dickey, p. 26)

IDEA FOR WINONA "CAME FROM A HIGHER SOURCE"

Thomas Kane said, "The root idea of Winona, so far as human knowledge extends, originated in the heart and brain of S. C. Dickey, D.D., during the years 1894 and 1895, but he believes with all his heart that its origin was from a vastly higher source. He believes that not only he, but the entire management and directory have been, are being, and will continue to be used, so long as they exercise humility, and earnestly seek Divine guidance along practical lines, to do a great work at Winona for God and country."

WINONA ASSEMBLY AND SUMMER SCHOOL INCORPORATES

The 1896 annual program noted that articles of incorporation had been filed in the office of Indiana Secretary of State J. William Owen on January 28, 1895, showing a capital stock investment of $100,000 and officially granting authority to "said Association to transact business under the provisions of said acts." Winona Assembly and Summer School was off and running.

The printed program for the 1896 edition of the Winona Assembly and Summer School describes the facilities in this way:

The Association has purchased 160 acres of land that stretches for a mile and a half along the eastern shore of the lake. The grounds include what has heretofore been known as

Spring Fountain Park. They have been beautified with small lakelets, arbors, flower-plots and winding walks, making it very attractive . . . Some fifteen acres, on a point extending out into the lake, have been prepared for athletic grounds. No better field for bicycling, running matches, base-ball and other outdoor sports can be found. It is overlooked by an amphitheatre capable of seating 2,500 people. Athletics will be a prominent feature of the Assembly this year.

An attractive feature of the grounds are the numerous springs which afford never-failing sources of surprise and interest to visitors. A pipe driven at any point to a depth of forty feet ensures a flowing artesian well. Some of these springs are medicinal in their qualities.

The following year, 1897, the program touted "the famous Northwestern Band and Orchestra of Ohio" which had been engaged for the season and advertised that *Messiah, Fair Ellen,* and a children's cantata would be rendered.

Sundays were strictly observed. The 1897 program states, "In keeping with the rules which obtain at all well-regulated Chautauquas, Sunday is strictly observed at Winona as a day set apart for worship and rest. Only those holding season tickets are admitted to the grounds. A fully organized Sunday school meets at 9:30 a.m., followed by church services at which some prominent minister will preach each Sunday. The crowning event of the Sabbath is the hillside service when, as twilight approaches, all gather in the open air for a service of song and prayer. In these informal meetings led by experienced workers, an opportunity for participation by all is given."

The program for the summer of 1900 describes the facilities, in part, this way: "Wide paths wind here and there through the park along the lake, near the hotel and large buildings. Near the Winona Hotel is located Froebel Hall, known to Winonians of the past as the Cyclorama Building . . . The circling hill lined with cottages on the left, the lily pond, the Winona spring, the Arbor spring, the beautiful beds of flowers all around, the lake at the right with the boat house and bath house, the buildings on further south present a view which once seen will never be forgotten."

After waxing eloquent about the various cottages and services that were available (ice is delivered at the door of every cottager), the grocery, the drug store, and the bookstore, the description continues:

> In the second story of Commercial Block are to be found fourteen recitation rooms used by the Summer School. The next building is the Double Café, with its lunch counter and dining rooms having a seating capacity of about 400. A view from the Café includes the tennis and croquet grounds, the arbor circle and the large maple tree with its 'maple water' flowing the year round.
>
> Adjacent to the Café is the Administration Building, which has been greatly improved by the erection of a new frontage facing eastward. Here the business of the Assembly is carried on in its general offices. Here will be found the post office, the summer school offices, the press rooms, news and souvenir stands, etc.
>
> To the south of the Administration Building is the beautiful floral island, a picture. . . . To the right is to be seen the athletic grounds, Science Hall, The Inn, one of the largest hotels in the state, containing about 250 rooms for guests; and the great Auditorium, where the lectures and entertainments are given with its opera chairs, its pipe organ and its perfect acoustic properties, often declared to be one of the best summer auditoriums in the United States.

Boating and cruising on the lake continued to be strong attractions. A report dated April 25, 1905, noted that a double-decked excursion boat would cruise Winona Lake the following conference season. Powered by steam, the boat was 85 feet long and could carry up to 500 people. It was made by the Racine Boat Company of Muskegon, Michigan, and was brought to Winona Lake in sections. Estimated cost of the craft was $8,000.

In addition to the physical attractions, attention was also given to education and culture. The Winona Assembly offered classes in Greek (both biblical and classical), Latin instruction with separate courses in Caesar, Virgil, and Cicero, advanced German studies of

Goethe and others, and much more, including work in French, English, history, economics and social science, mathematics, and physics, chemistry, botany, music, elocution, art, and physical culture.

It should be noted that not always was there harmony throughout Winona. In August of 1905, waiters at The Inn went on strike when five servers were brought in from Indianapolis to work during the annual Bible conference. The Inn's regular waiters were students or teachers who did not want to lose their jobs for a week.

The strike was settled when The Inn agreed to continue paying the regular waiters, who would receive $4 for the week, slightly more than their regular rate. The Inn, it was reported, expected to serve about 800 meals during the conference.

The charter date for the Winona Assembly was February 4, 1895. The first president was Charles H. Conner of New Albany, Indiana, who served three years. He was an elder in the Presbyterian church and was president of the Conner Steel Company of Louisville, Kentucky. He built the first cottage under Winona management, but that dwelling was destroyed in the disastrous fire of 1914.

The second president was Thomas Kane of Chicago, who was president of American Spiral Pipe Works. Kane was a well-to-do capitalist and devout layman, and he served as president of the board for almost a decade following Conner.

John M. Studebaker of South Bend, Indiana, was the third president of the Assembly. He was the oldest of five brothers who constituted the firm of Studebaker Brothers, the wagon (and later automobile) manufacturer in South Bend. Studebaker not only gave liberally of his finances, but he also gave much time in attending meetings and supervising building and maintenance of facilities. The Studebaker Spring, which is located in a grotto between the current Rodeheaver Auditorium and the Billy Sunday home, stands as a memorial to Studebaker's significant contribution to Winona.

H. J. Heinz of Pittsburgh, Pennsylvania, the entrepreneur, pickle promoter and ketchup king, was the fourth president of Winona Assembly. He is described as a "genius and far-seeing builder" whose main skill was advertising, which he exercised to great effect for Winona. Heinz provided many of the statues and artworks in the park, including *The Student*, a statue that was carved in Paris and still stands on the island in the swan pond adjoining the former adminis-tration building. In 1902 he donated a stone lion statue to Winona that formerly stood in the famous Walled City of Peking, China. A large bell from the Boxer Rebellion once was positioned east of the old 2,000-seat auditorium.

Subsequent presidents of the organization included Rev. Henry Webb Johnson, pastor of the First Presbyterian Church of South Bend; Mr. Harry H. Townley of Terre Haute, Indiana, one of the leaders of the state YMCA; and Edward A. K. Hackett, publisher of the *Fort Wayne Sentinel.*

Sol Dickey had met Dr. J. Wilbur Chapman, a Presbyterian pas-tor who would soon become known worldwide as an evangelist, in 1894 at the Denison Hotel in Indianapolis. Dickey later recalled, "I told him of my hope and plan to start Winona. Dr. Chapman evinced real interest and asked me to keep him posted in the de-velopment of the plan." Through the urging of evangelist Dwight L. Moody, Dickey re-connected with Chapman later and convinced him to accept the leadership of the Winona Bible Conference.

The first Winona Bible Conference opened on Wednesday, Au-gust 12, 1896.[6] On one of the first nights of the conference, which was attended by 300-400 Christian workers, there were terrible thun-der and winds which came up just at the opening hour. The roof of the auditorium was leaking, but the Bible conference was launched.

Chapman led the conference from 1896 until 1908, and he su-perintended the building of Strain Hall, Evangel Hall (later called Bethany Lodge) and the Kosciusko Lodge. He, along with publisher Hackett of Fort Wayne, founded the Winona Academy which gave an education to hundreds of boys of limited means and later was merged into Winona College. Chapman resigned in 1908 to go abroad on his expanding worldwide mission of evangelism.

Church historian Mark Sidwell noted, "The Winona Assem-bly and Summer School Association basked in the glory of its Bible Conference director. Although J. Wilbur Chapman became inter-

---

[6] Sidwell, p. 63

nationally famous as an evangelist after his service at Winona, he lent the organization the appeal and prestige of having a prominent pastor, notable evangelist, and popular hymnist[7] as its Bible Conference director. Winona profited from Chapman's achievements and the renown that they brought to Winona Lake."[8]

Of his involvement in Winona, Chapman himself remarked, "If I had missed my share in the Winona Bible Conference, I should have missed the best part of my ministry."[9]

In a speech given in August of 1919, Dickey also gave credit to Alexander McDonald, elder of the Third Presbyterian Church of Cincinnati and president of the Standard Oil Co. of Kentucky, as one of the founders of Winona. Dickey described Alexander as, "with Mr. Studebaker . . . one of the most generous friends Winona ever had." McDonald gave the money to purchase and build the dredge that created the canal. He bought the iron bridges which spanned the canal, and McDonald Island was named in his honor.

It was in the summer program for 1900 that Dickey's report as secretary and general manager described "Winona's Best Scheme."

Uncle John Thorpe, of Chicago, the landscape artist, who laid out the World's Fair Grounds, has presented to the directors a unique plan by which more than thirty acres of beautiful lots can be platted within a short distance of the Auditorium. His plan is to cut a canal eighty feet wide from the west end of the present bath house to the lake just in the rear of the Inn, about 400 yards north of the Indiana University Biological Station buildings thus making an island of the ground including and adjacent to the present half-mile race track.

He provides for two bridges, two boulevards eighty feet wide, an esplanade forty feet wide running around the entire shore, several promenades and about 300 fine building lots. The lake will be lowered one foot and kept at a certain level

---

[7] Two of Chapman's best-known compositions are *Our Great Savior* and *One Day*.

[8] Sidwell, p. 73

[9] Gaddis & Huffman, p. 96

by means of a dam at the outlet. The surface of the island will be raised about two feet by means of dredging, taking dirt from the canal and shore of present land. The lots will thus be more than four feet higher than the lake. A perfect sewerage system is found feasible and will be guaranteed.

The dredging and creation of the canal were actually accomplished two years later, in 1902, due largely to the largesse of McDonald.

The next year's report said that the need for funding was presented to McDonald, who "quickly grasped the situation and generously provided the necessary means." It was found that a dredge with a dipper of more than a cubic yard capacity could be operated at an expense, including coal, of only $10 a day, and so McDonald provided the needed dredge. As of February 20, 1901, it was reported that "a canal 25 feet wide and about five feet deep has been constructed across the peninsula, transforming it into an island." The plans called for a next cutting, which would widen the canal to 50 feet, with an intention of eventually making it 70 or possibly 80 feet in width.

TRANSPORTATION DEVELOPS

In an article on the Winona Railroad for the *Warsaw Times-Union* on July 15, 1986, local historian William Darr noted "Today the grassy area between Gatke's parking lot and the Winona Hotel gives little evidence that the trolleys made a loop, or circle, there and stopped at a large combination railroad station, office, and entrance gate to the grounds of Winona Lake."

Guests came by many methods. The Pennsylvania Railroad stopped at the Eagle Arcade, where passengers could disembark. They then entered town via the Arcade, which included a souvenir shop and restaurant.

News media reported in May, 1906, that workers had begun construction of a tunnel under the Pennsylvania Railroad tracks. This would allow passengers to board westbound trains without crossing the eastbound tracks. This underground tunnel-walkway came out behind the Eagle Arcade. It has now been filled in for some time. The current Argonne Road viaduct at the entrance to the town was built circa 1923.

The Big Four Railroad was met by a launch that brought passengers to Winona through a canal west of the present Lakeview Middle School (the old high school). The Interurban Electric Line, which was 64 miles long, ran near Winona. It was called the "connecting link" because it connected the interurbans from the northern half of Indiana to the central half. It connected with the Northern Indiana at Goshen and with the Union at Peru.

The powerhouse for the railroad and local streetcars was located near what later became the Litchfield Creamery, and it provided electricity for both Winona Lake and Warsaw.

Sources note that in 1925 the Warsaw-Winona Trolley carried 531,965 passengers—a record number for one year.

A steamer boat, *City of Warsaw*, carried 150 passengers on leisurely cruises around Eagle Lake. The Assembly also owned a golf course approximately where Argonne Road is now, as well as a souvenir store, restaurant, and a drug store.

Others whom Dickey credited with the building of Winona in the early days included Rev. William P. Kane, pastor of the First Presbyterian Church of Bloomington, Illinois, and later president of Wabash College; Governor James A. Mount of Indiana, who devoted much time to Winona (the Mount Memorial building was named in his honor); and Major W. J. Richards, founder of the *Indianapolis News*, who was an ardent supporter and friend of Winona.

Dickey and the Winona vision were attractive to wealthy people who espoused Winona's values. A news report from October 3, 1905, details the visit to Winona of Helen Gould, described as "a wealthy philanthropist from New York City."

Gould arrived in Warsaw by train and took the interurban to Winona Lake. She lodged in the Winona Hotel and rode around the lake on the steamer *The City of Warsaw*. After a reception for her that was attended by 500 people, she announced that she would turn a half-million dollars' worth of property in New York over to the Assembly.

The Presbyterian Building, later called the Westminster Hotel, was built in 1905, with a dedication service on May 19, 1905. Kosciusko Lodge was built about 1900 as a summer camp for Presbyterian youth, and continued to provide religious education for nearly 50 years.

Local news media also reported on February 22, 1906, that auto magnate J. M. Studebaker of South Bend had donated 100 golden pheasants to Winona Lake. The birds were to be placed in an aviary near Kosciusko Lodge, an inn at the south end of the park.

A KIND OF RELIGIOUS CHAUTAUQUA

Rev. Sol Dickey's vision for "a kind of religious Chautauqua" quickly grew in both popularity and scope. The Chautauqua movement originated as a summer program for Sunday School teachers at Chautauqua Lake, New York, in 1874, and the movement spread rapidly, reaching its peak about 1924.

The biographer of William Jennings Bryan, by all accounts one of the great luminary speakers of the Chautauqua circuit, reported that, "By 1900, over a hundred independent Chautauqua assemblies had sprung up in localities from southern California to New Hampshire. Most were scattered in such midsized, Midwestern communities as Marinette, Wisconsin, and Crete, Nebraska."[10]

The rising popularity of radios and automobiles eventually contributed to their decline, but for 50 years the Chautauquas provided the only satisfaction for cultural hunger in small communities.

The many cultural, spiritual, and natural attractions at Winona eventually drew an average of 250,000 visitors each summer during the "Golden Years" of 1896-1914. By 1910, the summer educational programs in literature, science, theology, and the arts, had been expanded to year-round schools in agriculture, technology, and the liberal arts. A school of theology was founded by Winona in New York City, and the Winona Technical Institute was begun in Indianapolis. At the same time, Winona's Bible Conference achieved national fame among Protestant church workers.

World-class artists and musicians were regularly brought in for performances at Winona. For example, on Monday, July 26, 1909, the New York Symphony Orchestra under the baton of Walter Damrosch began a series of twelve Winona Lake summer concerts.

---

[10] Kazin, p. 135

One of the summer programming highlights each year was the performance of the Indian passion play *Hiawatha,* dramatized from the familiar Longfellow poem of the same name. The performance was given on a floating stage just off McDonald Island, and the cast included a band of about 40 braves, squaws, and children from the Indian reservations of northern New York.

According to the 1909 summer program, "The story of Hiawatha, his wooing of the maiden of another tribe, the wedding ceremony, with songs, dances and feasts, the blight of the famine, the death of Minnehaha, and the farewell of Hiawatha are woven into a pictured story that is highly satisfactory to those who witness these performances."

"Stage embellishments" which added to the effectiveness included "wigwams, camp fires, and the general wildness of an Indian camp." The cast, between performances, "will make their camp on the Winona Lake front. There they will live in their wigwams as in primitive days, the braves and squaws at their daily tasks and diversions and the children at their pastimes. The camp will be open to visitors at given hours during each day."

Novelty acts, often contracted at considerable expense by Winona's management, added excitement and anticipation to the summer programming. One such event was the much-advertised arrival of *Airship Columbia*, a huge dirigible which flew briefly at Winona in August of 1906.

Owned by A. J. "Alf" Bodkin, a Kosciusko County native who lived and conducted his highly profitable business in Chicago, the dirigible arrived on a Pennsylvania Railroad car on Thursday, August 2, 1906. Getting the airship off the train car was described as "like unloading a circus." Off came the airbag, engine, propeller, steering mechanism, hydrogen-generating machine, and hundreds of gallons of sulfuric acid to be used in making the hydrogen that would fill the airbag. The ship had a 39-foot frame, and the airbag, constructed of "the finest Japanese silk," was about 100 feet long, oblong, and was valued at about $14,000.

The flight itself was somewhat of a bust, occurring around 5 p.m. on Friday, August 17. There were engine problems, and so the dirigible was aloft for only a few minutes, and was powered by a bicycle-like contraption that was pedaled by the pilot. Thousands of spectators, however, had visited the dirigible while it was tethered inside a large tent prior to the flight.

An indication of the level of activity at the park is gained from noting various activities occurring the same week as the dirigible's visit. Cadets from the Culver (Ind.) Military Academy were in camp on McDonald's Island that week. There was a convention of Indiana newspaper editors in town. A band comprised of paperboys from Indianapolis and a band made up of Canadians in Scottish kilts was in town for concerts. A number of church groups were having conferences that week, and there was a national choral contest. As many as 15,000 people were said to be on the grounds for at least some of the days that *Airship Columbia* was in Winona Lake.

"Venetian Night" was a great midsummer water festival when all the water craft owned by the Assembly and by individuals were afloat. The lake shores will be "ablaze with colored lights, music will be by Rogers' Band, and arrangements will be made to care for a great crowd of people," according to the printed summer program. A carnival queen was to be selected by popular vote, with the coronation of the queen occurring at a reception the night before the carnival.

And finally, another attraction who made repeated appearances was Col. Isaac Brown, "The Bird and Bee Man," who gave talks on birds and was available for early morning "rambles with nature lovers and for informal talks." The program promised that "he leads Winonians to where the birds are to be seen in the trees, and as they flit about, he tells of where they come from in the spring, how they live and make their homes in the park."

An advertised highlight of the 1910 season was the presentation of the Egyptian opera *Egypta*, which tells the story of Moses. William D. Chenery, author of the opera, was present to "drill the singers of the parts" and to "have personal charge of the production." It was noted that Mr. Chenery brought thousands of dollars' worth of scenery and electrical effects and a special stage was to be built on the lake for five Thursday-evening performances during the summer.

The next year he produced "a new and surpassing sacred opera, *Ahasuerus.*" In addition, a children's choir of more than 300 performed the operetta, *The House That Jack Built.*

The highlight of the 1911 program was noted aviator Glenn H. Curtiss, who appeared on July 14. Curtiss exhibited his "new hydroaeroplane" with the promise that he would "alight and rise both from the lake and from the land."

It was noted that Curtiss had recently won the Scientific American trophy in 1908, and in 1909 he had represented the USA in the first international race at Rheims, France. But perhaps his crowning feat had been a memorable flight down the Hudson River to New York City, "covering the distance of 150 miles in 152 minutes." The admission fee to see Curtiss at Winona was "only fifty cents."

Curtiss did, in fact, appear with his plane, but the performance was less than spectacular. He did make several short flights across Winona Lake, but never rose to significant altitude and never performed any aerial acrobatics of any kind. The highlight was taking Billy Sunday as a passenger, and a well-publicized photo shows Curtiss at the controls with a white-shirt bow-tie-wearing Billy Sunday alongside the pilot. One of the biographies of H. J. Heinz also describes his excitement at flying with Curtiss at Winona Lake.

William Jennings Bryan, according to a local newspaper report, was named president of the Winona Assembly and Bible Conference on January 25, 1912. J. M. Studebaker of South Bend was elected to its board of directors.

An article from the *Indianapolis Star* on Sunday, August 29, 1915, was entitled "Sunday Record Day at Winona." Second- and third-deck headlines screamed "Billy Sunday, Bryan and Schumann-Heink Main Attractions at Exercises Attended by Crowd of 20,000 Persons," "1,500 Autos Bring Visitors," and "Huge Overflow Meetings Held in Morning and Afternoon—Prof. E. O. Excell Leads Chorus of 600 Voices."

The article reported that with Billy Sunday, William Jennings Bryan, and Schumann-Heink as the main attractions, the Winona Bible Conference experienced the greatest day in its twenty years of existence. Twenty thousand persons were on the grounds. At least

7,500 of them came in automobiles from cities and towns within a radius of 100 miles. Actual counting showed more than 1,500 automobiles parked along the driveways. About Schumann-Heink, James Heaton's biographer noted, "She was allergic to flowers, and before the performance would scan the stage to be sure there were none there, because they bothered her singing voice."[11]

William Jennings Bryan was the morning speaker in the auditorium. He spoke to an audience of 6,000 persons. Billy Sunday addressed the overflow in one of the greatest outdoor meetings ever held at Winona. In the afternoon Mr. Bryan introduced Sunday in the auditorium, then went to the hillside to assist evangelist "Bob" Jones and other speakers in addressing the crowd that could not be accommodated inside. Meetings also were conducted at Indian Mound by the Rev. W. E. Biederwolf, and at another point by Mrs. W. A. Sunday and Mrs. William Asher.

Prof. Excell of Chicago led the chorus of more than 600 voices. Mme. Schumann-Heink, who came from New York to sing free of charge before the Bible conference, was in the audience.

Important personalities in the Assembly during these years included:

JOHN M. STUDEBAKER (1833-1917), one of the co-owners of the Studebaker Brothers Manufacturing Company of South Bend, Indiana, was one of Winona's leading supporters during the "Golden Years," investing both his time and money in the movement.

JAMES A. MOUNT (1843-1901), the former governor of Indiana, was an early supporter of Winona. The Mount Memorial Building was named in his honor. Mount was elected governor in 1896.

BENJAMIN HARRISON (1833-1901), ex-president of the United States, participated in one of the earliest religious conventions held at Winona, the 109th General Assembly of the Presbyterian Church, in 1897.

J. WILBUR CHAPMAN (1859-1918). At the urging of D. L. Moody, Sol Dickey convinced J. Wilbur Chapman to help begin the

---

[11] Heaton, p. 24

Winona Bible Conference. Dr. Chapman directed the Conference from 1896 to 1908, and brought it to national prominence. Prior to his work at Winona, Chapman was a popular evangelist and a Presbyterian pastor.

G. CAMPBELL MORGAN (1863-1945). Dr. Morgan was acknowledged to be one of Britain's greatest preachers during his ministry at Westminster Chapel in London. He spent many summers in Winona, speaking regularly at the Bible Conference and helping to found the Winona School of Theology in 1920.

ALEXANDER MCDONALD, (1836-1910). A very successful investor, he was a business partner in the oil industry with John D. Rockefeller and later became president of Standard Oil of Kentucky. He financed the digging of the canal in 1902. Venetian Nights were held annually along the canal banks under the direction of Captain Pine. These unique parades of beautiful floats attracted vast crowds to huge bleachers that had been moved into position along the canal. Boats donated by the Assembly were decorated by themes, and prizes were awarded. The last pageant was held in 1917, when a near-tragedy occurred. A float depicting the homes of a drunkard and a temperance man capsized when the drunkard fell overboard and the other passengers all rushed to his aid.

THE WINONA RAILROAD

On the day the Winona Railway ceased operations, May 31, 1952, a news article commented on its origin: The Winona Railroad came into operation in 1902 when the Pennsylvania Railroad announced that it was going to double-track its entire line from Chicago to Pittsburgh and the sidetrack on which a local train brought visitors to Winona from Warsaw would no longer be available.

By the summer of 1903, directors of the Winona Christian Assembly had completed a trolley line between the two towns. The 18 open cars ran on an hourly schedule, sometimes carrying 15,000 passengers in one day for special events at Winona.

Track ballasting material came from a gravel pit on the old Boss farm just east of Argonne Road. From this pit the Winona directors also sold gravel to the city of Warsaw for grading streets.

Goshen, Warsaw, Peru, and towns along the way voted subsidies totaling $170,000 on the condition that the Winona Interurban Railway build a high-speed electric railway north and south connecting with other interurban systems that had spread all over Indiana.

The north line to Goshen was started in 1905 with the first cars running by June of the following summer. The south section was completed in 1907. A large powerhouse, costing $200,000, was constructed where the remains of the Gatke Foundry now stand. It supplied the additional power needed for the 70-mile system and also provided steam heat and electricity to all the public buildings at Winona and about 50 private homes in the town. Electricity as well as water was supplied by the railroad to the city of Warsaw.

Planned expansions to Fort Wayne and Valparaiso were never built. All stock in the railroad was owned by the Assembly and all profits above the interest on the bonds went into improvement of Winona Lake as a Chautauqua and religious center.

SERIOUS FINANCIAL DIFFICULTY

The Winona movement's financial foundation was based upon the idea of "money-making altruism." The doctrines of this credo included:

First: Pay or amply provide for the prompt payment of all financial obligations;

Second: Take good care of one's business and property;

Third: Take good care of one's family;

Fourth: Provide moderately for increased business and rainy days to come;

Fifth: Do all the good possible with the remainder of the profits.

To these ends, numerous money-making Winona enterprises such as the Winona and Warsaw Railway Company, The Winona Interurban Railway Company, and the Winona Electric Light and Water Company had been developed.

With the coming of the automobile, the steady overall attendance at Winona events decreased, and the year 1915 saw the Assembly in serious financial difficulty. Evangelist Billy Sunday, who had been on the side of the creditors' committee in the settlement of Winona's financial troubles, was cheered when he announced that he had changed his mind and was ready to support the old management in its plan for reorganization. Mr. Bryan, who was to become president of the new Winona, gave added assurance of his support.

In July, 1916, the mortgage on the Goshen-Warsaw line was foreclosed and the road went into receivership. Theodore Frazer, who had become president of the Winona Light and Water company in 1910, headed that company until he went into the army in 1917, serving as a captain of engineers. Following World War I, Frazer returned to Warsaw to become secretary of the Dalton Foundries in June of 1924 and became associated with the Winona Railroad Co. He was vice president of the utility until 1932 when he was appointed receiver during the darkest days of the Depression.

Meanwhile interurban systems throughout the country were failing, but a shift to freight handling in 1924 aided Winona considerably. When Goshen residents petitioned to have the tracks in their city removed, passenger service to the Winona railroad's northernmost point ceased in 1934.

Now the only passenger service operated by the railroad was the three-mile run between Warsaw and Winona.

The last streetcar ran on July 4, 1938, and buses took over the passenger route after that. Theodore Frazer helped the railroad recover, and he became president of it in 1936. Under his leadership the railroad was modernized, becoming a diesel-powered freight feeder line in 1938.

In January 1945, Frazer announced the sale of the bonds, stocks, and physical assets of the 66-mile railroad to a syndicate from Chicago, which included Claude L. Jackson, who was named president of the railroad. Frazer died April 4, 1946.

Increasing operating costs after World War II, less demand for tank car shipping of oil, and smaller orders for coal shipments were factors in the company's decision to cease operations. The first petition in 1949 to abandon the New Paris-Warsaw section was denied by the Interstate Commerce Commission in 1950. However the resubmitted appeal in 1951 was granted and the train made its last run on May 31, 1952.

A large wreath was placed on the front of its giant engine and about 60 local dignitaries and Chamber of Commerce officials took the final 40-mile trip to the north terminus of the line and back again to Warsaw.

The train halted on Center Street in the block between Center and Indiana streets, with the engine headed west. Speeches were made by William Mollenhour of the *Times-Union* and WRSW staff, and others spoke as well.

William Darr, in a 1986 newspaper article on local railroads, noted that "The Winona Railroad was close to, or in, bankruptcy or receivership during much of its history. It operated under four names: Winona and Warsaw Railway, 1902-1905; Winona Interurban Railway, 1905-1924; Winona Service Company, 1924-1926; and the Winona Railroad Company, 1926-1952."

BETHANY CAMP

Bethany Camp was built on 10 acres originally owned by the Furlong family on the lakeshore where the Winona School of Theology and the Winona town park were later located. It included bungalows, a dining hall, gymnasium and auditorium. The original donors of many of the facilities were Mr. and Mrs. William Peterson of Chicago. An organization called the Bethany Girls Group (originally called the "Busy Girls") was founded in 1914 by Miss Carrie Stewart of Middleport, Ohio.[12] The group was formed to provide friendship and spiritual support to "girls" leaving the farm and moving to the big city to get jobs. "Girls" in that day were today's young ladies—technically adults.

The group was part of the Presbyterian Church and it appears to have remained in the Midwest. Carrie Stewart's sister Nellie was also a strong supporter of the Bethany Girls. The club's motto was "Fear not, for I am with you." In 1919, 500 women attended the camp.

The founder, Mrs. Carrie Stewart Besserer, died in February, 1936, at her home in Middleport, Ohio. She was 65 years old and

---

[12] Gaddis and Huffman say Bethany Girls was founded "about the year 1901," p. 51

had been ill for more than a year, but until that illness had continued to be active as the director of the Bethany Girls' organization.

A report from 1937 noted that Bethany Camp's land and facilities had been purchased by R. G. LeTourneau of Peoria, Ill., "to be continued as a camp of Christian training for boys and girls of high school and college age. It will be under the direction of Mrs. LeTourneau and a competent staff." Gaddis and Huffman recorded that the Winona School of Theology later purchased Bethany Camp from the LeTourneau Foundation and the 1948 session marked its first year on the new campus.

Bethany Camp would later host Brethren Youth Conferences, under the direction of Leo Polman, and it also was the on-site location for the Winona School of Theology. Even later, it would become the Winona Lake town park and house the city offices and police department.

In 1987 the Town of Winona Lake used the majority of an approximately $58,000 federal revenue sharing grant to renovate the town hall, to dredge the canal, and for the reforestation and cleanup of trees in the town.

WINONA LITERARY CLUB

One of the Winona institutions that dates from 1903 and is still going today is the Winona Literary Club. The group meets monthly, once counted "Ma" Sunday as an active member, and it celebrated its 100th anniversary in August of 2003 with a meeting in the fellowship hall of the Winona Lake Free Methodist Church.

Charlotte Mikesell (Mrs. D. Blaine Mikesell) chaired the meeting, which included a letter of congratulations from the town board and several musical selections. Past presidents in attendance were recognized by Peaches French, president, and they included Charlotte Mikesell, Laura Peugh, Ruth Allison, and Marilyn Roeber. Each was introduced and gave a few words about the history of the organization, and each received a corsage in appreciation.

The program, "A Skip Through Time," detailed the 100-year history of the club and was presented by Peaches French, Carole LaRue, Kathy Allison, Liz Milliman, Evelyn Mottweiler and Beverly Kent, who also sang a solo. There were 52 in attendance.

CHICAGO BOYS CLUB

The Chicago Boys Club was incorporated in 1902. It was founded in Chicago by John F. Atkinson, and first occupied rented quarters on South State Street in Chicago. The Chicago Boys Camp at Winona, sponsored by the Chicago Boys Club, was started in late 1910 on a large, wooded tract on Winona's south side (currently the biking trails and Stone Camp subdivision). It provided a vacation spot for boys from poor neighborhoods of Chicago who had known only the concrete, brick, and steel in the streets of a city. Its slogan was "The Golden Rule: A Measure of Character."

The camp was open for nearly 80 years, providing a place of solitude for the inner city children from Chicago to spend two weeks out of their summer. The camp had several buildings on-site, including a large dining hall, a caretaker's home, a maintenance building and many cabins. Foundations of these structures remain today, and are sprinkled throughout the 117 acres. In 1984, the name was changed to Boys and Girls Clubs of Chicago to acknowledge the many young women who were also participating in the clubs.

At this writing the property, though privately owned by Dr. Dane Miller, is open for use by mountain bikers, hikers, joggers, and others. There are 9.5 miles of pure flowing mountain bike single-track that wind around the trees, Cherry Creek, and open spaces of the old Chicago Boys Club property.

INDIANA UNIVERSITY BIOLOGICAL FIELD STATION

Indiana University professor Charles H. Eigenmann established the first inland biological station in the United States at Turkey Lake in Kosciusko County, Indiana, the summer of 1895.[13]

The university trustees permitted Eigenmann to use apparatus from the university's zoology department for a nine-week summer session with the understanding that there would be no cost to the university for operating the station. The first year, however, was such a success that thereafter the trustees provided permanent equipment.

---

[13] Kellams, Dina. "Summer Fun at the Biological Field Station" Posted on https://blogs.libraries.iub.edu/iubarchives/2011/05/31/summer-fun-at-the-biological-field-station

The purpose of the station was research and instruction in the biological sciences. Nineteen students attended the first year, 32 the second year, 63 the third, and 103 the fourth. At the end of the fourth year the station was moved to Eagle Lake (Winona Lake) where land was gifted by the Winona Christian Assembly along with funds for erecting two small, two-story frame buildings.

The 1920 announcement for the summer session outlined living arrangements for the students, which included tent camping, renting a room for $2-$4 a week, or staying at a local hotel with weekly rates of $10 and up. Boats could be rented.

In 1938 the formal instruction at the station ceased, a victim of the Depression. After that it was used primarily as a research center for faculty and graduate students. In 1960, the Department of Zoology proposed a new program in field biology which included building new facilities in Whitley and Noble counties. In 1965, the land at Winona Lake was sold back to the Winona Lake Bible Conference for $2,000.

CHAPTER 4
Winona Schools

*"I wish to wrest education from the outworn order of doddering
old teaching hacks as well as from the new-fangled order of cheap,
artificial teaching tricks, and entrust it to the eternal powers of
nature herself, to the light which God kindled and kept alive in the
hearts of fathers and mothers, to the interest of parents who desire
their children grow up in favor with God and men."*
Johann H. Pestalozzi

WINONA FEATURED CHAUTAUQUA PROGRAMMING AS WELL AS A BIBLE
conference, but Reverend Dickey and his directors eventually pur-
sued their third goal—the creation of specific schools. Dickey's man-
ner of developing Winona's schools was the reverse of D. L. Moody's
method at Northfield, Massachusetts. Moody built his Northfield
Girls' Seminary and Mount Herman School for Boys and then developed the summer conferences as a practical way to use the grounds
in the summer. By contrast, Rev. Dickey built his Chautauqua and
Bible conferences and then developed the schools to utilize the facilities for the other nine months of the year.

When they began starting schools in about 1902, Winona's
board chose the Pestalozzian Model as their educational standard.
This model was the forerunner of "applied learning" education in
that it emphasized "learning by doing." The method was named for
Johann H. Pestalozzi (1746-1827), a Swiss pedagogue and educational reformer.

Thomas Kane, in discussing Winona Schools, said, "The whole Winona Movement is practical as distinguished from theoretical education... only an exceptionally small proportion of American youth are or can be college-bred; the fact is that only about three per cent of them ever enter high school, and a still smaller proportion are high school graduates."

There were at least seven separate schools or institutions that comprised the educational segment of "The Winona Movement." They included

Winona Agricultural Institute
The Winona Technical Institute (Indianapolis)
The Winona Park School for Young Women
The Winona Academy
The Normal School
The Winona College
Winona Bible School (New York)

WINONA AGRICULTURAL INSTITUTE

The 1904 summer program carried information about the formation of the Winona Agricultural Institute. This college of agriculture combined practical courses with the development of moral and spiritual character. Its goal was to prepare students for positions as scientific farmers, farm managers, county agents, teachers of agriculture, stock raisers, farm bureau operators, horticulturalists, and for civil service work. The plan was to alternate classroom study with practical labor.

Literature announcing its founding said,

In August, 1901, the Winona Agricultural and Technical Institute, a corporation, was organized, the stock being owned and held by the Winona Assembly and Summer School. The WATI purchased 15 acres of the Wilcox farm and laid out the present campus on which is now erected the beautiful pressed brick building known as the Mount Memorial, and which will be completed not later than June 1 of this year; also the Strain Hall, a handsome brick dormitory, the munificent gift of an Eastern friend.

The WATI also purchased 50 acres of the Ross farm and platted same, calling it the Mount Memorial Addition, with the understanding that all of the proceeds from the sale of said lots are to be used in the payment for the construction of the Mount Memorial Building. About $30,000 of these lots have been sold, and it is hoped, ere the season of 1904 closes, to complete the sale of the remaining $30,000 of lots.

The school was opened in September, 1902, with 87 students and 12 in the faculty. The school finished its second year with a total enrollment of 116 students and a faculty of 14.

In addition to using the Presbyterian Building, Mount Memorial Building, and Strain Hall, the school also used The Daguerre building as a gymnasium. Built early in the century by the Daguerre Memorial Commission, it was named in honor of the French inventor of the daguerreotype photographic process.

WINONA TECHNICAL INSTITUTE (INDIANAPOLIS)

A separate institute, called the Winona Technical Institute at Indianapolis, was organized on abandoned arsenal grounds in the capital city, with the grounds and buildings obtained through auction in March of 1903. Dr. S. C. Dickey was authorized and empowered to act for the Winona group to secure donations of money sufficient to purchase the tract of land for the school.

An impressive group was assembled to back the school's start. Gaddis and Huffman said the board of 47 members included "fourteen corporation presidents, eleven presidents of banks or trust companies, five ministers, four publishers, several attorneys including the District Attorney for the Pennsylvania Railroad, a congressman and a physician."[14]

The grounds, comprised of 76 ¼ acres at 1500 E. Michigan Street in Indianapolis, were located one mile from the monument in the capital city. The buildings, which cost the government about $600,000, all of substantial brick and stone, and in first-class condition, with little changes were well adapted to the uses of a trade and technical school.

---

[14] Gaddis & Huffman, p 45.

"Tech," as Indianapolis residents now call it, did not begin as a school, but as a Civil War arsenal. Army planners chose the site in 1863 and the first soldiers arrived in 1865. The U.S. government used the arsenal to store heavy artillery, lighter arms, and some munitions until 1903. Many arsenals around the country were abandoned after the Spanish-American War, and the war department had made it clear that they contemplated the complete abandonment of the site in favor of the establishment of Fort Benjamin Harrison on a much larger tract of land.

The arsenal grounds were sold at public auction to an Indianapolis public trust on March 27, 1903, in order to keep the property intact as the site of a school or park. A campaign was begun by Sol Dickey and others to raise money for the purpose of procuring the property as the site of an arts and trade school to be conducted by the Winona Agricultural and Technical Institute. Some 4,000 donors, principally from the city of Indianapolis, contributed to the fund. The final abandonment of the arsenal was marked by the firing of the last sunrise gun on April 3, 1903.

A trade school was established in the fall of 1904, known as the Winona Technical Institute at Indianapolis, whose stock was owned and held by the Winona Assembly. A school of pharmacy started with 60 students, and an electrical school with 40 students. There were also schools for house and sign painting, printing, foundry operation, plumbing, carpentry, bricklaying, and more.

Unfortunately, despite their good intentions, they were unable to raise sufficient funds and the school was completely insolvent by 1910. A lawsuit ensued.

Documents of the suit laid out the history:

> …A group of men of large means, who were connected with or interested in the Winona Assembly and Summer School Association, a corporation conducting a Chautauqua and summer school at Winona Lake, Indiana, determined to establish an agricultural and technical school, the agricultural department of which should be at Winona Lake and the technical department at Indianapolis, provided the citizens of Indianapolis would purchase said tract of land from

the United States Government as a site on which to locate said technical department. Said group of men representing Winona interests held a meeting in Pittsburgh, Pa., on the 2nd day of March, 1902, and adopted the following resolution, to-wit: "That we will endow and manage a technical institute in Indianapolis provided the citizens of Indianapolis and vicinity will secure for us the United States Arsenal Grounds and buildings, free of cost or encumbrance, or provided they will secure grounds and buildings of equal suitability or value, and our executive committee is empowered to make all contracts in the matter."

The arrangement had been that when the school procured a sufficient endowment to guarantee the perpetuity of the school, the trustees should execute a deed to the Institute. When no endowment had been raised, a lawsuit was then brought by the trustees from whom the land was purchased. The court ordered that the real estate be conveyed to the Board of School Commissioners of the City of Indianapolis as trustee. An appeal failed and a final judgment was rendered May 22, 1916.

Historical documents show that "while the case was pending, the receiver carried on the Winona Technical Institute for a short time and then leased the property to the Board of School Commissioners of the City of Indianapolis." That board, which needed a third high school, was authorized to receive gifts in trust for school purposes, and in 1912 an overflow high school, vocational in character, was started on the site with Milo H. Stuart as principal.

Today Arsenal Technical High School, which considers its founding date to be 1912, enrolls 2,500 students. It is a public high school run by the Indianapolis Public Schools school system, and is the only school of its type in Indiana.

WINONA PARK SCHOOL FOR YOUNG WOMEN

The school for young women was one of several secondary schools to be opened by the Assembly. The Winona Park School for Young Women opened in 1905, and in 1906 the liberal arts curriculum of the Agricultural School was transformed into a separate male secondary school,

The Winona Academy. Girls' school classes were held at the Inn hotel, and Mount Memorial building was the location of the boys' school.

A flyer advertising the Winona Park School for Young Women proclaimed it "an interdenominational college preparatory school, with faculty of 12 members, all college graduates and experienced in their lines."

The school offered college preparatory, general and cultural courses, including music, art, elocution, domestic science, or normal training. Rose M. Clark was principal, and Jonathan Rigdon president.

THE WINONA ACADEMY

The Winona Academy was a school of Christian influence for boys aged 12-20. A booklet announcing the opening of the school in the 1906-1907 school year said, "It will be the purpose of the Academy to admit students who have completed the eighth year of our public school course and prepare them to enter the freshman class of the best colleges and universities of our country."

Solomon Dickey was listed as president, J. Wilbur Chapman as vice president, and Henry Ellsworth DuBois as principal. The announcement noted, "This is not a new school but simply a continuation under a new name of the academic studies of the Winona Agricultural Institute. The board of directors of the Winona Agricultural Institute, after a careful consideration of the matter, have decided to separate the agricultural and academic work as heretofore carried on in that school, thus continuing the two lines of work in two separate schools."

Promotional literature described the campus as the "most beautiful and healthful location in central west, 2 ¾ hours from Chicago." The school proudly claimed that its certificate admits to leading universities. Expenses were $350 per year. The Westminster (then called the Presbyterian Building) was the home of the Winona Academy.

THE NORMAL SCHOOL

A normal school was organized in 1908. Entrance requirements for the Normal School included graduation from a commissioned high school or other secondary school of equal rank. Publicity noted that the Winona Normal School had been approved by the State Teachers' Training Board for Class A and Class B certificate courses, for the one-year certificate course, and for the two-year course leading to the elementary professional certificate. Teachers who had 45 months' teaching experience could qualify for the elementary provisional certificate by completing the two-year course at Winona. Out of it grew Winona College.

Publicity for the Normal School in 1908 noted that it "prepares teachers for all the grades of public school or normal school work. It also offers courses in business, domestic science, telegraphy, law, piano, voice, Bible, physical culture, expression, and public speaking." Jonathan Rigdon was listed as president.

WINONA COLLEGE

The climax of Winona's school-building activities came in 1908. Sidwell points out that in that year the Indiana state legislature required "normal-school" (teacher education) coursework to extend beyond mere summer sessions.

To preserve its summer normal classes, the directors organized the year-round Winona Normal School. Immediately, the school incorporated the Agricultural School, and when it became Winona College a few years later, it also absorbed the Winona Academy and the Winona Conservatory of Music, which had been housed in Strain Hall. The college was organized around four departments—liberal arts, education, business, and music. Dr. Jonathan Rigdon was president. A department of household arts was added in 1914.

Winona College administrators were quite proud of the school's academic standing, noting that "Our college work ranks with the best. Our graduates are in demand." The 1912 publicity notes, "One of our graduates of 1911 was accepted by the University of Pennsylvania for graduate work and was offered a scholarship. . . Another went to the University of Illinois to work on his degree in engineering. The faculty gave him an equal standing with that of their own graduates." Sixty-one courses were offered the summer of 1913, ranging from Shakespeare to Plane Trigonometry to Commercial Law to Inorganic Chemistry.

A copy of the *Winona College News,* published bi-monthly by Winona College and Winona College Student Associations and dated Thursday, September 27, 1917, Vol. 1, No. 6, advertised "pleasant Friday evenings" as a fine lecture course for the winter. The purpose of the winter lecture course was to provide wholesome entertainment, as well as intelligent discussions and lectures and good music for the college folk and people of the park. The price was one dollar for the entire series of 10 entertainments and lectures. Samples included an illustrated lecture on "The Stars," a recital by the Winona Choral Society, an illustrated lecture on "Sweden," a reading entitled "The Sky Pilot" by Mrs. John Steele, a lecture on home economics and sanitation, and more.

This issue of the newsletter welcomed Dr. Charles Manchester to the college faculty. Dr. Manchester was a minister of the gospel and had filled pulpits at various times in his life, the last pastorate being in the Fort Wayne Church of God. It continued, "But the greater need of a struggling church or a struggling college prevented him from keeping a pastorate very long. His field is larger. At Winona College, Dr. Manchester will occupy the chair of history and will assist in other departments."

By the time this article is read, the publication stated, "Dr. and Mrs. Manchester will have become settled in their home, *The Wallace.* Two daughters, Miss Pansy and Miss Lois, are engaged as teachers in the college and high school work."

The First World War pretty much marked the end of Winona's schools. Summer courses had been maintained by Winona College for some time in the areas of agriculture, manual training, music, drawing, and primary methods in education. Dr. William Biederwolf had become president of the college in 1917, and E. O. Excell was chairman of the board of regents. First winter sessions were abandoned and then, two years later, in 1918, the entire operation was closed.

The Westminster became a hotel and the Mount Memorial building, after several unsuccessful attempts to start other schools, eventually became home to the Winona Lake School of Theology until it was sold to the Free Methodist Church to use as a publishing house.

WINONA BIBLE SCHOOL

In addition to its schools in Winona Lake, the Assembly also launched a Winona Bible School in New York City in 1905. The school appeared to be a cross between a Bible institute and a Bible college. Like the Technical School, however, the Bible School failed shortly after its founding and soon disappeared from Winona's literature.

Sidwell's analysis is that the schools were a headache for Winona's directors. Although they were intended by Dickey and others to be distinctively Christian, students did not always cooperate. Billy Sunday used to recall an incident in which the Winona park's watchman found two students so intoxicated that they could not find their way back to the school.

The Assembly also found the schools to be a financial drain on the organization. Many scholarships and loans were made to students to finance their tuition, and then the loans were not paid back.

For many years alumni of all the Winona schools had a reunion at Winona Lake each summer. A summary booklet containing updates on alumni was published each year. The 1939 booklet contained this summary:

> It is 37 years—1902—since the Winona Agricultural Institute opened. 33 years since the Academy and Aggie became separate schools, 31 years since the College opened. One by one the work of the schools merged with the College till we had only the College and Aggies. An unfortunate change of administration in 1917 closed W. C. A., and in the following winter, the College. The demand for summer work at Winona was so insistent that the summer school was reopened, and for some years ran as an extension division of Indiana U. The State dropped Winona after taking over Ball Teachers College, and the schools have never been reopened. In 1926 the five winter schools planned a week of reunion, each school taking a day. In 1929 it was voted to have ALL the schools come together for a weekend, and our first printed report went out that year, and has been an annual event.

CHAPTER 5

The Town Incorporates:
The Great Fire of 1914

"Fire is the best of servants; but what a master!"
Thomas Carlyle

THE TOWN OF WINONA LAKE WAS INCORPORATED JUNE 2, 1913. THE primary purpose for incorporating was to furnish adequate protection against fire for the buildings of the Assembly grounds and those of the immediate vicinity and also to effect an organization through which public improvements could be facilitated.

The town board minutes from October 20, 1913, indicate, "Moved by W. E. Lugenbeel, seconded by E. Johnston and motion carried, that the clerk be instructed to write Prof. R. L. Sackett of Purdue University as to his willingness to give the sewer system of Winona Lake a thorough investigation to ascertain the probable cost of putting in a new sewer system or remodeling the present system, also as to the expense of his services for so doing."

The sewer system was eventually installed but, as will be seen later, the debt load incurred by the improvements and infrastructure seriously threatened the financial solvency of Winona Lake in the early 1900s.

The town covered 200 acres, with the town limits beginning at the entrance to the Chautauqua grounds on the north and west, including the territory between Kings Highway and the lake and extending as far south as the Kosciusko Lodge, just south of Cherry Creek. The corporation site was divided into three wards. The population of Winona Lake at that time ranged from 600 in the winter months to 10,000 during the height of the Chautauqua activities in the summer. The water supply and electric lights enjoyed by the community were furnished by the Winona Electric Light and Water Company. Little did the founders realize how inadequate the fire protection would be when a disastrous fire hit the following year.

The president of the board of trustees at the time of the incorporation was George P. DeHoff (1913-16) and the clerk-treasurer was William G. Fluegel (1913-18).[15]

Winona's first major fire was the loss of the Strain Hall dormitory in 1913. This structure, located at the corner of Kings Highway and Seventh Street, had been built at a cost of $12,000 and it housed 24 boys with rooms for the matron and family. During the summer it had been used as a music hall. It was never rebuilt.

The town's most catastrophic fire occurred in April of 1914 when a leaf fire spread to a row of cottages on Chestnut Street.

Conflicting dates are given for the Great Fire of 1914. Gaddis and Huffman say the fire began at about 11 a.m. on April 18. A *New York Times* article (April 19, 1914) says that on April 16 fire completely destroyed 23 cottages at Lake Winona. According to a web-based history of the Winona Lake Fire Department, on April 11, 1914, at approximately 11 a.m., several men were burning leaves below the Chestnut Street Hill, south of the Winona Hotel. A sudden gust of wind carried flames and sparks from the leaves to cottages lining Chestnut Street. Within minutes, several of the cottages were burning.

Bill Collison, who was in the park, ran to ring the fire bell, which was mounted on a platform near the grocery store. The alarm brought every volunteer available. Al Cuffel, caretaker of the Winona Hotel, stationed himself on the roof with wet gunny sacks to beat out flying sparks.

People hurried to the scene of the fire. Two men, Philip Laurien and Victor Hatfield, brought from a barn located at the corner of 10th and College the town's only firefighting equipment—a hose reel on wheels. The hose reel was dragged to the scene, but by the time the men arrived, the fire was too advanced to stop. The water pres-

---

[15] Lemuel Royse's *History of Kosciusko County*

sure from the contraption was not strong enough to keep the fire from advancing to more cottages.

Men of the Warsaw fire department responded quickly to a call for help and worked desperately and heroically. Bucket brigades were formed to douse the sparks and embers which showered the roofs of the closely-packed cottages. Townspeople worked frantically to save whatever could be carried from the threatened buildings.

One elderly woman, Mrs. Nancy Snepp, was carrying a pile of clothing and was severely burned as she was almost trapped inside a burning house. Several firefighters were overcome by the gasses and smoke and two of the men suffered heart attacks.

With winds increasing and flames intensifying, all efforts were placed on saving the Winona Hotel. Marvin F. Howe, the Pennsylvania Railroad tower man, remained at his post even as he watched his home burn to the ground. Howe wired Fort Wayne for help. A special Pennsylvania Railroad company train carrying a complete fire company of 13 men arrived from Fort Wayne with pumping equipment in about 40 minutes.

While they waited for help to arrive, volunteers from Winona Lake, with the consent of the owners, dynamited several cottages in hopes of keeping the fire from spreading to the Winona Hotel. Two cottages were blown up, one being a small frame structure on the site of the Ball Home at Fourth and Chestnut Streets.

Historian Daniel Coplen noted that a cottage named *The Bennett,* which was one of the buildings blown up to stop the fire's advance, had been purchased only a few days earlier by evangelist O. A. Newlin, who at that very hour was in his attorney's office waiting to hand over the check that would pay for it. Coplen said, "He would spend $9,000 for what would soon be a pile of rubbish." The explosions which blew up the cottages shattered the windows of nearby homes. Among these was *Felsenheim,* aptly named "The Stone House" at the corner of Fourth and Chestnut, which later served as a Brethren missionary residence.

It was the home of the Fluegel family and had been constructed of cement blocks and was roofed with asbestos shingles. Although window frames and other wooden parts were charred badly, the house stood like a fortress when all the homes about it were burning. Later, a roofing company showed movies of the Fluegel home calling it "The House that Stopped the Fire."

When the special pumping equipment from Fort Wayne arrived on the train, hoses were strung from the lake to the Winona Hotel. A steam engine, carried on a flatcar, was moved to the pier, pumping water from the lake up to the area of the fire.

The hotel was saved, and several hours after firefighting efforts started, the blaze was under control. In the end, the losses in the town totaled more than $100,000 and 23 houses and cottages were destroyed by the fire. Four city blocks had been reduced to smoldering ash. Farmers living a mile east of the town had to beat out firebrands that landed on their barns and other buildings.

Some embers from the fire, still glowing, were carried as far as Barbee lakes.

Seeking to quiet the fears of constituents who may have heard of the fire, the summer program booklet for 1914 noted:

On Saturday, April 18, fire destroyed 23 houses at Winona. They were located near the Winona Hotel, and ten of them were winter homes. Seventy five per cent of the loss was recovered from the insurance companies, and rebuilding has already begun.

The new structures will not be crowded together as closely as before, and the general appearance of the entrance grounds will be very much improved. None of the Assembly property was injured, and the unfortunate event of the fire, although causing discomfort and loss to a few individuals, will not in any measure retard the progress of the season's activities. The municipal council has provided ample equipment for the protection of the buildings within the park, and the recurrence of a similar catastrophe, it is hoped, will not be possible.

A Fire Department is Organized

Winona had learned its lesson. The Great Fire prompted officials to organize the Winona Lake Volunteer Fire Department with Chaucy Eddington as chief. A horse-drawn wagon was purchased, and later a motor truck was purchased. The town's first fire station was erected south of the Winona Hotel on Park Avenue.

According to a newspaper article entitled "History of Fire Fighting in Warsaw and Winona Lake," published in October of 1950 and written by Vincent H. Gaddis, fire fighting in Winona Lake began back in 1905 under the direction of Tom Ross. There was no organized department. Whenever a fire broke out, every able-bodied man near the scene was expected to assist in extinguishing the blaze. The equipment consisted of two hand-drawn Ross carts and later a soda acid tank on wheels.

Other major fires at Winona include the partial loss of the Winona Hotel in 1925 and the destruction of the center wing of The Inn during the early 1930s.

A fire the afternoon of May 9, 1925, destroyed the east wing of the Winona Hotel, which at that point was owned by three men: Homer Rodeheaver, Lincoln Dickey of Cleveland, Ohio; and O. B. Stephenson of Chicago. Between one-third and one-half of the building was destroyed, with losses estimated at $15,000-$20,000. As many as 2,000 people showed up to watch firemen battle the blaze, which was fought with water pumped from Winona Lake.

The fire started in a chimney and was first noticed by some children playing nearby. The fire occurred only a few days before a convention of the Church of the Brethren, expected to attract as many as 10,000 people, many of whom planned to stay or eat at the hotel. In spite of the fire, the Brethren convention went off as planned.

The Inn, which had been first occupied in 1897, met its final end by an intentional fire on August 21, 1971. At 7:15 a.m. that day, firemen set fire to the building which had been a famous landmark in Winona Lake for nearly 60 years. It was built on grounds that used to house horse barns in the 1880s for the race track on the island. About 150 persons watched the early-morning blaze as firemen from Winona Lake and Warsaw kept the flames under control. Owners of the building, the Winona Christian Assembly, decided to have the building burned to make space for a parking lot.

A month after the Great Fire, on May 19, 1914, Winona Lake received its first fire engine. Purchased from the Howe Engine Co.

of Indianapolis, the gas-powered engine could pump water from the lake or from a fire hydrant. Equipped with 1,000 feet of hose, the pumper could throw a stream of water 138 feet high. The engine could be pulled by hand, by a team of horses, or by an automobile. It cost $2,100.

Over the years firefighting equipment was added and sophistication was gained with the addition of firefighting and lifesaving equipment. By the 1950s, the town had a Seagrave pumper truck and a Bean high-pressure fog truck, which was purchased in 1947 by popular subscription. In 1985, the town of Winona Lake paid for the shell and insulation of the building that now houses the fire trucks at the current fire station on the corner of Kings Highway and Rupe Drive. Members of the all-volunteer fire department then built the offices, kitchen, restrooms, and meeting room, including plumbing and electrical work that occupy about half of the building. After "living in the building" for a while, the department added an additional garage and sleeping quarters that are attached to the garage.

Today 32 members of the Winona Lake Volunteer Fire Department man two engines, one tanker, one quint, and two utility vehicles. The department provides other services including medical first responders, hazmat operations, and vehicle extrication. Typically, members of the department respond to more than 300 calls for service in a year.

CHAPTER 6

"The Glory Years" – (1895-1920)

". . . a kind of religious Chautauqua."
Dr. Solomon Dickey

IN 1895, SOLOMON DICKEY TRAVELED TO NORTHWESTERN NEW YORK
state in order to consult with Bishop John Heyl Vincent, a co-founder
of the nationally famous Chautauqua Institute. In 1874, Dr. Vincent
had joined with Akron, Ohio, businessman-inventor Lewis Miller
(Thomas Edison's father-in-law) to train Sunday school teachers of all
Protestant denominations in an attractive place during the summer.

Within a few years, however, the Chautauqua idea was extended
to include lectures, discussions, musical and theatrical performances,
and home readings. A large number of educational programs such as
the adult summer school, correspondence courses, and "great books"
discussion groups have their roots in Chautauqua.

The original Chautauqua Lake Sunday School Assembly had
been founded as an educational experiment in out-of-school, vacation learning. Immediately successful, it was soon broadened beyond
courses for Sunday school teachers to include academic subjects, music, art, and physical education.

The Chautauqua idea was explained by Dr. Vincent and Mr.
Miller:

> The whole of life is a school, with educating influences all
> the while at work. These agencies and influences should be
> wisely and continuously applied by and on behalf of each

individual. Intellectual activity must be continuous in order to promote intellectual health and efficiency.

Chautauqua provides a school for people out of school, who can no longer attend school, a college for one's home, and leads to the dedication of everyday life to educational purposes. The work is so carefully planned that by doing a little every day and following the provided weekly outline, the reader makes his odd moment tell to the best advantage.

Reading, reading, reading, page after page, chapter after chapter, book after book, one may gradually become absorbed in elevating themes, gain knowledge and power, brighten life, strengthen character, broaden one's work, and come into fellow kinship with noble souls.

Thus the reader improves the conversation at the fireside, sets a good example to the children and neighbors, trains the will power, and keeps the soul from deteriorating under the worry and hurry of this "busy age."

Solomon Dickey decided to pattern his "Winona Movement" after the successful formulas used at two already-established organizations—the Chautauqua Institution (New York) and Northfield Bible Conference (Massachusetts).

The Winona Movement would be educational, entertaining, and deeply spiritual. It would be more than a camp meeting but not quite Coney Island. Dr. Dickey's Winona was to be "a resort that will serve the needs of the whole man, aiding him physically, socially, mentally, and spiritually.

The great evangelist Dwight L. Moody had begun, in 1880, issuing an annual invitation for Christians to join him at Northfield:

Dear Friends and Fellow-Workers:

A General Conference of Christian Workers will be held at Northfield, August 1st to 20th, and all of God's people who are interested in the study of His Word, in the development of their own Christian lives, in a revival of the spiritual life of the Church, in the conversion of sinners, and in the evangelization of the world, are cordially invited to be present.

We are to have with us some of the most widely-known teachers of this country and England—men on whose labors God has already set his seal. There will be the great help that comes from close contact with hundreds of earnest men and women almost all of them engaged in some form of Christian work. The accommodations for boarding are ample and pleasant, and the expense moderate. I shall be glad to hear from all who are planning to come. May I not ask Christian people to begin now to pray for a special outpouring of the Spirit upon every meeting of the Conference?

Yours in the Master's Service,
D. L. Moody

Thousands annually accepted D. L. Moody's call to attend the Northfield conferences, including Dr. Dickey. Following his visit, Dickey resolved that Winona would be established on four cornerstones— the Fatherhood of God, the Deity of Jesus Christ, the Personality of the Holy Spirit, and the Divine Inspiration of the Bible. Also, as advised by Mr. Moody, all controversy in theological questions was excluded.

The name "Chautauqua" signified a location—the famous educational resort located on the shore of Lake Chautauqua in western New York. But it also stood for a national movement for self-improvement in "all things of life—art, science, society, religious, patriotism, and refinement." At Winona, Chautauqua described the outstanding secular programs of lectures, recitals, and plays, which were presented from 1896 until nearly 1940. Many leading personalities headlined the programming at Winona:

GLENN H. CURTISS (1878–1930), noted aviator, was a regular visitor and platform guest.

ADMIRAL RICHARD E. BYRD, JR. (1888–1957), the famed polar explorer, was the featured speaker on July 4, 1931. Local news media reported that, while in the area, Byrd took time to visit a girl in Warsaw who was one of his biggest fans.

WILLIAM JENNINGS BRYAN (1860-1925), a noted orator and statesman, was actively involved in Winona, including serving as its board president. Bryan spoke at Winona on numerous occasions and regularly vacationed in Dr. Dickey's Killarney Castle on the tip of McDonald Island. Bryan was best known for being a three-time Democratic Party presidential candidate, for delivering his "Cross of Gold" address, for resigning as Woodrow Wilson's Secretary of State to protest America's entrance into World War I, and for prosecuting the "Scopes Monkey Trial" in Dayton, Tennessee, in July of 1925.

JAMES HEATON (1879-1981) became affectionately known as "Mr. Chautauqua." A native of England who came to Indiana with his family when he was 10, Heaton was music director for several evangelists, including Biederwolf. He moved to Winona in 1908 and during summer seasons he operated the gatehouse to the park. He managed the platform programs from 1913 to 1938 and served on stage as Master of Ceremonies. He was a very capable singer and song leader.

HELEN KELLER (1880-1968). Although physically handicapped (deaf, blind, and mute), this author and lecturer inspired millions with her life of achievement. She spoke at Winona in 1915.

MRS. GEORGE PICKETT (1848-1931), widow of the Confederate general who led Pickett's Charge during the Battle of Gettysburg in 1863, participated in honoring Union veterans of the Civil War in a program at Winona in August of 1910. She was introduced by a Civil War veteran, Dr. Scott, who lived in Winona.

PAUL LAURENCE DUNBAR (1872-1906), one of America's best-known black poets. He read from his poetry at Winona in 1896 and 1897.

BOOKER T. WASHINGTON (1856-1915), black educator and social reformer. Washington spoke at Winona in 1897 on the topic, "The Negroe and Industrialization."

WILL ROGERS (1879-1935), America's best-loved humorist, newspaper columnist, and social observer, spoke at Winona in 1928 after relaxing for the day with Homer Rodeheaver at Rainbow Point, Rodeheaver's home. Shortly thereafter he wrote a newspaper column entitled "You Can Hear a Holy Trombone at Winona."

SGT. ALVIN YORK (1887-1964), America's most decorated and popular hero of World War I. A dedicated Christian, York spoke at Winona in 1943 on the topic, "Keeping the Bible in Education."

LOUISE HOMER (1871-1947) was an American operatic contralto who had an active international career in concert halls and opera houses from 1895 until her retirement in 1932. She sang with the Metropolitan Opera from 1900 to 1919 and again from 1927 to 1929. Composer Samuel Barber was her nephew.

AMELITA GALLI-CURCI (1882-1963) was an Italian operatic soprano. She was one of the best-known coloratura singers of the early 20th century and her gramophone records sold in large numbers.

MISCHA ELMAN (1891-1967), Russian violinist, famed for his passionate style and beautiful tone.

JOHN PHILIP SOUSA (1854-1932) was known as the "March King" because of his many outstanding musical compositions, including *The Stars and Stripes Forever.*

REV. RUSSELL CONWELL (1843-1925), popular lecturer best known for "Acres of Diamonds," a speech he delivered more than 6,000 times over 55 years. Kosciusko County historian George A. Nye, in one of his volumes of county history, quotes an individual: "Russell H. Conwell gives his lecture 'Acres of Diamonds' at Winona on July 27, 1898. . . Used to wear a cape for an overcoat. Was a large man."

THOMAS R. MARSHALL (1854-1925), a native of nearby North Manchester, Indiana, was the 27th governor of Indiana and later became vice-president of the U.S. under Woodrow Wilson. He spoke at Winona frequently.

COL. HERBERT PETRIE'S WHITE HUSSARS were popular guests at Winona, playing eight out of ten years. They were a unique organization of colorfully uniformed brass musicians advertised as "an operatic and symphonic ensemble." Mr. and Mrs. Petrie made Winona their home for a number of years. Petrie also founded and hosted the Petrie Band Camp. During World War I, Major Petrie attended performances at the Penthouse Theatre in Fort Lawton,

Washington, the country's first theatre-in-the-round. When he returned to Warsaw, he remained so interested in the idea that he was determined to recreate the experience in his home town. In 1956, he founded the Wagon Wheel theater-in-the-round and Wagon Wheel restaurant. Mildred Petrie taught speech and drama in Warsaw High School until the 1960s.

JAMES WHITCOMB RILEY (1849-1916), "The "Hoosier Poet" lectured and recited his poetry at Winona on numerous occasions.

EFREM ZIMBALIST, SR. (1889-1985). The Russian-born violinist performed at Winona several summers during the 1930s.

ERNESTINE SHUMANN-HEINK (1861-1936), the most important contralto of her day, sang at the Metropolitan Opera from 1899-1932. She was a celebrated Austrian, later American, operatic contralto, noted for the power, beauty, tonal richness, flexibility, and wide range of her voice.

JANE ADDAMS (1860-1935), social worker, reformer, and humanitarian. Addams was one of numerous female lecturers at Winona. She spoke at Winona in 1897.

CAMP WINONA

Winona Lake is tied to a bit of the history of World War I through Camp Winona, a military camp that helped the war effort by training truck drivers and mechanics. The camp was active from August 1918 until the war ended in November of that year.

The camp was located in front of what is currently the Rodeheaver Auditorium and the Remnant Trust on Park Avenue in Winona Lake. Men were housed in the Winona and Westminster hotels, and in The Inn, a facility (no longer extant) in the 1000 block of Park Avenue. The Mount Memorial building was used as the company headquarters. The Marshall Home, once located in the 1100 block of Park Ave., and the Otterbein (present site of the Free Methodist Church) were used as the camp's hospitals. Warsaw's McDonald Hospital was utilized for the most seriously ill soldiers.

According to local historian William Darr, the greatest hardship that faced Camp Winona was illness. The entire nation was being ravaged by the Spanish influenza, and Camp Winona, despite attempts at quarantine, suffered 18 deaths from pneumonia and influenza.

The Armistice of November 11, 1918, was joyously celebrated in Warsaw and Winona Lake, and Camp Winona ceased to exist on Saturday, November 23, 1918. Special cars and trains of the Winona Interurban Railroad were contracted to transport 732 men and military material to Indianapolis. Camp Winona, Warsaw/Winona Lake's only military base, became a memory. No monument today marks its existence.

FINANCIAL CRISES

Winona's first major financial crisis was the bankruptcy of 1915. Sol Dickey laid the primary blame for Winona's financial troubles on the building of the interurban railway from Peru to Goshen. The increased use of automobiles, and the opposition of the legislature to all railroads, he said, made the Winona directors' investment of about $1.5 million of their own funds still insufficient to generate enough revenue to pay the interest and provide revenue.

Gaddis and Huffman portrayed the despair Dickey faced:

> Dr. Dickey, alone in his study, reviewed the years. He remembered that night of storm when Winona had been dedicated to God amidst the flash of lightning and the roll of thunder; he remembered all the early struggles, the steady growth and the outpourings of spiritual power. And from out of the past, dimly across the marching decades, he heard again the words of wise old Dwight L. Moody: "Always you must build and plan on faith, not doubt." On his knees, in humble consecration, Dr. Dickey laid his burden on the altar. And somewhere, far beyond this world of test and trial and struggle and strife, his prayer that Winona be saved was heard.[16]

Dr. Dickey and other faithful friends—chief among them Chicago song publisher E. O. Excell—banded together in sacrificial financial and personal commitment, and in 1915 reorganized under a new

---

[16] Gaddis & Huffman, p. 58

charter as The Winona Assembly and Bible Conference. Dickey noted that the directors of the Winona Assembly personally furnished about three-fourths of the funding necessary to get the operation going again. By the time Dickey died in 1920, he had seen the newly organized Assembly draw thousands of attendees and he also saw the start of the construction of the Billy Sunday Tabernacle and the founding of the Winona Lake School of Theology.

In 1922, Dr. William E. Biederwolf took over from Mel Trotter, the converted alcoholic who had directed the conference for a short time, and became the director of the Bible Conference, a position he held until his death in 1939. Biederwolf, as a teenager, had come to faith under Sol Dickey's pastorate at Dickey's church in Monticello, Indiana. An evangelist who first appeared on the Winona platform in 1902, Biederwolf had graduated from Princeton during its years of rigorous orthodox theology. In a time period when bitter doctrinal fights were raging between orthodox and liberal theologians, he guided Winona to a strongly fundamentalist position, determined that it would stand firmly for "the Old Book and the Old Faith."

Bob Jones, founder of the school that carries his name and a noted fundamentalist leader, was a Biederwolf fan. Bob Jones, Jr., noted, "He [Biederwolf] was one of the two or three evangelists whose pulpit style incorporated most of the elements of great preaching. His scholarship was broad; his use of the English language was concise, accurate, and powerful; his sympathies were deep; his heart was warm; and his doctrinal position was firm and solidly scriptural though he was not given to extremes of interpretation and rode no hobbies."[17]

A second financial crisis developed in the late 1920s when plans were approved to pave streets and improve the Winona sewer system. Because the Assembly owned so much property, its tax bill was large and it was thrown into heavy debt. Then, in the 1930s, the gate system was abolished and the loss of that revenue made Winona's financial problems more acute. At the time, the country was suffering through the Great Depression, which caused a drop in attendance that compounded the crisis.

---

[17] Jones, p. 99

Those difficulties resulted in another reorganization in 1937-38. This time, Winona became the Winona Lake Christian Assembly with R. G. LeTourneau as president, Arthur W. McKee executive manager, and J. Palmer Muntz as director of the Bible conference. W. E. Biederwolf, who had raised much of the money necessary for this latest re-invention of the Assembly, died in 1939.

Over the next several years the organization offered a reduced Chautauqua program, but in 1943 even that was discontinued. After that, the Assembly focused on Bible, missionary, and Youth for Christ conferences and eventually became primarily a conference center that rented out facilities to groups who wished to convene for one or several weeks at a time at the choice Winona location.

CHAPTER 7

Winona's Most Famous Resident – "Baseball Evangelist" Billy Sunday

"If you don't like what I have to say, don't take it up with me . . .
take it up with God!"
Rev. Billy Sunday

NESTLED IN THE PARK AND PERCHED ATOP A HILL JUST BEYOND THE
Rodeheaver Auditorium in Winona Lake is a home dedicated to per-
petuating the legacy of Winona Lake's most famous resident of the
past—the "baseball evangelist" Billy Sunday.

Who was this man? Why did he choose Winona Lake as his
home? What is the lasting legacy of his lifetime?

Billy Sunday was the Billy Graham of his day. Although his popularity peaked during the years 1908-1920, he had a 39-year career as
a platform evangelist, speaking in person to more than 100 million
people. His career included at least 548 separate revival campaigns
or speaking appearances that ranged over 40 states. Shortly before his
death, he estimated for one magazine reporter that he had delivered
nearly 20,000 sermons over his lifetime—an average of 42 per month.

A Broadway-type musical on his life dubbed him "Billy One,"
with the obvious inference that Billy Graham would be "Billy Two."
Both had deep and lasting connections with Winona Lake—it was
here that Billy Graham's early employer Youth for Christ was founded, and it was also from a prayer meeting in the Rainbow Room of
the Westminster Hotel (now Westminster Hall) that Graham's well-
known 1949 Los Angeles crusade was launched, catapulting Graham
into the nation's attention.

Graham, incidentally, remembered attending a Billy Sunday meeting when Graham was five years old. One writer recorded that in 1923, young Billy was taken to a large revival campaign held in Charlotte, North Carolina. Frank, the father, told his five-year-old son, "Be quiet, or the evangelist will call your name from the platform."

Years later, Billy Graham acknowledged, "I sat there frightened to death."[18]

The former curator of the Billy Sunday Museum and Home in Winona Lake, William Firstenberger, documented 870,075 converts to Christianity from 1896 to 1935 as a result of Billy Sunday's campaigns. Sunday averaged 7,312 converts per revival, Firstenberg reports in his book, *In Rare Form: A Pictorial History of Baseball Evangelist Billy Sunday.*

"Billy One" was a friend of the rich and famous, and many of them regularly visited him at his Winona Lake home or contributed financially to the Christian Assembly programs to which Sunday lent his name and his fame.

In 1908, according to *Kosciusko County: A Pictorial History* by Daniel Coplen, it was said "the fact that Winona was the home of baseball evangelist Billy Sunday gave it more publicity than any other thing. If people living in Warsaw would tell abroad that they lived near Winona, their listeners would perk up their ears and say, 'Why that's the home of Billy Sunday.'"

Like Graham who followed him, Sunday's main legacy was his lifetime of preaching the "old-time gospel" and calling sinners to repentance. In city after city his advance team would enter early, organize the local churches and townspeople, arrange for cavernous temporary "tabernacles" to be built, and ready the locale for a revival.

When Sunday arrived, the crowds would come. A song leader, choir, soloists, and instrumentalists would warm up the crowd with popular gospel songs of the day. For many years Winona Lake resident Homer Rodeheaver with his famous trombone performed this up-front function for Sunday. Of Billy Sunday, Rodeheaver said in

---

[18] Blue, Scott A. "Prime-Time Religion: The Life and Evangelistic Methodology of William Ashley Sunday." *Journal of Evangelism and Missions,* Spring, 2002, p. 77

his book *Twenty Years with Billy Sunday,* "He was one of our greatest evangelistic thinkers—a brilliant man."

At the appropriate time, Sunday would come onstage and deliver an athletic, blistering message punctuated with slang, props, and enthusiasm. Often he would speak to segmented audiences—his "women-only" meetings were famous. Frequently he would rail against the evils of alcoholism—Sunday was a strong proponent of Prohibition.

But always there was a call for people to leave their lives of sin, to devote themselves to God, and to "hit the sawdust trail." This meant making a public confession of faith by coming to the front of the meeting—walking down sawdust-covered aisles to have prayer with the evangelist and be given follow-up literature on how to live the Christian life.

HITTING THE SAWDUST TRAIL

Mrs. Sunday one time detailed the origin of the phrase "hit the sawdust trail." She and Billy were in Bellingham, Washington, for meetings and were invited to go see some of the dense, virgin timber forest of the region. "You couldn't see the sky when you got inside under those trees, they were so close together," she explained. "If you didn't have a guide, you would get lost, because every side looked just alike."

The men whose job it was to go into the forest and scale the timber—find out how many feet of lumber could be cut from a certain area—would carry great sacks of sawdust with ropes around them which they threw over their head and left shoulder. As they would pass from one spot to another, they would reach into the sacks and take a big handful of sawdust, swishing it along ahead of them. They continued, making a sawdust trail from where they entered the forest to where they would stop at night.

When their work was completed, they would say, "Well, I'm ready to go home. I'll be all right if I can just hit that sawdust trail." So they would look around, find it, and follow the sawdust trail until they got out of the forest and back home to safety. The sawdust trail, Ma Sunday explained, represented coming from what would have been a lost condition to a saved condition—from a dark, uninteresting and unsatisfactory place to back home, to light, and comfort with friends and family.

One tabernacle building in which Sunday spoke was a temporary building and had a sawdust floor to help dampen sound. A newspaper the next morning ran a headline saying that a certain number of people hit the sawdust trail in the Billy Sunday Tabernacle the night before.

"That was the first time we had ever heard it used in connection with people accepting the Lord Jesus as their Savior," recalled Mrs. Sunday, but the newspapers picked up the phrase and ever after the symbol of conversion was "hitting the sawdust trail."

Sunday's preaching style won him an enormous amount of newspaper and media coverage. One archivist who helped catalogue his papers and memorabilia noted, "He used colorful and slangy language and entertained and instructed his audiences with mimicry, impersonations, as well as memorable epigrams and anecdotes. His messages laid great stress on every human being's need for personal salvation through Jesus Christ and on the authority and reliability of the Bible. He was also a strong critic of alcoholic beverages and favored their prohibition in his most famous sermon, *Get on the Water Wagon.*"

Robert F. Martin, author of *Hero of the Heartland: Billy Sunday and the Transformation of American Society, 1862-1935,* said Sunday was "one of the most acrobatic evangelists of the age." One newspaper columnist estimated that Sunday traveled about a mile during each sermon—this physicality was likely an outgrowth of Sunday's earlier career as a professional baseball player.

NEVER KNEW HIS FATHER

William Ashley Sunday, an Iowa farm boy who had spent part of his childhood in an orphanage, was an unlikely candidate to become friends with the rich and powerful, and to have such an impact on his world.

Born November 19, 1862, near Ames, Iowa, Sunday never knew his father, who enlisted in the Iowa Infantry Volunteers four months before Sunday was born. The father died a month after Sunday's birth of an unknown disease contracted in Missouri while on duty, leaving Sunday's mother a widow with three sons.

The provider on the family farm was Sunday's grandfather, Squire, whom Billy admired for his versatility and mechanical skills. Billy's grandmother made his clothes, and later in life Billy said, "they were ill-fitting affairs but they were warm. You couldn't tell from looking at my pants whether I was coming or going."

Through circumstances that are not entirely clear, but likely due to internal tensions in the family and difficulties on the farm, Sunday and his older brother were sent to live at the Soldier's Orphanage in Glenwood, Iowa, when Billy was 13. After several years there, he obtained work as a stable boy, tending ponies for a man in Nevada, Iowa, who gave Sunday a home and the opportunity to attend school.

There Sunday began to emerge as an excellent athlete. As a teenager, he beat all runners at a Fourth of July race, including the adults. He began to play baseball, and was known for his tremendous speed stealing bases and catching fly balls.

Future Baseball Hall-of-Famer Adrian "Cap" Anson, player/manager of the Chicago White Stockings (now the Chicago Cubs), saw Sunday play in Marshalltown, Iowa, and gave him a tryout for the Chicago team. In a race with the team's fastest player, Sunday won by 15 feet.

"Winning that race opened the hearts of the players to me," Sunday said years later. "I will always be thankful to Cap for giving me that chance to show off to the best advantage."

Sunday was signed, and became a member of the Chicago White Stockings, the premier team of the league, in 1883. That began a major-league career that would last for eight years with three different teams (Chicago, Pittsburgh, and Philadelphia).

Sunday was usually the lead-off batter, because of his speed. Never a strong hitter, he had a lifetime batting average of .248, and he is reputed to have struck out his first 13 times at bat. But his speed would unnerve infielders, who would frequently overthrow the first basemen in their haste. Sunday was the first player ever to circle the bases in fewer than 14 seconds. There are conflicting reports on his statistics, but it was often reported that in one year he stole 94 bases, a record later beaten by the legendary Ty Cobb, who stole 96.

Often noted was a race in August of 1885 that pitted Sunday against the famed Arlie Latham, champion sprinter of the Saint Louis Browns. In a hundred-yard dash, Billy bested the speedster by a full ten feet.

It was about this time that Sunday began to exhibit signs of dissatisfaction with the direction his life was going. Professional athletes then—as now—were known to be a "rough crowd" whose lives on the road were not marked by high moral tone and fidelity.

A Life-Altering Conversion

The official date of Sunday's conversion to Christianity has been lost to history (he could not recall the exact date himself), but clearly an experience with the Pacific Garden Mission in Chicago about 1886 or 1887 altered his life forever.

He is reported to have been standing on a corner in Chicago with some of his teammates after a night of drinking, when a gospel wagon from the mission came by. Musicians sang hymns Sunday had heard his mother sing when he was a boy, and when the music stopped an ex-con named Harry Monroe spoke about lives that had been changed at the mission. Sunday, touched by this experience, turned to his friends saying, "Boys, I'm bidding the old life goodbye."

He began attending services at the mission regularly, and after one of these services he committed his life to Jesus Christ and was "born again." Later in life he recalled, "I will never pass that spot without stopping, taking off my hat, and thanking God for saving and keeping me."

On September 5, 1888, Sunday married Helen "Nell" Thompson, the daughter of a well-known Chicago Presbyterian businessman. The wedding took place in the Thompson family home in Chicago. That afternoon they took the train to Pittsburgh, Pennsylvania, where Billy played ball on September 6. Billy and Nell lived for 22 years in the Chicago brownstone at 64 Throop Street, directly adjacent to the site of their wedding.

After five full seasons with the White Stockings, Sunday was traded to the Pittsburgh Alleghenies (later renamed the Pittsburgh Pirates), where he played two and a half years before moving to the Philadelphia Phillies in a midseason trade in 1890.

Almost immediately after his conversion, Sunday changed his behavior patterns off the field and began spending free time at Chicago's YMCA in a Bible study class. With his fame as a player rising, Sunday was often asked to speak in churches and at YMCAs. He played baseball for another four years after his conversion, but apparently was no longer living the lifestyle of the typical professional ballplayer.

Just as his dollar-value as a player was peaking, Sunday decided to leave the game and serve God full-time. Both Philadelphia and Cincinnati offered him lucrative contracts for the 1891 season, but instead of "going for the gold," Sunday instead took a full-time position with the YMCA at $83.33 a month, a fraction of what he would have earned in baseball.

For the next two-and-a-half years, working for the YMCA in Chicago, Sunday visited the homes of the poor, learned firsthand how alcohol could destroy a life, and became convinced that salvation through Jesus Christ was the only answer for personal and societal peace.

ADVANCE MAN FOR J. WILBUR CHAPMAN

In 1894 the well-known evangelist J. Wilbur Chapman offered Sunday a position as advance man for Chapman's revival circuit, making him responsible to travel ahead of Chapman, setting up all details of the meetings to come. Chapman had first heard of Winona while conducting evangelistic meetings in Indianapolis in 1894, and his "camp meeting" at Winona the following year marked the beginning of his association with Winona Lake.

Working for Chapman, author William Firstenberger says, gave Sunday a "hands-on course in how to run evangelistic campaigns." During his two years with Chapman, Sunday learned much about preaching, crusade organization, stylistic flair necessary to keep an audience's attention, and much more. Chapman also was Sunday's link with Winona Lake, although Sunday had known of Winona Lake because his maternal grandparents met and married in Kosciusko County in the early 1800s.

Chapman was one of the early founders of Winona Lake as a center for religious conferences and Chautauqua performances in the mid-1890s, and also served for a time as the director of the Winona Lake Bible Conference. He encouraged Sunday to bring his young family to Winona Lake and to participate in the lecture series.

Sunday was suddenly unemployed in December of 1895 when Chapman decided to return to a pastoral position in Philadelphia. But only days after learning of his unemployment, Sunday received a telegram from three preachers in Garner, Iowa, who asked him to lead a week-long revival there. He accepted, had 268 converts to Christianity in eight days, and his new career as a traveling evangelist was launched.

Sunday's popular style and flair for showmanship grew his reputation quickly, and soon he branched out from the Midwest to hold campaigns for tens of thousands of people in cities such as Philadelphia, Baltimore, and New York. Soon tents, churches, and opera houses were unable to hold the crowds he drew, and so citizens of host cities would gather money and build large wooden tabernacles to house his meetings. The largest of these held up to 20,000 people, and after the evangelist left town, the structure would be torn down and the wood sold to pay for expenses of the meeting.

With no amplification systems available, the tabernacle platforms were constructed with a voice-projection device described by one writer as " a huge upside-down sugar scoop" along with baffles in the ceiling built to project the sound. The floors were covered with sawdust to deaden the sound of people walking on a wooden floor, and so those who "walked the sawdust trail" to find salvation were popularly referred to as "trailhitters."

And the trailhitters came in throngs. In Youngstown, Ohio, 80,000 people came forward to be saved. In Columbus, Ohio, there were 181,000; in Philadelphia 42,000; in Boston 64,000; and in New York 95,000. Even by today's standards, the numbers are staggering. Perhaps Sunday's peak was the 1917 spring campaign in New

York City in which the evangelist preached to more than 1.5 million people during a four-month period.

A New York newspaper reporter wrote, "Sunday was in excellent condition yesterday, and in the best of spirits. Clad in a two-piece sack suit, with a pleated white silk shirt, a bow tie, and low shoes of patent leather. He raced up and down the green-carpeted platform during his sermons, waving his hands, kicking up one knee now and again like a walking horse, brandishing a chair, standing with one foot on the chair and another on the pulpit, bending over backward like a springy sword blade, bobbing back and forth and waving a handkerchief between his legs as he reeled off one of his amazing long lists of vituperative epithets."

A typical outburst was Sunday's description of the Apostle Paul, "Paul, that stoop-shouldered, dim-eyed, wrinkle-browed, white-haired gospel veteran was full of the Holy Spirit; he was on the firing line for years and never dipped his colors. He knew that a man must be a child of God."

Among Sunday's close circle of friends and supporters were a "Who's Who" of the day's industrial and retailing barons. They included John D. Rockefeller, Jr., Alexander McDonald, John Studebaker, H. J. Heinz, Henry Leland, S. S. Kresge, and John Wanamaker.

Sunday was active in the presidential campaigns of Herbert Hoover and other politicians and was especially effective in leading to the Prohibition era in the U.S. He was credited by many as being influential in the adoption of Prohibition in 1919, and he strongly continued to support its reintroduction after its repeal in 1933. His fame peaked during World War I, and he strongly supported the war effort, urging young men to enlist and encouraging all Americans to buy war bonds and to conserve food and fuel.

Sunday's letters, which are catalogued and archived in the Morgan Library on the Grace College and Seminary campus in Winona Lake, contain personal letters from an amazing array of people including Connie Mack, Theodore Roosevelt, Frank Kellogg, William Jennings Bryan, Calvin Coolidge, William Mayo, Bob Jones, Sr., J. C. Penney, Cecil B. DeMille, and many more.

THE WINONA LAKE COTTAGE

Though they had lived and raised their family in Chicago, the Sundays had come to Winona Lake for more than 15 years during the summers, and even bought a cottage at Winona in 1900. Billy Sunday annually spoke at the Winona Bible Conference and helped direct the series, and felt that the relaxed atmosphere of Winona enabled him to be "free to be an average citizen, dress down in old clothes, and do yard work."

The Sunday's first cottage, named *Illinois,* was not large enough nor properly fitted to be a year-round home, so they moved it to an adjacent lot, sold it, and built a new 2,500-square-foot Arts and Crafts-style bungalow in its place at 1111 Sunday Lane.

Commanding a prime location on the bluff overlooking the park and lake, and located just 500 feet from the Winona Auditorium (now replaced by the Rodeheaver Auditorium), the new home was built in 1911. It was named *Mount Hood,* presumably a reference to the Hood River valley region of Oregon where the Sundays also owned a rustic retreat cabin and fruit orchard farm.

A thorough description of the home and its contents is included in Firstenberger's book, and the home is now open to tours, staffed by trained docents who give interpretive talks on the Sundays and their life in Winona Lake.

For all his social and spiritual impact, Sunday experienced great disappointment in the lives of his children. Helen Sunday, the oldest of the Sunday children and their only daughter, lived continuously in fragile health and had a disease that likely was multiple sclerosis. She died in October of 1932 and is buried in Sturgis, Michigan, in the family plot of her husband, newspaper publisher Mark Haines.

George M. Sunday, the eldest son, later worked for his father as a secretary, but eventually was caught in many of the vices against which his father preached. He died in California in 1933 of complications from a fall off the balcony of a high-rise apartment. His death was never identified as murder, accident, or suicide. His ex-wife Harriet, whom he divorced in 1930, was a Unity minister with her own church in Burbank, California. She died of a heart attack at her resort cabin in Lake Arrowhead, California, in early July, 1960, at the age of 68.

William Ashley Sunday, Jr., briefly played piano for the Sunday revival team, but eventually also followed a trail of destructive habits and failed marriages and died in 1938 in a driving accident near Palm Springs, California.

Paul Thompson Sunday, who graduated from Warsaw (Indiana) High School in 1925, was the only Sunday child to attend public high school (the others graduated from private schools). Also known for a wild life full of high-risk activities, Paul Sunday was one of four who died in a military plane crash in 1944 at age 36 while serving as a test pilot for the Lockheed Aircraft Corporation.

Billy Sunday's mother, Mary Jane "Jennie" Corey, was born in Syracuse, Indiana, in 1841. Her family moved to Iowa when she was seven years old. She died while living with Sunday and his wife, Nell, in Winona Lake in 1913.

Billy Sunday himself died of a heart attack at his brother-in-law's home in Chicago on November 6, 1935, just two weeks short of his seventy-third birthday. Only ten days previously, he had delivered his final sermon to a packed church in Mishawaka, Indiana, where 41 people responded to his last altar call for salvation. His wife, Nell, was 67 at the time of his death.

Helen "Ma" Sunday, who had been so instrumental as a financial manager and organizer for her husband's campaigns, continued heavy involvement in civic, religious, and Winona Lake affairs. After Billy's death she traveled extensively, speaking frequently, helping raise money for rescue missions and other Christian causes. She was active in the work of Bob Jones University, Youth for Christ, and the Voice of the Andes radio station. In the early '50s she spoke at some of Billy Graham's crusades. In the booklet *Remarkable 'Ma' Sunday* by Opal Cording Overmyer, a friend of Mrs. Sunday described her, saying, "she hopped around the country like a human flea."

Ma Sunday had a heart attack in 1948, but lived another nine years, dying on February 20, 1957. She was buried alongside Billy and their three boys in the southeast section of Forest Home Cemetery on the outskirts of Chicago. One biographer noted that she had outlived everyone in the Mount Hood household.

When she died, the local newspaper recorded that, according to an inventory filed by Mrs. Daisy Lou Baum of Winona Lake, executrix of the estate, real estate, books, papers, and mementos of the Sundays, located in Winona Lake, had been willed to the Winona Christian Assembly, with the home to be made into a Billy Sunday memorial.

For most of his life, Billy Sunday had vocal critics as well as defenders. Some church leaders thought him too simplistic in his theology. Secular journalists accused him of being a tool used by the ruling elite to defuse lower class discontent.

Sunday's popularity waned in his latter years, and he was even the subject of derision. Some felt Sinclair Lewis' scathing 1927 satire, *Elmer Gantry*, was a thinly-disguised poke at the baseball evangelist. Sunday himself vehemently denounced the book's intentions. Frank Sinatra, in a song written by Fred Fisher, sang about "Chicago, Chicago, the town that Billy Sunday couldn't shut down."

For a time, there was a Billy Sunday Visitors Center on Park Avenue in Winona Lake which chronicled the life of Sunday through displays, exhibits, and memorabilia. The Visitors Center was constructed to resemble the original 7,500-seat Billy Sunday Tabernacle built in 1920 where countless evangelistic revivals, services, and events were held until its demolition in 1992.

The site of the tabernacle is now "Tabernacle Field," and it became for a time the home of the Winona Blue Laws vintage base ball team. In 2010 the Sunday memorabilia were moved to the Reneker Museum of Winona History in Westminster Hall, and the former Billy Sunday Visitors Center was re-fitted to house the Remnant Trust collection of valuable documents.

TITLES OF WELL-KNOWN SUNDAY SERMONS

"Booze"
"Chickens Come Home to Roost"
"Devil's Boomerang, or Hot Cakes Off the Griddle"
"Fighting Saints"
"Here We Are Midst Plenty"

"If Christ Came to New York"
"Reasonableness of Christianity"
"Secret of Failure"
"Timid Women"
"What Must I Do to be Saved?"
"Why Some Men Fail in Ministry"
"Women Possess Keen Intuitive Sense"

BILLY SUNDAY QUOTES

"The web of this nation is made from the thread spun in the home."

"When you finally reach home plate, the Great Umpire will call you either 'Safe' or 'Out.' Which will it be, boys?"

"I know about as much theology as a jack rabbit."

"At Kansas City, Kansas, before the saloons were closed, they were getting ready to build an addition to the jail. Now the doors swing idly on the hinges and there is nobody to lock in the jails"

"Christianity means a lot more than church membership."

"I challenge you to show me where the saloon has ever helped business, education, church, morals, or anything we hold dear."

"If you don't do your part, don't blame God."

"Jesus Christ was God's revenue officer."

"More men fail through lack of purpose than lack of talent."

"The saloon is a liar. It promises good cheer and sends sorrow."

"You might as well try and dam Niagara Falls with toothpicks as to stop the reform wave sweeping our land."

"Trying to run a church without revivals can be done—when you can run a gasoline engine on buttermilk."

"Some of the biggest lies ever told are to be found on gravestones."

THE IMPACT OF ONE MAN'S LIFE

The following sequence is often cited as an example of the impact one life can have:

- In 1855, a Sunday School teacher, Mr. Kimball, led a Boston shoe clerk to give his life to Christ. The clerk, Dwight L. Moody, became an evangelist.

- In England in 1879, Dwight L. Moody awakened evangelistic zeal in the heart of Fredrick B. Meyer, pastor of a small church.

- F. B. Meyer, preaching to an American college campus, brought to Christ a student named J. Wilbur Chapman.

- J. Wilbur Chapman, engaged in YMCA work, employed a former baseball player, Billy Sunday, to do evangelistic work.

- Billy Sunday held a revival in Charlotte, North Carolina. A group of local men were so enthusiastic afterward that they planned another evangelistic campaign, bringing Mordecai Hamm to town to preach.

- During Mordecai Hamm's revival, a young man named Billy Graham heard the Gospel and yielded his life to Christ

Only Eternity will reveal the tremendous impact of that one Sunday School teacher, Mr. Kimball, who invested his life in the lives of others.

SUNDAY FESTIVALS

In the late 1990s and early 2000s, there was a resurgence of interest in Winona Lake history in general, and Billy Sunday in particular. A part-festival, part-conference held in June of 2002, for example, appealed to both the scholarly and the fun-loving. The two-day event featured authors and researchers who have written on Billy Sunday, free tours of the Sunday home, and re-enactment performances by Billy Sunday impersonators.

On the first day, a 19th century-style base ball game was held on Tabernacle Field (former site of the Billy Sunday Tabernacle) between the Hobart Deep River Grinders and the Elkhart Bonneyville Millers, followed by a "feats of strength pentathlon" which included a base race, sawdust shoveling, water chugging, fast talking, and ice cream sundae eating.

Local thespians Kathleen Allison (as "Ma" Sunday), Steve Grill (as Billy Sunday) and Brent Wilcoxson (as Homer Rodeheaver) performed in "Down the Sawdust Trail." Authors, biographers, and filmmakers interested in Sunday gave lectures and demonstrations of their work. And three professional actors/impersonators, each with a different emphasis, gave performances to help interpret Sunday and his times.

JOHN HUFFMAN REFLECTS

The archives of the Billy Graham Center on the campus of Wheaton College in Wheaton, Illinois, contain a treasure trove of materials that relate to Winona's religious history. One particularly pertinent interview was with John A. Huffman, Sr., who followed his father, Jasper, as president of the Winona School of Theology. The interview was conducted in 1988 by Robert Shuster, who was Director of the Billy Graham Center Archives at Wheaton College until 2002. Edited portions are reproduced here with the permission of the Billy Graham Archives.[19]

SHUSTER: You mention that when you were about sixteen your family had a summer home at Winona.

HUFFMAN: We lived in the summertime at Winona from 1920 on. I was eight years old at that time. A multimillionaire from Cincinnati had a beautiful home in Winona called *Aloha Cottage* which he turned over to our family for its use in the summertime. We didn't own that home, but with the exception of a couple of years when father put me on the farm where he thought every boy ought to be for a couple of years to become a man, from the time I was eight years old until 1970 I was at Winona every summer in one capacity or another.

SHUSTER: Were you acquainted with the Billy Sunday family?

HUFFMAN: Yes. Billy Sunday's family had all left Winona Lake except the youngest son, Paul. We got a glimpse of him now and then.

---

[19] Used by written permission from the Archives of the Billy Graham Center, Wheaton, Illinois. The transcript has been edited for readability. The full-text original transcript is available at http://www2.wheaton.edu/bgc/archives/trans/389t01.htm.

He had a canoe down at Rodeheaver's Rainbow Point and we knew when the canoe was out, Paul was in it.

SHUSTER: How did you first meet the family?

HUFFMAN: We knew where they lived, and it was sort of a sacred shrine. There's a main boulevard from the entrance right through toward the Chicago Boys' Camp. As you went through the entrance there was the lake. To the left was the Winona Hotel and then you went down past the beach swimming area and to the left you had the Billy Sunday Tabernacle, to the right the business section. You get down to the other end of town, and there's a hill and a crossroad going up called Evangel Hill. At the top of Evangel Hill was the Billy Sunday cottage. It was a modest cottage by present measurements, but was then considered a very fine cottage. It overlooked the lake over the house tops.

By special permission Billy had an irrigation system piped in from the lake, so when water couldn't be used from the city system to sprinkle lawns, his lawns were sprinkled. There was a cascading little creek coming through his lawn on down toward the lake and a beautiful garden. There was shrubbery around the place so that you couldn't actually get on the Billy Sunday lawn but you could pass by the walk to the edge of it.

My first actual glimpse of Billy Sunday was peeking through the shrubs when he was out working in his lawn. He was a very retiring person and home to him was home. He wanted nothing of phone calls or reporters. We had a way of knowing when he was home because they didn't have air conditioning in those days and it was a cottage-type house. There was a gable end at the front looking down toward the Administration Boulevard. When Billy Sunday was home in the summer time, that window up in the gable end was open. By having that open they got some ventilation.

One of my first glimpses of Billy Sunday was when he umpired a baseball game. He did that regularly. He was a famous baseball player and baseball was a strong sport in those days. He would once a year umpire a baseball game at Winona Lake played between the Winona Lake and the Warsaw teams.

My father had just been made the president of Winona Lake School of Theology and then Dr. Biederwolf himself decided to introduce my dad to Billy Sunday between innings, which was a bad time to do it. He took my father out on the playing field when Billy was out at the pitcher's spot and Biederwolf tried to get Billy's attention to introduce him to my dad. He said, "Billy, I want you to meet the new dean of our school of theology." Billy stuck his hand out, shook hands, looked exactly the opposite direction and said, "I'm glad to meet you." He wanted the game to go on—he didn't want to be stopped. He was a rare character and his life was very interesting. Ma Sunday was the power behind the throne.

SHUSTER: How do you mean that?

HUFFMAN: She made the decisions in his life and she sat on the platform to see that things went right. She maneuvered . . . and Billy depended very much upon Ma Sunday for decisions. To illustrate, he was being booked for a great meeting in Boston. It was during the close of the war period [1916].

War hysteria still was alive. Billy always retreated to Winona between campaigns. That's where he rested; that's where he felt comfortable. He got a telegram from the Unitarians inviting him to speak at a Unitarian meeting to take place the night before the big campaign started in Boston. Ma Sunday used to tell this story and got great delight in telling it, that Billy came in and he was trembling and he said, "Ma, look at this, look at this." She said, "What?" He said, "This is a telegram from the Unitarians Association in Boston wanting me to preach to them." He said, "There's only one thing I can preach to that bunch of hell-bound sinners, it's, 'For there is no other name under heaven whereby a man must be saved.'" [Acts 4:12].

She said, "Good." He said, "You mean it?" She said, "Good." So he wired back that he would appear there. Well, it was a frame-up on him. The Unitarians were going to put the campaign down and lick it before it started by making a fool out of Billy. The story is he got there, and they had a hall which was to be an imitation of the Billy Sunday campaign tabernacle. Sawdust was sprinkled up and down the center aisle, an altar at the head, and everything was just like Billy would have it.

He got up and simply preached the gospel, and it was so effective that it completely undid what they attempted to do. Many Unitarian ministers were there; some of them were converted; all of them were interested. It backfired on them. Instead of people staying away from this phony operation, it became one of the biggest campaigns of Billy Sunday's whole career.

SHUSTER: You mention that he was rather a retiring man and also a great athlete?

HUFFMAN: Ma Sunday stated that there's only one constructive thing he ever did in the home that she could remember. He hung a little clock on the wall and she said, "I'll never let anyone touch that because that's the only constructive thing he's ever done in this home." But yes, he had a baseball running record that was not exceeded for many years. He was fast on his feet and he was a fielder but he also had conviction. He refused to sign a contract with a team that wanted him if he would have had to play on Sunday, and he wouldn't do it. He was a popular player. And he preached like he played. He would wind up just as though he was throwing from outfield into the base and he would go through all the motions of running the bases. He was athletic in the pulpit.

SHUSTER: What was he like to talk to, just man-to-man?

HUFFMAN: Hard to talk to, to carry on a conversation. I tried once but I didn't get to him. Ma interfered.

SHUSTER: When you were still a boy?

HUFFMAN: I was twelve years old, maybe. I used to go around selling printed Christmas cards with your name on it. I got my samples and walked that long flight of steps up the hill to his house. I stood there, pounded on the front door, and a maid came to the door and wanted to know what I wanted. "I want to see Mr. Sunday." She said, "Just a moment." Then Ma Sunday showed up—big, pleasant face, jolly person. She said, "What do you want, Sonny?" I said, "Well, I want to see Mr. Sunday." She said, "He's very busy, you can't see him. But what can I do for you?" So I told what my purpose was. She said, "Well, let's see your samples." So she sat on the swing with me, went through the whole book and looked at every card, and she said, "Sonny, I'm sorry but I can't buy any cards from you for two reasons. We don't have any money to pay for cards and we have so many friends we wouldn't know where to start sending or to stop." That's as close as I got to him in that attempt.

When my girlfriend (who's been my wife now for fifty-three years) was a freshman at Marion College and I was a junior, she came to visit and I took her to Winona Lake. I wanted her to see the great Billy Sunday. The window was open and I saw some movements behind the shrubbery where he worked on the lawn when he was there.

I knew where there was a gap in the shrubs and so I took her along the main walk. I saw him and she peeked in. And there he was—no shirt, no undershirt, no socks, no shoes—just a pair of slacks or shorts. They were blue with a great big green patch in the seat. He was not a big person—he was a wiry person but he had a big, hairy, broad chest. And she got the real view of the great Billy Sunday.

One time I was walking by and he was working in there sprinkling and some kids came by. He just waited 'til they got right in that gap in that fence and he turned the hose on them. Just gave them a soaking [laughs] and off they went. He was very nonsocial off the platform.

SHUSTER: Did you have opportunity to see him preach?

HUFFMAN: I heard him preach twice. Once at the Billy Sunday Tabernacle and once in Fort Wayne, Indiana, at the Fort Wayne Gospel Temple.

That was an echo of the old Billy. Billy's prime was less than twelve years. He grew up in Iowa, and for years he never left the state. He never did leave the country—he never preached outside the United States, not even in Canada to my knowledge and never abroad. He lost his fortune toward the end of his life through a business deal with one of his sons. He had good insurance for Ma when he left, but he had to get out and work. So he'd go out on one-night stands. He always preached at Winona once a year, at least, in the

Billy Sunday Tabernacle and it was usually a fund-raising thing for Winona Lake. He gave all the money to Winona. For years he was the financial backer of Winona Lake.

SHUSTER: What stands out in your mind about his preaching?

HUFFMAN: How athletic he was, how fast he was. There's a record available of his preaching. He was high pitched, and a whirlwind of a preacher. He was all over the place. He was on the chair; he was smashing a chair; he was taking off his coat throwing it to Ma and she'd catch it—Ma was always behind him. Rodeheaver was the Cliff Barrows.

SHUSTER: Rodeheaver was?

HUFFMAN: Yes, Rodeheaver was the Cliff Barrows, the platform manager. He was also the choir director, the master of ceremonies. He had everything in control. They had places to take care of the babies; they weren't supposed to be in the audience. But there was a baby in the Fort Wayne Gospel Temple which seated three thousand people. Billy [had] just started to preach [and] a baby started yelling and he stopped and stared and simply stood piercingly looking in the direction that noise came from. He spotted the mother and said, "I'm not going to say one more word until the young heifer walks out with that bawling calf." Billy was crude but people never forgot what he said. During the war, he said, "If you turn hell upside down, you'll find printed on the bottom Made in Germany." Another quote was, "If Al Smith would run against the Devil for the presidency of the United States, I'd vote for the Devil." You never forgot what he said, but he was deadly earnest, endeavoring to win people to Christ.

SHUSTER: What about Ma Sunday and how would you describe her?

HUFFMAN: Very gracious, very humble. You'd often see her going away from a meal at the hotel with a little bag. She'd take food home.

Very generous, but very, very thrifty and very self-sacrificing. Often you'd see her going about the campus at Winona picking up sticks. She had a lot of firewood for the winter stacked up and most of it she gathered.

SHUSTER: Did you get to know Homer Rodeheaver at all?

HUFFMAN: Yes, we knew Rodeheaver very well.

SHUSTER: How would you describe him?

HUFFMAN: A "sanctified playboy." He was a million-dollar personality when a million dollars meant something. He could play an audience. He always had his trombone on his arm and that was his inseparable companion. He spared his voice with it, he led singing with it, and he did a fair job of playing. He had a gift of having appropriate stories at just the moment of crisis. He didn't hesitate to use them again and again and again. Someone one time said to him, "Why tell the same old stories all the time?" He said, "They work." And he said, "Half of the people that are there have never heard them before and the half that have heard them like them."

He was a great personality and very shrewd. He owned hundreds and hundreds of copyrights and that's where the money came from.

SHUSTER: And did he also write songs?

HUFFMAN: Not much. I only know of one or two songs he wrote but he popularized songs.

The author of *The Old Rugged Cross,* George Bennard, said, "Rodeheaver is the most gracious man I've ever known." He said, "I was having the hardest sledding and he knew it and came to me one time and he said, 'George, many people have come to me and said, 'Is it true that Rodeheaver bought *The Old Rugged Cross* for fifty dollars or something like that and made thousands on it?'" George said, "It's nobody's business what he bought it for or what he's made on it. He satisfies me and it ought to satisfy them. I have no complaints." Then he told me that he was having a hard time saving his home and Rodeheaver found out about it and sent him a check to pay his home off. So there are two sides to that story.

CHAPTER 8

Winona in the 1920s

"Oh how strenuous is life! I know a little of it. Men 'ought always to pray, and not to faint.' How fierce the battle! I know something of the conflict, but I ought not faint, because I can pray."
Dr. G. Campbell Morgan

A TIME OF TOUGH TRANSITIONS

ACCORDING TO GADDIS AND HUFFMAN, "SOON AFTER THE FIRST World War the peak of Billy Sunday's influence passed. A decline followed. Churches no longer could be organized. The day of tabernacle evangelism was over and Sunday went into semi-retirement. From time to time he emerged from his quiet Indiana home to hold small meetings or to visit the scenes of his great successes of yesterday" (p. 75).

There was, however, plenty of continuing activity in Sunday's adopted town of Winona Lake. This era saw the establishment of the Winona Lake School of Theology, the Rodeheaver School of Sacred Music, and the Conference on Prophecy and the Jews, as well as the continuation of Chautauqua programming under the direction of James Heaton. Billy Sunday and Homer Rodeheaver became prominent in Winona Lake public life and drew large crowds to meetings when they appeared locally.

After years of success, financial problems again arose in the town. There was a virulent outbreak of typhoid fever in July of 1925, which led to the sealing of several of the park's natural springs. This, of course, caused some negative publicity.

Therefore Winona launched into the construction of a new sewer system and sewage disposal plant (outdoor toilets had been prohibited, beginning in 1924). Historians later agreed that these improvements marked the beginning of Winona's new financial difficulties. Debt grew. The onset of the Depression worsened the financial situation. Chautauqua programming, which had gradually declined through the years, came to an end in 1938-1940 after contracts already in place had been honored. Religious modernism continued to influence and divide. Conflicts arose on the board, and Biederwolf had to fight off an attempt to oust him as director of the conference.

Once again, there was reorganization. William Biederwolf and his staunch ally, J. Palmer Muntz, a Baptist pastor from New York, brought the Winona Lake Christian Assembly into being in 1939. Biederwolf, who was an athlete, scholar (Princeton), evangelist, pastor, and author, directed the Bible conference from 1922 to 1939. He was known for his diligent study of Scripture and his warm, direct preaching style. It was his invitation to Alva McClain and Herman Hoyt that ultimately resulted in the newly founded Grace Theological Seminary relocating to Winona Lake from Akron, Ohio, in 1939.

Biederwolf opened the 1924 Bible conference with this prayer:

We thank Thee for Winona. In these days when so many are either willfully or unwittingly seeking to undermine the holy faith of our fathers, may the institution stand Gibralter-like in defense of those essential things of Thy Word which constitute the unsearchable richness of the infinite mercy of God in Jesus Christ, who is King of kings and Lord of lords, Who in the beginning was with God and was God, and Whom we adore and worship.

The year 1920 saw both the death of Sol Dickey and the beginning of construction on the Billy Sunday Tabernacle. Dickey died in a friend's house in DeLand, Florida, on December 22. His family brought the body back to Warsaw for burial. Later, in 1938, the Assembly erected a small monument with a bronze bust of Dickey in front of the Billy Sunday Tabernacle—a monument that still stands there today immediately across Park Avenue facing the post office.

The Winona Lake gates were dismantled in 1930, and it became possible for residents and visitors to attend events without charge. Among the popular speakers at Winona were the British evangelist Gipsy Smith (1860-1947), who attracted large and enthusiastic crowds, and Dr. Bob Jones and his son, Bob, Jr. Both Dr. Bobs were regular speakers at Winona for many years and Dr. Bob Jones, Jr., was a member of the board of directors from about 1940-1960.

Bob Jones, Jr. recalled fondly his Winona Lake experience. He said, "Among the greatest privileges I had as my father's son was to get to know many of the great evangelists, Bible teachers and preachers . . . it was at Winona Lake, Indiana, that I came in contact with the great majority of them."[20]

Jones' mother, however, was not so impressed. He recalled, "My mother hated the place. The backwaters of the lake bred mosquitoes. The climate, she declared, was the worst imaginable—one day was insufferably hot without a breath of air; the next was damp, cold, and rainy. Mother complained that whatever clothes she took were always the wrong ones."

"Some years we would stay in the big, rambling hotel," Jones recalled. "Other years we would rent a house. Between trying to fight mosquitoes and keep house in an inconvenient and inadequately furnished summer place and keeping a sharp eye on this active boy, she had her hands full, and it is no wonder that she looked on the annual visit to Winona as a penance and not a vacation."[21]

Transportation to Winona was enhanced by The Winona Flyer, a limited-stop train that ran between Goshen and Indianapolis. Passengers riding the Flyer could travel directly to Winona without having to change cars. Top speed was in excess of 70 mph.

The roque courts were a popular recreational spot in Winona, where a form of croquet was played from 1920 until 1939. Regional tournaments were often held at this splendid facility located at the center of the island. Roque is an American variant of croquet played on a hard, smooth surface. Popular in the first quarter of the 20th

---

[20] Jones, p. 87

[21] Jones, p. 88

century and billed "the Game of the Century" by its enthusiasts, it was an Olympic sport in the 1904 Summer Games, replacing croquet from the previous games. A news report from July of 1928 noted that a roque tourney at Winona lake drew contestants from New Jersey, Florida, Ohio, Illinois, California, and Indiana.

Another attraction on the lakefront was the famous sliding board at Homer Rodeheaver's home, Rainbow Point. Katherine Carmichael, noted pianist and Rody's neighbor, was often seen entering the water on a toboggan. For a privileged few, the highlight of a visit to Winona Lake was a trip down Homer Rodeheaver's slide. It extended from the upper level of Rainbow Point's veranda and stretched out to the lake. Visitors could sail out and land in the lake more than twenty feet below. Will Rogers is reported to have talked about the slide as he crossed the continent on his circuits, and he featured it in a newspaper column. As a result, the crowds of people wanting to enjoy the slide became so great that Rodeheaver feared it might collapse the house. The slide was taken down for safety's sake, much to the disappointment of all.

THE WINONA LAKE SCHOOL OF THEOLOGY

The Winona Lake School of Theology was founded in 1920 and it enrolled theology students until 1970, when it was moved to the Chicago area and changed its name. Notable alumni include James Strauss, D. James Kennedy and Dwight Zeller.

The school was founded by G. Campbell Morgan, a well-known pastor of his day who had recently left Westminster Chapel in London, England, to spend time in the United States. He led the school in 1920 and 1921, and was succeeded for the year 1922 by George W. Taft, president of Northern Baptist Seminary in Illinois. In 1923, William Biederwolf became head of the school.

Presidents of the Winona Lake School of Theology included Dr. William E. Biederwolf, Dr. G. Campbell Morgan, Dr. Jasper A. Huffman, and Jasper's son, Dr. John A. Huffman.

The school had separated itself from the other Winona institutions in 1935, and thereafter operated separately, but in a closely-related fashion to the Winona summer programming.

Although Biederwolf held the title of president of the school until his death in 1939, in reality the school was shaped and organized by Jasper Huffman, who had been serving as the dean of Marion College in Marion, Indiana, when Biederwolf persuaded him to become dean of the Winona theological school.

Jasper Abraham Huffman (1880-1970) was born in Elkhart, Indiana. He became a scholar, publisher, educator, biblical archeologist, and activist for higher education within his own church denomination. Jasper served as president of the Winona School of Theology from Biederwolf's death in 1939 until 1954, when Huffman's son, John Adam Huffman, succeeded him, serving as president from 1954 to 1970. The younger Huffman revealed more insights in this transcribed conversation between himself and Wheaton College archivist Robert Shuster, conducted at the Billy Graham Center at Wheaton College on April 14, 1988.[22]

HUFFMAN: Dr. G. Campbell Morgan came occasionally to Winona Lake as a Bible conference speaker and always was very popular with ministers. In 1920, when the great British preacher and scholar was there, the facilities of Bethany Girls Camp were opened to Dr. Morgan in a special program where ministers who were really interested in Bible study could come and take a serious Bible training course over a period of two and a half weeks.

Dr. Morgan's course was so popular they had two sessions a day. That auditorium was filled with ministers, some 600 meeting daily. In his inimitable way he put a big blackboard up and charted the outline of his lecture, and they were eager for it. Father was brought there as director of the summer school in 1928 and spent all of his summers from then on until many years later developing that and putting it on a real curriculum basis.

SHUSTER: What was Dr. Biederwolf's connection?

HUFFMAN: Dr. Biederwolf at the time was the head of the Bible conference and he was known as the director of the Winona Lake School of Theology. Biederwolf was a brilliant man, a Princeton

---

[22] These edited excerpts are used by permission, with the full interview available at: http://www2.wheaton.edu/bgc/archives/trans/389t01.htm.

man, and yet he was an evangelist primarily. He realized he didn't have the qualifications to set up a curriculum for a theological seminary but he was behind the scenes getting money and support for the institution all through his remaining years.

SHUSTER: Did your family move to Winona Lake or did you live there?

HUFFMAN: We had a summer place at Winona Lake from 1928 on. I was born in 1912, so I grew up at Winona Lake. It was a long season. It had closed gates and was known as a Chautauqua center, bringing in some of the greatest talent of the country. The Billy Sunday Tabernacle, which conservatively seated 7,500 people, was filled and they ran a very intensive program of about ten Bible conference services a day. It was America's greatest Bible conference center.

SHUSTER: What was the attraction about Winona Lake?

HUFFMAN: It was in good proximity to Midwestern populace. It was on the Pennsylvania Railroad. Fast trains from New York to Chicago went right through Winona Lake, with a station there. And it was a very beautiful lake and had facilities for taking care of thousands of people in the summertime. Most everyone that lived on Winona Lake in those days had property that was income property in the summer months. Many of them lived on the income from the summer.

You couldn't get into Winona without a pass. You couldn't own property at Winona Lake in those days unless you signed the covenant: you'd have no Sunday boating, no Sunday swimming, no card playing, no smoking, no drinking on the premises, and the property owners were responsible to see that their guests behaved accordingly or they were ousted.

SHUSTER: You mentioned that Winona had closed gates. What did you mean by that?

HUFFMAN: Literally, there was a fence around the entire compound and there were only one or two entrances. The main entrance always had a gate teller, and gates went up and down. You had to show your pass or you didn't get in.

SHUSTER: And the purpose of that was?

HUFFMAN: To maintain a standard. It was never officially Presbyterian, but it was dominated by Presbyterians and in those days Presbyterianism was quite puritan. These were the standards of the church at that time. When Prohibition went out, the municipality of Winona Lake had to decide whether it was going to continue with closed gates. There was no post office, no government recognition. Or, they could let down the bars on these restriction which were becoming pretty much Blue Laws [laws against activities on Sunday]. That was one of the hardest decisions the fathers had to make when my dad was on the board as secretary. In those days many of us would never go to the theater, but we got the best pictures at Winona Lake, such as *Ben Hur* and *King of Kings* when they had made the run in theaters.

THE HUFFMAN LEGACY

Jasper Abraham Huffman, who did much to develop the Winona School of Theology curriculum, was a farm boy who started preaching at eighteen years of age and was one of the early ministers in what was then known as the Mennonite Brethren in Christ Church. It later changed its name to the United Missionary Church and after that it united with the Missionary Church Association of Fort Wayne, Indiana. The two combined churches are known now as the Missionary Church.

In the early 1900s, Jasper Huffman envisioned a denominational institution for higher education. In the years that followed, he worked at several Christian colleges before Bethel College in Mishawaka, Indiana, opened its doors to 94 students in 1947. Huffman was asked to be the first president, but he declined, instead accepting positions as professor and dean of Bible. The Bethel College administration building is named for Jasper A. Huffman, and he is credited as one of the founding fathers of Bethel and the person responsible for the college's name.

John A. Huffman, Sr. succeeded his father at the Winona School of Theology. He was born in Dayton, Ohio, and wanted to be a band director when he was growing up but felt a call to the ministry. He received his bachelor's degree from Marion College (now Indiana Wesleyan University) and graduated from Boston Divinity School of Theology. He went on to complete graduate courses at Boston University and Harvard University.

Huffman became the first assistant pastor that Park Street Church in Boston ever had and from there was given his own church in Cambridge, Massachusetts. In the mid-1940s, Huffman was one of the founding members of the National Association of Evangelicals and was the founding editor of the organization's publication, the *United Evangelical Action* magazine.

In 1954, he and his wife moved back to the Midwest where he became president of the Winona Lake Summer School of Theology. During the summer months they lived at Winona and the remainder of the year they lived in Wheaton, Illinois. He organized the Flying Seminar and led many groups on 31-day pilgrimages to the Holy Land and places of the Bible. In his semiretirement, he served as associate pastor in churches in Florida, California, and at the First Presbyterian Church in Glen Ellyn, Illinois, until his retirement in 1997.

Rev. John Abram Huffman died at age 92 on May 22, 2004, in Windsor Park Manor in Torrey Johnson Health Care Center in Carol Stream, Illinois, of complications from a stroke. Huffman was the last living member of the National Association of Evangelicals' founders committee.

THE HUFFMAN PUBLISHING BUSINESS

Knute Larson, who for many years pastored The Chapel in Akron, Ohio, worked with the Huffman family in their publishing business when Larson was attending Grace College and Grace Theological Seminary.

Larson recalled,

S. Lambert Huffman was one of the action-driven sons of Dr. Jasper Huffman, a theologian-contemporary of Alva McClain and co-founder of the Missionary Church. Lambert, who helped to influence the move of a Bible school in

Cleveland to become Malone College in Canton, Ohio, was always looking for business-ministries to spread his influence, and he bought Higley Press, located in Berne, Indiana, moved it to Winona to become Higley-Huffman Press. In two years he named it Lambert Huffman Publishers. He put it in 'the castle,' right next to his residence at the point of the island, and started to expand its publications.

Stretching for the best in popular writing in that day, he enticed Ken Anderson, Christian film-writer and director with Gospel Films in Muskegon, Michigan, to come be the managing editor of the company. When Ken Anderson knew within months of moving to Warsaw that editing took too much patience and time away from his creative side, he left the publishing house to start Ken Anderson Films, with the full approval and partnership of Lambert Huffman. Ken [had] hired me as proofreader [so when he left] Lambert handed me the managing editor job when I was 19.

Larson did that for seven years while finishing Grace College, Grace Theological Seminary, and for two years while he was youth pastor with Ken Ashman at the Grace Brethren Church in Wooster, Ohio.

In each of the 52 *Higley Commentary* lessons Larson included a short homily on the lesson's memory verse by Christian leaders. These included Winona Lake teachers and theologians such as Herman Hoyt and other professors at Grace Theological Seminary, as well as ministry leaders including Ted Engstrom, Warren Wiersbe, John Walvoord, Mel Johnson, Christian Weiss, and V. Raymond Edman.

Other authors included Theodore Epp, Vernon Grounds, Harold Lindsell, Joe Bayly, Don Hillis, and F.F. Bruce. Leaders of denominations and other seminaries, and many Grace Brethren pastors, friends of Larson, also wrote for the commentaries.

The main products of these publishers were the *Higley Commentary*, a 500-page book produced every year for teachers of the International Uniform Lessons, popular in many flavors of churches: Presbyterian and Pentecostal, Methodist and Baptist, and independent. They went all over the United States, shipped from the castle, and later, after growth, from the warehouse behind the building housing Ken Anderson films.

Huffman Publishers also did quarterlies for primary, junior, junior high, senior high, and adults—all of these for the students taught by a teacher studying the *Higley Commentary*.

If you looked up mover-shaker in a dictionary, you would find Lambert's picture. He was from the Friends movement—his wife's brother was Everett Cattell, who became president of Malone after serving in India as a Friends missionary. Lambert was a writer, a singer, who dabbled in theology, loved healthy socials, and tried to tumble anyone who would ski behind his fast Winona motor boat.

His more studious hobby was studying the life of Samuel Johnson, who produced a large dictionary among other works. Lambert wrote a biography on Johnson entitled *The Magnificent Delinquent: The Tragic but Tender Story of Samuel Johnson and his Wife, Tetty.*

Huffman later moved to Florida, taking the business along, and there he sold it to others who still produce the *Higley Commentary*.

John A. Huffman, Sr. provided further commentary on the Huffman family and on S. Lambert Huffman: "My other brother was a Christian businessman. He said that he lived what we boys preached. He wasn't a preacher, didn't feel called to preach. But he was very creative. He lived in Canton, Ohio, most of his adult life and he was a man of conviction. He became assistant business manager of a roller bearing company. He resigned his job during the war.

"And then he also purchased the Higley Publishing Company and published the *Higley Commentaries*. He also was one of the founders of Malone College and Miami Bible College. He was very active. He was a starter--he got things started and then he moved on."

CHAPTER 9

Winona's Heritage of Sacred Music

*"I go around to churches and tell people there is no use of their
sitting there like a lot of sour crabapples scaring people away. We
Christians have a right to be happy. So come on friends, let's make
the world a brighter and better place."*
Homer Rodeheaver

FROM THE EARLIEST DAYS OF THE WINONA ASSEMBLY, SACRED MUSIC
has been a vital part of Winona Lake programming. Music instruction was part of the curriculum from the very start, and music was
always an integral part of the worship that took place each summer.

The 1906 summer program, for example, notes that congregational singing would be led by Prof. Edwin Othello Excell (1851-
1921), commonly known as E. O. Excell, a prominent American
publisher, composer, song leader, and singer of music for church,
Sunday school, and evangelistic meetings during the late nineteenth
and early twentieth centuries. He was described as "a leader of religious choruses and as a later-day writer of hymns," and the program
declared "no one is more widely known over America than E. O.
Excell, and it is doubtful if there is a leader who can get more song
out of a congregation. A powerful singer himself, he seems to impel
others to sing."

Excell compiled or contributed to about ninety secular and
sacred song books and is estimated to have written, composed, or
arranged more than 2,000 of the songs he published. The music
publishing business he started in 1881 and that eventually bore his

name, was the highest volume producer of hymnbooks in America at the time of his death. The most popular Excell compositions at the time were *I'll Be a Sunbeam* and *Count Your Blessings.*

Excell also served as vice president and board member of the Winona Assembly for a number of years. The annual "Winona Choral Contest" he conducted featured contests for mixed, men's and women's choruses, quartets, duets, vocal and piano soloists and recitationists. Prizes to be distributed totalled $1,300.

One of the regular advertisers in the summer programs was M. P. Moller Pipe Organs of Hagerstown, Maryland. Advertising that "We have built more than 800 pipe organs for churches in every state in the Union," the company proudly noted that it was "builder of the large two manual organ at Winona Assembly."

A newspaper report from July of 1936 notes that "There are 165 choral directors from prominent churches and colleges throughout the United States attending the Christiansen Choral School, just opened in the Westminster Hotel at Winona Lake." The article noted that the school was under the leadership of Dr. F. Melius Christiansen of St. Olaf College, Northfield, Minnesota, and that in addition to pupils and instructors from 33 states, several others attended from Canada and Hawaii. Warsaw High School had 35 students participating in demonstrations of Miss Carol M. Pitts' class in voice diction, according to the report.

HOMER RODEHEAVER

Without question, the dominant figure in sacred music in the history of Winona Lake was Homer Rodeheaver (1880–1955), who had a brilliant and colorful career as a song leader, evangelist, gospel song writer and publisher, and philanthropist.

Rodeheaver was born on a small farm in Hocking County, Ohio, near Union Furnace, to Thurman Hall and Fannie Armstrong Rodeheaver on Oct. 4, 1880. His father, who had fought with the Union forces during the Civil War, operated a small sawmill at the time of his son's birth.

The infant Rodeheaver at six months was frail and not expected to live when the family migrated to Newcomb, Tennessee. He gradually regained strength and health in the Cumberland mountain air and sunshine. There his father expanded his sawmill business into a furniture manufacturing plant.

Rodeheaver often cited the times as a small child in his Tennessee home when he would place chairs in the form of an audience in the sitting room, then get up on another and sing and preach to this self-made congregation. His parents were loyal Methodists and they were instrumental in establishing his early association with both church and Sunday school. Today at Newcomb there is a little brick church named "Rodeheaver Chapel" in his honor.

His first public appearances were in Tennessee as a member of his brother Yumbert's church quartet. Yumbert was the first to teach his younger brother to play various musical instruments, including the drum, clarinet, and trombone.

Rodeheaver's mother died when he was eight years old. Five years later his father married Bettie Newman of Knoxville. She was the mother of Ruth and Jack Rodeheaver.

The evangelist first ventured into business when he was nine years old. His father owned an old gray, blind horse. The youngster found a discarded sled near his father's sawmill, hitched it to the horse, and propositioned his uncle for a draying job. His uncle paid him 10 cents per load to haul grocery supplies from the railroad station to his nearby store. Later Rodeheaver obtained another horse and wagon and expanded his dray business to haul lumber, coal, and other supplies.

Soon he became a four-mule team owner at a still-tender age, delivering food and other supplies across the Cumberland mountain range to and from his father's mill. Later he worked in his father's furniture factory for 25 cents per day. When he was 11 years old, fire destroyed his father's plant, leaving the family virtually destitute. However, the father and his three sons rebuilt the factory.

ENLISTS IN ARMY

When he was 16, Rodeheaver and his older brother enlisted in the Spanish-American War, serving with the Tennessee Fourth Regiment in Cuba.

After the war Rodeheaver entered Ohio Wesleyan University. There he worked his way through college by waiting on tables, gathering other students' laundry for a local firm, shoveling snow, emptying garbage cans, and singing in church choirs. For the next few years he was in and out of college, in and out of coal mines, logging camps, and sawmills, striving for a formal music education.

While a student at Ohio Wesleyan, Rodeheaver got his initial taste of evangelistic work. Dr. R. A. Walton was conducting a meeting at nearby Mount Gilead. His song leader had become ill. Walton telephoned the university for a student fill-in. School authorities recommended Rodeheaver and gave him a leave of absence to attend the meeting. The meeting lasted three weeks.

It was through Dr. Walton that Rodeheaver first met Dr. William E. Biederwolf. He accepted an invitation to join Biederwolf's evangelistic group as song leader for a two-week engagement in Springfield, Missouri. He stayed on that job for five years.

JOINS BILLY SUNDAY

One day in 1909 the famed Billy Sunday attended a revival campaign in Kansas where Homer Rodeheaver was serving as song leader. Sunday wrote to Biederwolf about his desire to hire Rodeheaver away from Biederwolf to join the Sunday team, and the following year, 1910, Sunday and Rodeheaver started on a 20-year career of "soul-winning through sermon and song." They had formed the most famous revival team of the century.

Sunday and Rodeheaver were destined to preach and sing to countless millions, to win converts by the hundreds of thousands, to battle the liquor traffic until their very names struck terror into the hearts of brewers and distillers. They stirred the nation to a spiritual quickening that packed the churches, purged cities of corruption, and enthroned Christ in unnumbered thousands of homes across the nation. It was always a team of these two consecrated men, who complemented each other, both spectacular in performance, humble in spirit, both passionately in love with evangelism.

During his around-the-nation trek with Billy Sunday, Rodeheaver's famed trombone averted crowd panic on several occasions.

In Kansas a severe wind storm struck in the middle of the closing meeting of a revival campaign. Lightning, thunder and heavy rains, as well as near-hurricane winds, caused chaos under the big canvas. Winds began to pull the big tent poles. The top and sides began to sag. One of the quarter poles fell, striking a woman on the head.

The crowd began to panic, and nearly everyone jumped up to run. Rodeheaver picked up his trombone and began to play. The crowd quieted down. He was able to maintain the crowd's attention until the storm ended. Newspapers headlined Rodeheaver's action.

A similar incident occurred in Toledo, Ohio, when a section of bleachers crumbled in the armory where a meeting was being held. Again Rodeheaver's trombone saved the day.

An incident that Rodeheaver never got over occurred on a cold February Sunday in 1952 when Rodeheaver and music editor Roland Felts were ministering at a Methodist church in Vandalia, Illinois.

Rodeheaver and Felts went out to dinner with the pastor and some other friends. Since they were to return for the evening service, Rodeheaver left his trombone under the piano at the church. When they returned from dinner, the trombone was missing, and it was never found.

Rodeheaver's biographer Bert Wilhoit reported, "This was a great loss to Rodeheaver. Not only was this the trombone that had gone around the world with him several times, but it was the only trombone he felt comfortable using. The Conn Company of Elkhart, Indiana, had previously presented him with a new trombone. Rody had tried to use it, but the bell was too large and the positions were different. Now he took it up again, but his playing was never the same. As a result, he more often held the new trombone over his shoulder, rather than actually using it. His appearance on the platform was not the same as before."[23]

One historian described Rodeheaver's function in a Sunday crusade meeting this way: "He strode onto the platform, strong but cherubic in appearance, his dark hair and black, bushy eyebrows accentuated by his white suit . . . For a half-hour or more before Sun-

---

[23] Wilhoit, p. 88

day came to the platform, Rodeheaver, a genial and enthusiastic master of ceremonies, warmed up the crowd., presiding over a colorful panoply of sights and sounds. In his soft Tennessee accent, he greeted delegations of Elks, Rotarians, automobile mechanics, laundry workers, college students, and many others, numbering from a dozen to four thousand. He asked them to sing their favorite hymn or secular song. . . Rodeheaver was a veritable one-man parade on the platform. He carried his trombone as though it were glued to his body, pointed it, twisted it, tucked it under his arm."[24]

PUBLISHES SONGS

While he was traveling with Billy Sunday, the song leader noted the most popular gospel songs and purchased the copyrights to words and music. Although he had written between 40 and 50 songs himself, Rodeheaver's greatest success came through popularizing the songs of others.

The most popular songs that he promoted included *The Old Rugged Cross,* written by George Bennard, and *In the Garden,* by C. Austin Miles. Both sold a record million and a half copies in 1915.

Other gospel songs popularized by Rodeheaver included *Brighten the Corner Where You Are, I Walk With the King, If Your Heart Keeps Right, Living For Jesus, Sing, Smile and Pray,* and *Beyond the Sunset.* Rodeheaver also contributed to the popularization of many of the old Negro spirituals.

Homer Rodeheaver believed in a happy Christianity. Behind his slow southern humor lay a seriousness concerning Christianity. His ability to move audiences from laughter to prayer to serious thought concerning their own souls, his dramatic readings, his practical object lessons, his songs of salvation were all wrapped up in Christian living.

There was something of the Paul and Timothy relationship between Sunday and Rodeheaver. The affection of the older man for the younger was deep and abiding, while the devotion of Homer to Billy was inspiring. Despite the difference in their ages, there was an

---

[24] Becker, p. 43

In 1881 the three Beyer brothers (from left: J.F., C.C., and J.E.) bought the land which is now the town of Winona Lake from Julius Boss. They built a creamery and developed a butter and egg business, but also saw the area's recreational potential. They began developing Spring Fountain Park which drew thousands of visitors before being sold to Solomon Dickey and the Presbyterian Church in 1894.

Sol Dickey and the Presbyterians changed the name from Eagle Lake to Winona Lake in 1895. Visitors arriving at the train station entered Winona via the Eagle Arcade building, which included a restaurant and souvenir shop.

Winona's most eccentric structure, Killarney Castle, was built on Esplanade at the point of McDonald Island in 1902 by Solomon Dickey. It was Dickey's home and later served as a publishing office, apartments, and as a private 12-room residence. William Jennings Bryan stayed in the front turreted bedroom when in Winona serving as Assembly board member and president.

The Cyclorama, located between the Eagle Lake Hotel and the boathouse, displayed a painting of Civil War battles on 15,000 square feet of canvas. The painting was later changed to scenes from the life of Christ. The Cyclorama was torn down to make way for construction of the Billy Sunday Tabernacle in 1920.

The Presbyterian Building—later known as the Westminster Hotel and International Friendship House—was built in 1905 and for many years housed Homer Rodeheaver's music publishing company. Billy Graham's 1949 Los Angeles crusade was launched from an all-night prayer meeting in the Westminster's Rainbow Room. Today it includes the Reneker Museum of Winona History.

The roque courts, located at the center of the island, were a popular recreational spot in Winona, where a form of croquet was played from 1920 until 1939. Popular in the first quarter of the 20th century and billed "the Game of the Century" by its enthusiasts, roque was an Olympic sport in the 1904 Summer Games.

Mount Memorial, named for Indiana's 24th governor, James A. Mount, originally was built in 1905 as the main building for the Winona Agricultural Institute. Later it housed the headquarters and publishing house of the Free Methodist Church and was the first Winona Lake location for Grace Theological Seminary.

The Billy Sunday Tabernacle, completed in 1920, seated 7,500 and for many years served as the main venue for Bible conferences, Youth for Christ conventions, local commencement services, and much more. It eventually deteriorated beyond repair and was razed on March 15, 1992.

Billy Sunday (1862-1935) was a professional baseball player-turned evangelist who made Winona Lake his permanent home in 1911. In his 39-year career as an evangelist, Sunday preached to more than 100 million persons in 548 separate revival campaigns.

Billy Sunday, his wife Helen "Ma" Sunday, and their children built the Mount Hood cottage overlooking Garfield Park in 1911 and the family occupied it until Mrs. Sunday's death in 1957. Today the home is preserved with many of the original furnishings and artifacts as a museum and tourist attraction.

(left) Homer Rodeheaver (1880-1955) and his ever-present trombone provided an attractive and engaging song service warmup to the preaching appearances of Billy Sunday. A genius at obtaining copyrights and publishing gospel music, Rodeheaver headed the Rodeheaver Hall-Mack Company which for many years was the world's leading gospel music publishing house, headquartered in the Westminster Hotel.

(above) Rainbow Point, the distinctive waterfront home of Homer Rodeheaver, was distinguished by the long slide from the rooftop to Winona Lake. When humorist Will Rogers commented on it in a newspaper column, the crowds of onlookers and sightseers became so great the slide was taken down for safety's sake.

Paul Lowman and his three pet lions were a familiar sight around Winona Lake from 1936-1939. The first and oldest lion, Jerry I, was the only one who learned to waterski behind Lowman's Chris-Craft speedboat.

The young evangelist Billy Graham was the first full-time employee of Youth For Christ, which was founded in Winona Lake in 1944. The prayer meeting that launched Graham's famous 1949 Los Angeles crusade was held in the Rainbow Room of the Westminster Hotel. Graham frequently returned to Winona Lake to speak, drawing huge crowds as his fame grew.

abiding companionship. For 20 years they campaigned together in practically every large city in America.

LIVING AT WINONA

For 35 years Rodeheaver made his home and headquarters at Winona Lake. Here he directed his annual Sacred Music Conference which was always climaxed in the huge Billy Sunday Tabernacle with his famous Sacred Music Festival. Hundreds of choir directors, evangelistic song leaders, soloists and others in the religious music field came for training each summer.

The Rodeheaver Publishers of Sacred Music was founded in 1910 in Chicago by the three Rodeheaver brothers. The firm's longest-term employee, George Sanville, for many years the manager, was with Homer Rodeheaver for 42 years. B. D. Ackley, music editor, had been with the company since 1935, but first associated with the firm beginning in 1910.

The original company was founded as a means to serve Billy Sunday's campaigns with music. James Thomas, Rodeheaver's brother-in-law, was secretary-treasurer. The firm opened an eastern office in Philadelphia in 1912. In 1938 the three brothers purchased the Hall-Mack Publishing Co., of Philadelphia, merging it to become the Rodeheaver Hall-Mack Co.

The firm's headquarters was moved to the Westminster Hotel at Winona Lake in 1941. A western branch office was established in Inglewood, California, in 1948. Rodeheaver's business associate, George Sanville, described Rodeheaver as "the best platform man the nation has ever known."

Sanville, who was born March 21, 1879, in Chester, Pennsylvania, spent more than 50 years in active work in the promotion of religious hymnbooks and sacred music. He was introduced to the business of making songbooks in 1900. In 1906 he became manager of the Praise Publishing Company in Philadelphia, and the company's first songbook was reported to have reached a sale of 250,000 copies.

In 1912 Homer Rodeheaver bought out the Praise Publishing Company and Sanville became manager of the Rodeheaver firm's office in Philadelphia. From that time until his death in 1957, Sanville served as manager of the Rodeheaver Company, moving with it to Winona Lake where he lived in an apartment at the Westminster Hotel.

In addition to publication of religious songbooks, the firm made gospel recordings and printed special piano arrangements of sheet music. Its *Old Fashioned Revival Hour* songbooks and recordings were used each week by 750 radio stations throughout the nation.

Printing was done in Chicago, and the firm also maintained offices in Los Angeles. The company sold a million hymnbooks annually, making and publishing the Billy Graham hymnbook, among others.

The trademark of the company was a rainbow bent over a bar of music from the song, *If Your Heart Keeps Right.* This symbol was found on Rodeheaver's business cards, his stationery, his dishes at Rainbow Point, and in a rug woven for him by a converted Chinese Christian in Peking. It was even branded on the cattle at Rodeheaver's Florida ranch.

Rodeheaver and his sister, Ruth, completed the first of his new technicolor movie series, *Miracles Thru Song,* early in the spring of 1955 in Hollywood. The series includes selections *When Malindy Sings, Heartaches,* and *Somebody Cares. Miracles Thru Song* was premiered in the Pasadena Civic Auditorium the September before Rodeheaver's death in 1955. He had plans for other such movies when he died.

DREAM COMES TRUE

Homer Rodeheaver's most ambitious dream, Rainbow Boys Ranch, became a reality about 12 miles south of Palatka, Florida, on the historic St. Johns River. Here Rodeheaver donated a 790-acre tract of land in 1950 to the founding of this project for homeless, abandoned, neglected, or under-privileged boys. The land had been converted into an extensive settlement where a wholesome home environment with religious, school, and vocational training was given to boys ages 12 to 16, who were accepted for training and rehabilitation.

There were many boys who, because of death, desertion, divorce, parental disability, or dysfunctional home situation, had no home of their own. These youngsters were given a second chance in life and an opportunity to build a strong foundation for the future.

Rodeheaver's dream continues to flourish through the accomplishments of the boys who grow into better men because of his foresight. His favorite saying was, "It's better to build boys than to mend men."

Rodeheaver participated in many sports, but horseback riding was his favorite. He was instrumental in the formation of the Tennessee Walking Horse Association at Shelbyville, of which Winona Lake's Stanley Arnolt was at one time president. He also loved to fish and hunt and to play tennis and golf. His obituary noted that the week before he died, "he arose from his sick bed to watch the TV presentation of the Sugar Ray Robinson-Bobo Olson heavyweight fight."

Rodeheaver's friends, ranging from Poet Edgar Guest and Coca Cola's Asa Candler, Jr., to cowboys, student preachers, and underprivileged children, always found in him a symbol of loyalty and Christianity. When he was introduced to the late John D. Rockefeller, Sr., on a golf course, the two men delayed their golf game long enough to sing, *I'll Go Where You Want Me to Go, Dear Lord.*

Rodeheaver's favorite Scripture was Colossians 3:16: "Let the word of Christ dwell in you richly in all wisdom; teaching and admonishing one another in psalms and hymns and spiritual songs, singing with grace in your hearts to the Lord." (KJV)

As a song composer Rodeheaver wrote *Good Night and Good Morning, Somebody Cares, Forgive Me for Forgetting, Then Jesus Came, Confidence,* and many others.

The program for the centennial celebration of Billy Sunday's first crusade described crusade singing as featuring "bright, buoyant gospel songs and Homer Rodeheaver demonstrated his sense of crowd control and spiritual purpose by the way he organized the music before the sermon. By the time Billy Sunday preached, the diverse crowd had been unified by Rody; the irritations of tiring travel and long lines giving way to feelings of celebration and crusade excitement."

Rodeheaver's selections for crusade choirs included gospel songs such as *Sail On!, Brighten the Corner Where You Are,* and *In the Garden,* as well as standard hymns of the church. He used great masterpieces such as Handel's "Hallelujah Chorus" from *Messiah* and Mozart's "Glorious Is Thy Name."

When Sunday's theme was temperance, the choir might sing *De Brewer's Big Hosses* or another number from the "Temperance" section of the topical index in the songbook. During larger crusades, when the choir loft would seat 2,000 singers, the 5,000 choristers would rotate evenings of participation.

Of all the music coordinated by Homer Rodeheaver, some of the most memorable moments came when he lifted his melodious baritone voice in ministry. In 1913, his duet with Mrs. Virginia Asher made a new song, *The Old Rugged Cross,* one of the most popular of its era. The Asher-Rodeheaver recordings of the song sold more than a million records by 1936.

NOT WITHOUT CONFLICT

Though he was the master of song, Rodeheaver was not always in harmony with his associates. Later in his career he became disenchanted with many of Sunday's practices, which ultimately led to his breaking off the partnership. He also was involved in a well-publicized feud with music editor B. D. Ackley, who accused Rodeheaver of having too much profit motive and threatened to publish damning evidence to that effect.

The incident that drew the most publicity, however, was a lawsuit filed by Georgia Jay of Chicago in May of 1912, in which she sued Rodeheaver for breach of promise for failing to marry her.

She contended that she and Rodeheaver became engaged while he was involved in a ten-week revival at Sioux City in 1909, but that he did not follow through on his proposal. Her testimony included reports of taxicab rides, long strolls, and discussions of future plans with Rodeheaver. She said she moved to Chicago to be closer to him and took a job as a stenographer at a law office, but Rodeheaver never came through on his promise to marry her because marriage would interfere with his career. She sought damages of $50,000.

The suit ended several years later when a jury in the Circuit Court awarded $20,000 damages to Jay. News reports called it "$20,000 Heart Balm." Rodeheaver never did marry.

Homer Alvin Rodeheaver died at age 75 at his picturesque Rainbow Point home on Winona Lake. Convalescing from a heart attack suffered earlier in the week, Rodeheaver had a cerebral hemorrhage and died at 10:55 a.m. on December 18, 1955.

At his bedside were his sister, Ruth Rodeheaver Thomas; her husband, James Thomas, brother-in-law and close business associate; and Rodeheaver's private nurse, Bertha H. Wilkinson, of the Florida Sanitarium and Hospital at Orlando.

Dr. John L. Hillery, a Warsaw physician, was summoned to Rainbow Point Sunday morning when Rodeheaver was first stricken. He attributed the cerebral hemorrhage to the heart attack the week before. Bruce Howe, Winona Lake fire chief and business employee, attempted to revive Rodeheaver with an inhalator brought to his bedside by Paul Landis of Landis funeral service.

ILL TWO YEARS

Rodeheaver had become ill with a heart condition two years earlier. Though in his early seventies, he steadfastly refused to reduce a most rigorous business pace despite warnings from doctors and pleadings by family members and business associates.

Rodeheaver had a second heart attack while in Florida on an evangelistic tour; and a third a year later during presentation of his annual Sacred Music Conference at Winona Lake.

A week before he died, Rodeheaver attended an evening service of the Winona Lake Presbyterian Church. Following this service he stayed on to show a two-hour preview film of a new series of gospel moving pictures he had made during the previous spring in Hollywood.

A few days later, Rodeheaver and party—back home for a brief Christmas holiday rest at Rainbow Point—attended a junior class play in the Warsaw High School auditorium. En route home that night he became ill with another heart seizure that ultimately led to his death.

Two older brothers who were associated with Rodeheaver in the sacred music publishing business preceded him in death. Dr. Joseph Newton (J. N.) Rodeheaver, affiliated at one time as an instructor with the Northern Baptist Theological Seminary in Chicago, died in January, 1946.

A second brother, Yumbert Parks Rodeheaver, died in August, 1950. A half-brother, Howard Jackson (Jack) Rodeheaver, died in an airplane crash in Warsaw in 1921.

OTHER COMPOSERS

In addition to all the songs Rodeheaver brought to the public's attention, a number of other well-known hymns and hymn writers have had connections with Winona Lake.

JUDSON VAN DEVENTER

Judson Wheeler Van DeVenter, for example, was the writer of the gospel song *I Surrender All.* Born in 1855 near Dundee, Michigan, Van DeVenter attended Hillsdale College, then taught art in Sharon, Pennsylvania.

In 1880, when he was 24, he married Malissa Miller. In 1886, he was living in Sharon, Pennsylvania, and acquired a passport. He planned to go to the British Isles, France, Switzerland, Italy, Germany, Holland, and Belgium. He used the passport to tour Europe and visit art galleries and museums and other resources to study painting.

He was active as a layman in the Episcopal-Methodist Church and became very active in the evangelistic meetings held in his church. Seeing his abilities, his friends urged him to quit his job and become an evangelist. For five years he wavered between the ministry and seeking recognition as an artist.

One day, while sitting in a meeting at the home of evangelist George Sebring in Ohio, Judson Van DeVenter decided to lay everything on the line and give everything over to the Lord.

"At last the pivotal hour of my life came," he later wrote, "and I surrendered all. A new day was ushered into my life. I became an evangelist and discovered deep down in my soul a talent hitherto unknown to me. God had hidden a song in my heart, and touching a tender chord, He caused me to sing."

The song that Judson Van DeVenter wrote has become one of the most popular American hymns.

All to Jesus I surrender,
All to Him I freely give;
I will ever love and trust Him,
In His presence daily live.
I surrender all, I surrender all.
All to Thee my blessed Savior,
I surrender all.

Having finally surrendered his life completely to Christ. He decided to switch to a career in evangelism and worked with J. Wilbur Chapman and others in America and England. Later, he traveled extensively throughout the United States, England, and Scotland as an evangelist, assisted by the singer Winfield S. Weeden.

The Van DeVenters had several children, including a daughter who died at age 20. By 1910, the couple had been married for 30 years and were living in St. Petersburg, Florida, where Judson owned a photography shop and worked with his son, also a photographer. A number of the extant historical photographs of Winona Lake conference activity during his lifetime were captured in Van DeVenter's photography.

They moved to Tampa, Florida, around 1923. He was professor of hymnology at the Florida Bible Institute (now Trinity Bible College) for four years. In 1924, his wife died at the age of 65.

In 1925, when he was 66, he married Carolyn, 47, who was a pianist and music teacher. Judson had a radio program called *The Gospel in Song and Story.*

In the 1930s he was a regular visitor to the Florida Bible Institute. Billy Graham credited Van DeVenter with having influenced him in his preaching, and mentioned the great time students had in the evangelist's home for fellowship and singing.

Judson Wheeler Van DeVenter died July 17, 1939, in Temple Terrace, Florida, at age 83. Though he wrote quite a number of hymns, only a couple remain in use today.

THOMAS O. CHISHOLM

Thomas O. Chisholm wrote a poem in 1923 about God's faithfulness over his lifetime. He sent it to William Runyan in Kansas, who was affiliated with the Moody Bible Institute and Hope Publishing Company. Runyan set the poem to music, and it was published that same year by Hope Publishing Company and became popular among church groups as the hymn, *Great Is Thy Faithfulness.*

The biblical lyrics reference Lamentations 3:22. The song was exposed to wide audiences after becoming popular with Dr. William Henry Houghton of the Moody Bible Institute and Billy Graham, who used the song frequently in his international crusades. This hymn was the school song of Philadelphia College of Bible (now Philadelphia Biblical University).

Thomas Obediah Chisholm was born July 29, 1866, in Franklin, Kentucky. He was educated in a small country schoolhouse. At age 16, he got his teaching certificate and became the teacher of the same country school he had attended as a boy. At age 21, he became associate editor of the weekly newspaper, *The Franklin Favorite.*

His life was forever changed in 1893 when, at a revival meeting under the ministry of Dr. Henry Clay Morrison, he turned his life over to Christ. Morrison then persuaded Chisholm to move to Louisville to become the editor of his periodical, the *Pentecostal Herald.*

Chisholm was ordained a Methodist minister in 1903 and served a brief pastorate at Scottsville, Kentucky. In poor health, he moved his family to a farm near Winona Lake, Indiana.

Hymnology historian K. W. Osbeck notes, "After 1909 he became a life insurance agent in Winona Lake and later in Vineland, New Jersey."[25]

In 1916, Chisholm moved to Vineland, New Jersey, where he worked as an insurance salesman. He retired in 1953 and moved into the Methodist Home for the Aged in Ocean Grove, New Jersey, living there until his death on February 29, 1960.

Although he suffered from poor health his entire life, Chisholm was determined not to focus on his sufferings but rather on the faithfulness of his Lord. He once said in a letter written to a friend, "My income has not been large at any time due to impaired health in the earlier years until now...I must not fail to record here the unfailing

---

[25] Osbeck, p. 84

faithfulness of a covenant-keeping God and that He has given me many wonderful displays of His providing care, for which I am filled with astonishing gratefulness."

In his lifetime Thomas Chisholm wrote more than 1,200 poems, of which 800 were published, and many were set to music. *Great Is Thy Faithfulness* was published in 1923 and remains one of his best-known hymns. According to Chisholm, it was not written for any specific purpose other than to share the biblical truth of his faithful God and Father.

VIRGIL AND BLANCHE BROCK

The most widely accepted version of the history of the gospel song *Beyond the Sunset* is that songwriter Virgil Brock wrote all four verses of the song during a dinner at Homer Rodeheaver's Rainbow Point when a blind cousin said that guests' description of clouds over the lake had helped him see "beyond the sunset." The blind guest is identified as Horace L. Burr.[26]

Another version of the song's origin says it was composed on the porch of *The Hillside*, a residence owned by Brock and located directly behind the Billy Sunday Tabernacle at the end of the Swiss Terrace. Other accounts say the song was composed at Rainbow Point with Blanche Brock sitting at a nearby piano, picking out the melody her husband, Virgil, was singing.

Warsaw Times-Union reporter Emmaline Boyd, reporting on an entertaining evening of sacred music held at the home of Mr. and Mrs. Lambert Huffman on the island in late January, 1964, said that, "One of the most stirring events of the evening was the performance of Virgil Brock singing one of his songs which has become world-famous—*Beyond the Sunset.*"

Boyd went on to report, "Brock has spent most of his life as an evangelist and has travelled all over the world in his work." She said Brock explained that a hillbilly singer in Wheeling, West Virginia, used *Beyond the Sunset* in a radio show, and the song was picked up by a famous vaudeville performer who included it in his act, and it was then popularized by Jo Stafford and Gordon McRae.

---

[26] Rizk, p. 10

Boyd reported that Brock told the group gathered in the Huff-man home "that he wrote it at dinner one evening after he, with a group of friends, was viewing a beautiful sunset at Rainbow Point. His nephew present, who was a remarkable blind person, mentioned that this was the most beautiful sunset he had ever 'seen.'"

Brock asked him how he could "see" a sunset and the nephew answered, "Why, I can see beyond the sunset." Boyd reported that this is what inspired Brock to compose the song that evening.

Jane Gordon Cook and Paula Heckman, in their coffee table photo book *Winona Lake Summers*, debunk the entire legend and say that *Beyond the Sunset* was actually written by B. D. Ackley. It was penned by Ackley, they say, at a gathering in Katherine Carmichael's home and inadvertently left on a table. Brock picked it up, according to Cook and Heckman, and later published it in his name.

Local news media announced on March 13, 1978, that "An end of an era came with the death of Dr. Virgil Brock, composer of more than 500 gospel songs and close associate of song leader and vocalist Homer Rodeheaver for many years." The 91-year-old former Winona Lake evangelist and composer died at Youth Haven Ranch, Rives Junction, Michigan, where he had resided for the past six years. A massive grave marker at Oakwood Cemetery in Warsaw showcases an engraved copy of the words and music to the Brocks' best-known composition.

B. D. AND A.H. ACKLEY

The names of the two Ackley brothers, Alfred Henry and Bentley D., have long been prominent in the gospel music field. Both were long-time associates with the Rodeheaver Publishing Company in the compilation and promotion of gospel music, and each contributed many songs to these publications.

Alfred Henry Ackley was born on January 21, 1887, at Spring Hill, Pennsylvania. He received a thorough education in music, including study in composition at the Royal Academy of Music in London, England. As a performer, he was recognized as an accomplished cellist. He studied under Alfred Walker at the Royal Academy, and with the famous cellist Hans Kronold. Following graduation from Westminster Theological Seminary, he was ordained to the Presbyterian ministry in 1914.

While serving Presbyterian pastorates in Pennsylvania and California, Ackley always maintained a keen interest in the writing of hymns and hymn tunes. It is estimated that he wrote well over 1,000 gospel songs and hymns in addition to aiding in the compilation of various hymnals and songbooks for the Rodeheaver Company. In recognition of his contribution to sacred music, he was awarded the honorary Doctor of Sacred Music degree from John Brown University. Ackley died at Whittier, California, on July 3, 1960.

His brother, Bentley DeForest, "B. D." Ackley, was born September 27, 1872, in Spring Hill, Pennsylvania, and died September 3, 1958, in Winona Lake, Indiana. He also was a prodigious American musician and gospel composer.

As a young man, B. D. had already learned several instruments, including the melodeon, piano, cornet, clarinet, and piccolo. After moving to New York City in 1888, he began playing the organ in churches.

"I met B. D. Ackley," fellow evangelist Dr. Oswald J. Smith recalled, "in Buffalo, New York, where he was minister of music in the Churchill Tabernacle when I was preaching there one time. The first hymn I wrote with B. D. Ackley was *Joy In Serving Jesus* in 1931. From the time I met him and his brother, I stopped writing music altogether. They could write so much better."

In a newspaper interview from April of 1952, the 79-year-old B. D. Ackley declared, "Music is really just my hobby. I'm primarily a businessman." Ackley not only composed music, but he was widely known for his ability as an accompanist.

While serving as pianist and private secretary with Billy Sunday, B.D. found an outlet for his musical compositions. Some of his gospel songs were introduced in Sunday's meetings, and many became overnight successes. Among his best-known compositions are *Sunrise, If Your Heart Keeps Right, I Walk With the King,* and *Jesus, I Am Coming Home.*

Ackley left a business position in 1907 to join the evangelistic party of Robert E. (Bob) Johnson in Minnesota, but after only three meetings, Johnson was short on bookings. In 1910 Ackley joined Billy Sunday as a combination accompanist and private secretary, a position he held for eight years. He began working with Homer Rodeheaver in 1910. As a composer and editor with the Rodeheaver Company, he wrote more than 3,000 gospel tunes.

In 1915 he was called back to Philadelphia by department store magnate John Wanamaker, who wanted to back the publishing of a gospel songbook. *Hymns of Blessing* sold out its first printing of 50,000 almost immediately, and went into a second printing.

Following further evangelistic work with "Cyclone" Mack, George Wood Anderson, and others, Ackley went to work for the Rodeheaver Company. Later this organization became the Rodeheaver Hall-Mack Company, and Ackley moved with the organization to Winona Lake in 1941.

The majority of B. D. Ackley's publications were written in collaboration with his brother, Alfred H. Ackley, who for many years pastored the First Congregational Church of Escondido, California. At least 500 songs were produced from this collaboration.

B. D. Ackley died in 1958, at age 85, and is buried in Oakwood Cemetery, Warsaw, Indiana. He was a member of the Winona Lake Presbyterian Church and the Masonic Lodge. His will stipulated that any royalty payments from the Rodeheaver Company should go to the Rodeheaver Boys Ranch at Palatka, Florida. Household goods were left to his daughter, Mrs. Herbert (Gertrude) Dye, of Winona Lake.

B. D. Ackley's piano was donated to the Town of Winona Lake in March of 2011 by Ackley's grandson, Dan Dye, in honor of Ackley's grandchildren. A news report of the gift noted that Ackley started his career with Billy Sunday and ended his career working with Homer Rodeheaver at the Rodeheaver Hall-Mack Co. The piano was Ackley's instrument at which he wrote more than 3,000 compositions. The piano is on display at the Winona Lake Senior Center, along with photographs of Ackley and Rodeheaver.

Dr. Alfred H. Ackley, B. D.'s brother, died at age 73 in early July, 1960, in Whittier, California. He was a summer resident of Winona Lake for many years and was chaplain of the Rodeheaver School of Sacred Music.

Among A. H. Ackley's best-known compositions are *He Lives, Heartaches, At the End of the Road, God's Tomorrow,* and *The Song of the Soul Set Free.* A minister for the United Presbyterian Church, A. H. Ackley served pastorates in Pennsylvania and California. He and his wife, Alice, had two sons, Richard and William.

W. ROLAND FELTS

W. Roland Felts, a native of Nashville, Tennessee, exhibited unusual musical prowess early in life. At age 15 he was a church organist and pianist and later he became music director of a local radio station in Nashville. He also sang with a well-known local quartet.

During the summer of 1951, Felts met Homer Rodeheaver during a week of camp meetings at Lake Junaluska Conference and Retreat Center, a Methodist conference grounds nestled in the Great Smoky Mountains of Western North Carolina. Felts, who had recently been discharged from the military, was serving as an accompanist and did not have employment for the coming fall. Rodeheaver suggested that Felts come to Winona Lake, travel with him, and work in the music company.

Felts moved to the Winona Lake/Warsaw area in 1957. After finishing a degree at Asbury College in Kentucky, Felts became associate music director of the company, working closely with B. D. Ackley. Upon Ackley's death, Felts served as music editor until the sale of the Rodeheaver Hall-Mack Company to Word, Inc., in 1969. He was a composer, arranger, editor, and keyboard artist.

In 1967, he began teaching at Grace College as an associate professor, teaching voice and music history. He was a choir director and church organist through the years at various local churches, including Winona Lake Grace Brethren Church and Trinity United Methodist Church of Warsaw, Indiana.

About working with Homer Rodeheaver, Felts said, "It was a pleasure to live as closely as I did with Rody during those years. I found him to be a considerate, charming, personable Christian, a gentleman of the highest order. Having known and worked with a person like Rody has been a lasting influence on my life."

Felts died on June 14, 2012, at the age of 88. He and his wife Verna, who taught piano for many years at Grace College, had two children.

Virginia Healey Asher

Virginia Healey Asher (1869 – 1937), gospel singer and evangelist to women, was one of the most influential women—after "Ma" Sunday—of the Billy Sunday/Homer Rodeheaver era.

Born in Chicago to Irish Catholic parents, she was permitted by her parents to attend services at Moody Church, then pastored by R. A. Torrey, an associate of evangelist Dwight L. Moody. Healey was converted to Christianity at the age of eleven and shortly thereafter became involved in the church's Sunday school ministry. She had a fine contralto voice and received some professional training from George F. Root.

In the service of Moody Church she met her future husband, William Asher, who had been converted at the same evangelistic meeting as Healey, and they were married on December 14, 1887. Their only child died at birth. Virginia Asher attended classes at the precursor of Moody Bible Institute.

The couple held open-air evangelistic meetings near the original Ferris wheel, built for the World's Columbian Exposition in Chicago (also known as the Chicago World's Fair) in 1893. Their success there led to William Asher's being called as assistant pastor of Jefferson Park Presbyterian Church, where both Ashers worked for five years during the pastorate of J. Frank Talmadge. During this period, professional baseball player and future evangelist Billy Sunday attended services at the church.

The Ashers moved to Duluth, Minnesota, where they evangelized in the slums and at Duluth Bethel, a ministry to seamen, miners, and lumberjacks in the frontier port city. The Ashers then became assistants in the evangelistic campaigns of J. Wilbur Chapman, for whom Billy Sunday eventually became the advance man. The ministry of the Ashers focused on sailors, prisoners, and the working poor until ill health forced Virginia to move permanently to Winona Lake, where both Chapman and Sunday owned cottages.

By the first decade of the twentieth century, the evangelistic ministry of Billy Sunday had grown dramatically in both size and income, and Sunday's wife, Nell, began to travel with her husband and manage the campaign staff. Nell Sunday first hired two female Bible teachers, Grace Saxe and Francis Miller, and then in 1911 invited the Ashers to become part of the organization.

Virginia Asher took charge of the ministry to shop girls, hospital employees, and factory operatives—any women who worked outside their homes. She organized local churchwomen to serve as hostesses at luncheons for these young women, and spoke to them about such sins as promiscuity and drinking. They were also strongly encouraged to attend the Billy Sunday services in the evenings.

At the evangelistic services, Virginia Asher often sang duets with music director Homer Rodeheaver. Their early recordings popularized such gospel songs as *The Old Rugged Cross* and *In the Garden.* Meanwhile, William Asher began to serve as Sunday's advance man and fundraiser. He and his wife were often geographically separated, which they accepted as a necessary part of their ministry.

At the end of a series of Sunday meetings in a city, Virginia Asher organized "businesswomen's councils" to continue Bible studies and evangelistic work after the Sunday organization had left for another campaign. At the suggestion of a member in Washington, D.C., Mrs. Asher formed a national council to create a permanent organization. The first meeting was held at Winona Lake in 1922. In 1923 Mrs. Asher was elected honorary president and chaplain of the National Federation of the Virginia Asher Business Women's Councils.

The National Council grew rapidly. In 1925 it voted to build a hospital for lepers in Soonchun, Korea. Other interests of the Council included the Pocket Testament League, work with Jews in Warsaw, Poland, and support of a camp cottage, *The Villa*, at Winona Lake for rest and recreation of business girls. Emphasis continued to be on Bible study as the primary activity of the groups.

Ill health forced Virginia Asher's retirement, and she died at age 67 in May 1937, at Winona Lake, where the Ashers had lived since the early 1920s. The Ashers are buried in Oakwood Cemetery in Warsaw, Indiana, and their gravesite includes an old rugged cross and the words to the song, mounted on a plaque.

ACQUIRED COPYRIGHTS

Although Homer Rodeheaver did not write a large volume of music himself, he was a genius at acquiring copyrights of works by other authors and composers and nurturing them to become the best-known hymns and gospel songs of his day.

Bert Wilhoit, in his biography of Rodeheaver, lists a number of composers and hymn writers whose work was published and promoted by Rodeheaver Hall-Mack. They include:

- George Bennard (*The Old Rugged Cross*)

- Charles H. Gabriel (*The Way of the Cross Leads Home, Since Jesus Came into My Heart, O, That Will be Glory*)

- C. Austin Miles (*In the Garden, Dwelling in Beulah Land*)

- Fannie Edna Stafford (*Somebody Cares*)

- Oswald J. Smith (*Song of the Soul Set Free, Then Jesus Came, The Glory of His Presence*)

- Harry A. Ironside (*Overshadowed*)

- Haldor Lillenas (*Wonderful Grace of Jesus, It Is Glory Just to Walk with Him[music]*)

- Ira B. Wilson (*Make Me a Blessing[text]*)

- George S. Schuler (*Oh, What a Day!, Make Me a Blessing[music]*)

- Charles F. Weigle (*No One Ever Cared for Me Like Jesus*)

- George Webster (*I Need Jesus, Throw Out the Lifeline*)

- Paul Rader (*Only Believe*)

- William C. Poole (*Sunrise Tomorrow*)

- Avis B. Christiansen (*It Is Glory Just to Walk with Him[text], Precious Hiding Place*)

- George Duffield (*Stand Up, Stand Up for Jesus[text]*)

- Lelia N. Morris (*Sweeter As the Years Go By, Nearer, Still Nearer, Let Jesus Come Into Your Heart*)

- Will L. Thompson (*Softly and Tenderly*)

- James Rowe (*I Walk With the King[text], Love Lifted Me[text]*)
- Frank E. Graeff (*Does Jesus Care?)*

THE SECOND WAVE

*The World's Largest
Bible Conference*

CHAPTER 10
The Winona Lake Christian Assembly (1939-1968)

"Furnishing an audience, huge in its proportions and national, increasingly international, in its geography, and unexcelled in the high character and influence, personally and collectively, the Winona Bible Conference offers a platform which every sincere man with a great message eagerly covets for his cause's sake. Nowhere else can he get such a hearing from inter-denominational leaders . . . Winona must have the best and the best must have Winona."
Ira Landrith

IN MARCH OF 1939, A "NEW ORGANIZATION FOR WINONA" WAS AN-
nounced with Dr. W. E. Biederwolf as the president. Biederwolf fell
ill shortly after the 1938 conference and, after spending months in
the hospital, died on September 3, 1939. Biederwolf had been president of the association, president of the Winona School of Theology,
and director of the Bible conference. Historian Mark Sidwell said,
"No single man either before or after him wielded as much authority
at Winona Lake as Biederwolf did at that time."[27] Perhaps the last
great act of his noteworthy career was to reorganize and transform
Winona to position it for the future.

Arthur W. McKee, a musical evangelist, who had worked with
Gipsy Smith and William Ward Ayer, was engaged as general manager for the Winona Lake Christian Assembly to replace James Hea-

---

[27] Sidwell, p. 175

ton, serving from 1938 until 1946.[28] A new board of directors was announced. J. Palmer Muntz began a twenty-year career (longer than any other man) as director of the Winona Lake Bible Conference in 1939. By almost all accounts, the decade of the 1940s was one of growing success, with the conference reaching its peak late in the decade.

The Bible conference movement in America, in general, refers to a number of large nondenominational conferences that were begun in the latter part of the nineteenth century. With the goal of combining relaxing vacations for families along with inspiring biblical teaching and music, a number of such conferences were founded in the late 1800s and early 1900s. The two generative conferences which church historians generally agree started the movement were D. L. Moody's Northfield Conference, founded in 1893 in Moody's hometown in Massachusetts, and the Niagara Bible Conference. The Niagara Conference began as the "Believers' Meeting for Bible Study" in 1876 in Massachusetts, but eventually settled on annual meetings located at Niagara-on-the-Lake, Ontario, Canada.

In his biography of Moody, *The Life & Work of Dwight Lyman Moody*, J. Wilbur Chapman said "This is a day in which God is using in a very remarkable way what is known as the Bible Conference."[29] Chapman credited both the Northfield and the Niagara conferences, and praised Moody's participation in making the Winona conference a success.

Chapman said, referring to Winona's conference, "For five years the Christians of the middle and western states in increasing numbers have gathered there for the same kind of work that was done at Northfield. Mr. Moody has ever contributed to the effectiveness of the conference by sending such speakers as the Rev. G. H. C. MacGregor, the Rev. G. Campbell Morgan, the Rev. F. B. Meyer, and the Rev. J. G. Cunningham. The gathering has increased from thirty-five the first year, to more than 1,500 at the last annual meeting. I desire personally to say that Winona owes to Mr. Moody more than it can ever repay."[30]

---

[28] After a short tenure of John Ironside as manager, McKee served again from 1948 until his sudden death in early 1953.

[29] http://www.biblebelievers.com/moody/15.html

[30] ibid

The 1939 season at Winona featured three hotels--the Winona, the Westminster, and the Inn. Speakers for the 1939 program included Dr. Walter L. Wilson, president of Kansas City Bible College; Dr. Charles L. Feinberg from Dallas Theological Seminary; Mr. R. G. LeTourneau of Peoria, Illinois; Rev. Peter Deyneka of the Russian Gospel Mission; Dr. Will Houghton, president of Moody Bible Institute; and Dr. Harry A. Ironside, of Moody Memorial Church in Chicago.

R. G. LeTourneau—A Leader for 17 Years

Robert G. LeTourneau entered the picture of the Winona Lake Christian Assembly in the reorganization of 1938 and, in all, he gave 17 years of leadership as a director and as chairman of the board of directors. LeTourneau, who was exceedingly generous to the Assembly, led from 1938 until 1955, when the offices of the presidency of the corporation and the office of board chair were separated. J. Palmer Muntz at that time became president of the corporation and Paul Bauman was named chairman of the board of directors.

LeTourneau was born on a farm near Richford, Vermont, on November 30, 1888. The family soon moved to Duluth, Minnesota, where Robert spent his boyhood until he was 15, when the family moved to Portland, Oregon. Tiring of school, he served a four-year apprenticeship as a molder in a foundry. Later he went to San Francisco, and after the earthquake, settled in Stockton, California, where he lived until 1917. Here he developed his knack for mechanical work and began a construction business.

He married Evelyn Peterson on August 29, 1917, and after a year of service with the government he entered the business which became the foundation of the first of the LeTourneau enterprises, LeTourneau Incorporated. This was the forerunner of larger plants in Peoria, Illinois; Toccoa, Georgia; and later in Australia. The plants manufactured large and powerful machines for farm work, road improvement, and earth moving.

The LeTourneau organization employed about 3,000 workers at one time, with sales of more than $10 million a year. LeTourneau was known for his practice of living on one-tenth of his earnings and giving nine-tenths to God. His LeTourneau Foundation at one time was reported to be the twelfth largest foundation in the nation and the largest religious foundation.

With his wife, Evelyn, he founded what became LeTourneau University, a private Christian university in Longview, Texas. He was known as a devoted Christian and generous philanthropist to Christian causes, including a camp and conference grounds that carry his name, "LeTourneau Christian Center." He was sometimes called "God's businessman." His story has inspired thousands through books including *God Runs My Business* and *Mover of Men & Mountains*.

LeTourneau's aircraft was the subject for a story in the *Warsaw Daily Times* newspaper in August of 1947. The article, written by the paper's aviation columnist, William Mollenhour, said, "The fastest airplane to be seen at a Warsaw airport to date is R. G. LeTourneau's converted A-26. This plane is identical to the one Bill Odom used to make his speed-dash around the world. R. G. and his genial pilot, Roy Barnwell, were doing an even 350 miles per hour when they first appeared over Smith Field last weekend."

Mollenhour pointed out that the aircraft had been remodeled to include sleeping cots and "a wonderful observation seat in the plexiglass nose." As an afterthought, Mollenhour noted that LeTourneau's plane "has 4,000 horsepower and lands at 100 to 120 miles per hour."

In addition to the contribution of all his time and expertise and general financial support with gifts and loans, LeTourneau also assisted the operation by purchasing the Inn Hotel and Bethany Youth Camp. LeTourneau's wife personally oversaw the operation of Bethany Camp for nearly a decade.

THE J. PALMER MUNTZ YEARS

J. Palmer Muntz (1897-1958) enjoyed the longest and most financially successful tenure as Bible Conference director, from 1938 until 1958. A native of New York, he was converted at age 13 and became acquainted with the Bible conference movement through attending, as a teenager, sessions at R. A. Torrey's Montrose Bible Conference in Pennsylvania. After attending seminary, Muntz began the first of several pastorates in New York, including the Cazenovia Park Baptist Church of Buffalo, New York.

Although he had no national reputation and no long history of association with Winona, Muntz, at age 42, was elected by the board as director of the Bible conference. He began incrementally lengthening the conference from 10-12 days until the entire program lasted eight weeks.

During the decade of the 1940s, the World's Greatest Bible Conference grew and became the centerpiece of the summer season in Winona. The Chautauqua programs had consistently declined and lost money, and were discontinued entirely in 1943. But the decision was more than financial. Sidwell noted, "The sense of urgency that swept American Christians during and after World War II—resulting in everything from expanded foreign missions to evangelistic organizations such as Youth for Christ—made 'Non-Christian' lectures and concerts seem extraneous."[31]

Christian organizations located and became well-established in the town, including the Rodeheaver Hall-Mack Co., the Free Methodist Church of North America, and Grace College and Theological Seminary. Billy Graham spoke several times in the Tabernacle at Youth for Christ meetings. Crowds were large.

The conference gained additional national and international exposure through the growing medium of Christian radio. Early in the 1940s, WMBI, the radio station affiliated with Moody Bible Institute, offered free radio time to Winona for many of the conference sessions. The conference still had to bear some of the technical costs, including leasing the necessary phone lines to Chicago, but the publicity was priceless. Muntz later called the WMBI broadcasts, "the best stroke ever done for Winona's publicity."

Moody Bible Institute for a number of years conducted "Moody Week" at Winona during the month of June, just before the opening of the annual Bible conference. One of its interesting features was the "Excursion," by which the Pennsylvania Railroad brought hundreds

---

[31] Sidwell, p. 184

of people from Chicago to Winona Lake for the Saturday program of Moody Week.

The decade of the 1940s was unquestionably the most successful in Winona Lake's history. One church historian noted, "The quality of the personnel running Winona, the larger and more efficient operation of concessions, the growing crowds, and the move of new organizations to the area all combined to push Winona to its height in popularity and fame."[32]

The "efficient operation of concessions" included a number of business enterprises that were either owned and operated by the Assembly, or from which the Assembly earned percentages or rental fees. Assembly-owned businesses included a bakery, a bowling alley, a shuffleboard court, a grocery store, a gas station, a roller skating rink and several restaurants, including the cafeteria (where the Boat-House restaurant is currently located) and the Eskimo Inn, as well as a successful restaurant in the Winona Hotel.

Although this decade was one of the most successful in conference history, problems were brewing.

During the decade of the 1950s, the roster of conference speakers and musicians included the best-known names of the day. Crowds were still growing, with attendance of more than 23,000 in one day sometimes reported.[33] But operational problems, interpersonal conflicts, personnel changes, denominational controversies, and theological debates were beginning to take their toll.

Muntz and LeTourneau were at odds during this time, and there was rapid turnover in leadership—five different individuals served as executive director during the 1950s. After a short tenure by John Ironside, Arthur McKee returned for two years until he died. Louise Alfors became acting manager through the 1952 and 1953 seasons, followed by Robert Hughes, who lasted three years. In 1956 John Andrews, Jr. was named to succeed Hughes, but he lasted only two years, to be replaced in 1958 by Gordon Beck.

---

[32] Sidwell, p. 189

[33] Larson, Mel. "Behind the Scenes at Winona Lake." *Moody Monthly* magazine, May, 1954, p. 13.

LeTourneau finally backed away from involvement in Winona's affairs in about 1956. The directors elected Mrs. Billy Sunday as president, but she died shortly thereafter and Paul Bauman, from the Grace Brethren, was elected the new chairman of the board. J. Palmer Muntz resigned as director of the Bible conference on May 30, 1958. He was honored with a "J. Palmer Muntz Day" in 1958, an event which featured Billy Graham as speaker and was attended by between ten and fifteen thousand people. Alva J. McClain, president and founder of Grace Theological Seminary, gave an address on Muntz's contributions to Winona Lake and presented gold watches to Muntz and his wife on behalf of the board.

A POTENTIAL BILLY GRAHAM TAKEOVER?

Winona's relationship with Billy Graham took an interesting turn about this time. Graham, who had been hired by Youth for Christ as a staff evangelist shortly after its founding in Winona Lake in 1944, became an occasional speaker in Winona for Youth for Christ events and later for the Bible conference itself. Graham felt a deep affection for J. Palmer Muntz, who was directing the conference and in fact, when Graham resigned as president of Northwestern College (St. Paul, Minnesota) in 1951, he tried to persuade Muntz to succeed him as president.

The board of the Bible conference apparently hoped the Assembly might profit from its affiliation with Graham—perhaps as it had with Billy Sunday in an earlier day—and in 1956 it elected Graham as a director of the Assembly.

After speaking at the "J. Palmer Muntz Day" in 1958, Graham rode to the airport with Charles Pitts, one of his board members. Pitts was a wealthy Toronto businessman who also served on the board of the Winona Lake Christian Assembly. Graham suggested to Pitts that the Graham organization help Winona in some way—perhaps by air conditioning the Billy Sunday Tabernacle. Pitts suggested, in return, that the Graham association invest in Winona in return for a controlling interest in the Assembly.

Muntz and Pitts both agreed on the desirability, but differed as to technique. Muntz suggested the Graham association invest heavily in Winona, which would give them significant voting power on the Assembly board. Pitts, however, wanted the old board to resign first, and then turn complete control over to the Billy Graham group.

A number of sessions were scheduled to come to agreement, but it never happened. The Assembly finally rejected the offer in the fall of 1959. One can only speculate what Winona might have become if the Billy Graham Evangelistic Association had become the owner-operator as the decade of the 1960s was dawning.

With Gordon Beck still in place as the resident manager, a number of attempts were made to upgrade facilities, including the razing of the old auditorium and the building of the new Rodeheaver Auditorium and the refurbishing of several floors of the Winona Hotel. A proposal to build a new, modern motel was deemed too expensive.

Sidwell noted, "Although the new and redecorated structures were popular with visitors, they did not attract the larger crowds that Winona Lake needed to survive. By the mid-sixties, the Assembly was actually in a state of undeclared insolvency."[34]

During the decade of the 1960s, major changes came not only to Winona, but to the whole country. Families could travel more easily to newer, more exciting tourist destinations. Bible conferences began to decline. Winona's buildings were old and in need of costly maintenance. The debt was enormous. Gordon Beck's tenure ended in 1965, and he was followed by Toledo businessman Waldo Yeager, who was named Executive Manager for the final years of the Assembly's existence.

THE WINONA MOVEMENT COMES TO AN END

There was one more reorganization. In 1968, the Winona Lake Christian Assembly was facing bankruptcy for the third time in its history. The directors of the Assembly were at the end of their rope, and had begun to talk liquidation.

Grace's president, Dr. Herman A. Hoyt, was present for the discussion and he recalled, "I timidly interrupted the conversation to explain that Grace Theological Seminary and Grace College would

---

[34] Sidwell, p. 240

be hurt. I explained that I was not thinking of the financial side, but rather the moral and spiritual. I explained that one of the reasons that Grace Theological Seminary had moved to Winona Lake in 1939 was because of the moral and spiritual atmosphere provided by this great Bible conference."

Hoyt recalled, "Mr. Conner, a businessman from Indianapolis, responded with amazing pointedness: 'Then, why don't you take it over?' I threw my hands in the air and responded that this was not what I had in mind, but the other men took up this idea. They discussed it at great length, and finally insisted that I should think the matter over and come back to the meeting in the morning with some answer. The idea took fire and was fanned by the Spirit of God working in these men."[35]

Part of the rationale included the fact that the Assembly used its facilities only during the three months of the summer. Grace presumably could use many of the same facilities during the other nine months, which coincided with the school year. There was also a general compatibility of religious beliefs and principles between the organizations.

Consequently, on August 23, 1968, the officers of Grace College and Seminary and the Winona Lake Christian Assembly entered into an agreement which became effective September 30 of that year. The agreement called for the Assembly articles of incorporation to be amended so that a majority of the members of the Assembly board were to come from the Grace board. In turn, Grace agreed to guarantee the payment of all outstanding debts and liabilities of the Assembly, which amounted to $694,539.36 as of the effective date of the agreement. On August 23, 1968, the Assembly accepted the offer. Properties worth in excess of $1 million, including 25 acres plus buildings, were transferred to Grace as were the liabilities and debts of the Assembly. The newly-formed board included 12 members of the Grace board and four members from the former Assembly board. The Assembly's director, Waldo Yeager, resigned immediately.

---

[35] Hoyt, Herman A. "Miracle at Winona." *Brethren Missionary Herald,* October 19, 1968, p. 22.

Yeager, one of the transitional Christian Assembly leaders, was executive director of the Assembly from 1965 to 1968. His son, Waldo E. Yeager, now living in Florida, recalled, "My father, Waldo Yeager, was on the Christian Business Men's Committee (CBMC) as well as on the Winona Lake board in the late 50s/early 60s. By the early 1960s I had assumed the leadership of the family business, Cortland Produce Co. Inc., freeing my father up to do speaking as a layman around the world with CBMC and for involvement on the CBMC and Winona Lake boards."

Waldo E. Yeager recalled that while his father was serving on the Winona board as vice chairman, the chairman, Harry Smith, a banker with Bank of America in San Francisco, died, ushering his father in as chairman.

Yeager said, "It was during that time the board determined that Winona was in serious financial and operational condition and asked my father to assume the position as the executive director of Winona over the following three or four years."

Paul Johnson was a Detroit Christian businessman whom the elder Yeager had recruited to join the Winona board. The plan was for Yeager and Johnson to arrange with Dr. Herman Hoyt to have Grace College take over the ownership and operation of Winona Lake Christian Assembly, with all of the Winona board resigning at that time. The elder Yeager died in 2000.

Grace managed the Assembly for twenty years. The pattern of frequent financial deficits persisted, even with the increased income produced from Grace's rental of various Assembly facilities. Furthermore, aggressive attempts to raise major dollars during the final several years fell far short of meeting the needs to upgrade the deteriorating and outdated facilities. Consequently, Grace found it necessary to close the Bible Conference as of September 30, 1988.

After more than seventy years, the Winona Movement, as envisioned and developed by Solomon Dickey, came to an end.

Under the leadership of Grace College and Seminary some programming continued. Groups continued to rent facilities at Winona by the week for conferences on prophecy, Jewish evangelism, a gathering of Christian magicians, an organization formed to evangelize in Russia, and more. Bible conferences continued for a time but were reduced to four weeks in 1969 and then to three weeks in 1970. Eventually they were phased out altogether.

A series of leaders continued to fight the losing battle of deteriorating buildings and declining market. As president of Grace Schools, Dr. Herman Hoyt fulfilled a dual role of leading both the educational institutions and the Christian Assembly. Over the years a number of individuals were named to lead what was left of the conference planning and facilities rental operation.

Ron Busch was named executive director of the Winona Lake Christian Assembly by President Homer A. Kent, Jr., in 1984 and he served until 1988, when the conferences closed. Busch had been assistant director of the Gull Lake Bible Conference in Hickory Corners, Michigan, for 12 summers and he was a board member for RBC Ministries (Radio Bible Class until a renaming in 1994). Busch had been a professor of communication at Grand Rapids Baptist College (now Cornerstone University) in Michigan prior to becoming director of the Winona conference. Busch died on October 11, 2004, at the age of 58 in Michigan from complications of diabetes and a surgery that took place on October 7.

Several key transitions took place during the years the "World's Largest Bible Conference" was at its height.

The fledgling Grace Theological Seminary had moved to Winona Lake from Akron, Ohio, in 1939 and soon realized the need for training undergraduates to prepare them to enter the seminary's graduate programs. Grace College was founded in 1948 as a two-year school and was expanded to a four-year liberal arts college in 1954.

The world headquarters of the Free Methodist Church, which had occupied the Mount Memorial building since 1935, moved to Indianapolis in 1990, leaving the local Free Methodist church as the denomination's only presence in the community. Its Light and Life bookstore was sold to local banker Brad Brail, who moved the retail store from Winona to a shopping plaza on Rt. 30 East, and eventually closed the business.

The Rodeheaver School of Music, once so popular with gospel musicians everywhere, declined significantly in its appeal and programming and eventually ceased operating. Its earlier popularity was demonstrated in a newspaper report from August of 1962 which indicated that a near-capacity crowd of about 5,000 was expected to jam Winona Lake's Billy Sunday Tabernacle to witness the annual music festival. The event was described as "a glittering extravaganza of gospel songs, excerpts from oratorios, spirituals and choral anthems programmed as a climax to the Rodeheaver Sacred Music Conference in Winona Lake."

The religious musical spectacular was under the direction of James E. Thomas, president of the Rodeheaver Company, and featured a 200-voice mixed choir, festival band, and "many of the nation's finest gospel singers, both a men's and women's chorus."

CHAPTER 11
Winona's Influence Spreads Worldwide.

*"There is prodigious room within the boundaries of theological or-
thodoxy for a surprising variety of spiritual expressions."*
Kenneth Boa

A NUMBER OF ORGANIZATIONS—MANY OF THEM CHRISTIAN MINIS-
tries—were either founded in Winona Lake or considered Winona
as a main operating base. Winona's reach was truly worldwide, and
many of the Winona Lake-based organizations or groups with their
roots in Winona continue to impact the world.

ORIENTAL MISSIONARY SOCIETY
The Oriental Missionary Society (OMS) had a presence in Winona
Lake for many years as one of its five regional offices. OMS began
ministry in Japan in 1901. Today, OMS ministers throughout Africa, Asia, the Caribbean, Europe, and Latin America.

When Charles and Lettie Cowman, Ernest and Julia Kilbourne,
and Juji and Katsuko Nakada began the work of OMS, they believed
the best way to reach a nation for Christ was through its own sons
and daughters. So they opened a Bible training school and trained
the Japanese to serve as church planters and pastors.

In David Hall's (ed.) book *Lived Religion in America: Toward
a History of Practice*, it is noted, "The Oriental Missionary Society,
founded by the Cowmans in 1901, originally worked primarily in
Japan and China. Around the time missionaries were kicked out of

China, the organization became the Overseas Missionary Society and it is now called OMS International."

The Cowmans served overseas from 1901 to 1917, when Charles Cowman's ill health forced them to return to the United States. During the next six years, Mrs. Cowman nursed her husband until his death. Out of Mrs. Cowman's experiences and heartbreak came her first book, *Streams in the Desert,* followed by its companion, *Springs in the Valley.*

During the next twenty-five years Mrs. Cowman inspired several nationwide Scripture distribution campaigns and wrote seven more books. Finally, on Easter Sunday in 1960, at the age of ninety, Mrs. Cowman met face-to-face the God she had served so faithfully for nearly a century.

After her husband's death she became a frequent speaker at the Winona Lake Bible Conference, as well as during weeklong summer missionary meetings sponsored by the OMS. The organization owned a home on Kings Highway, where Mrs. Cowman lived during the summer.

In the 1970s, OMS changed its name to OMS International to better reflect its global ministry. Then, in January 2010, the name was again changed to One Mission Society.

The principle of "one ministry giving birth to another" is exemplified in the story of Dick and Margaret Hillis, missionaries to China who were forced to flee China in 1950 because of escalating war in that country.

Shortly thereafter, just ten days after their sixth child was born, Dick Hillis was invited to attend a conference in Winona Lake. During an evening service in the Billy Sunday Tabernacle, Bob Pierce challenged Dick Hillis for ministry in Formosa and invited him to come forward so they could pray for him. A group of young men gathered around Hillis, including Billy Graham, and within three months Dick Hillis was part of a team on their way to Formosa.

Several years later, Hillis and his team developed a whole-nation strategy and joined hands with the Oriental Missionary Society to preach the gospel in every village on the island before the communists could take over. The president of Taiwan, General Chiang Kai-Shek, invited Hillis to preach the gospel to the armed forces.

Dick and a colleague, Ellsworth Culver, also developed a new sports evangelism ministry called Venture for Victory (VV). Don Odle, basketball coach at Taylor University in Upland, Indiana, was asked to direct the new sports ministry and bring the first Venture for Victory team to Taiwan.

One of the earliest Venture for Victory players was Bud Stanley Schaeffer, a Wheaton College alumnus who had been a standout high school player in Michigan City, Indiana (he was inducted into the Indiana Sports Hall of Fame in 1970), and who played professionally for a short time with the Boston Whirlwinds.

Grace College head basketball coach Jim Kessler recalls, "Bud, while playing in Manila before a standing-room-only crowd, was struck with the idea of what a great opportunity it could be to share the gospel with thousands who regularly assembled to watch American boys play basketball in friendly games in an international venue."

"This greatly influenced his decision," Kessler said, "to join that first team in a 'venture for victory.'"

For 12 years, Schaeffer and his growing family lived in the Philippines, where he directed and coordinated Venture for Victory basketball teams, camp work, and sports clinics. Those people who made religious commitments at games were encouraged to sign up for a Bible correspondence course available through Orient Crusades. Schaeffer also coached the 1956 National Olympic basketball squad from Taiwan, using the neutral Portuguese name of Formosa ("Beautiful Island") because of the protest of the People's Republic of China against Taiwan's participation in the games.

Orient Crusades changed its name to Overseas Crusades and in 1967 they asked Schaeffer to return to the U.S. and head a new division of the organization known as Sports Ambassadors. Athletic teams of basketball and baseball players, both men and women, were recruited and sent to countries all over the world, including South America, Australia, Europe, and the Far East.

Coach Jim Kessler of the Grace College Lancers said, "Bud 'The Cat' Schaeffer, as he was known all over the Philippines and Taiwan, is a great old saint of God and a true pioneer in sports missions, especially in the Orient."

Kessler now frequently partners with Sports Ambassadors to take Grace College basketball teams on mission trips. including a trip to the Philippines in July and August of 2008. On that trip the Grace athletes played 25 basketball games in 18 days, gave testimonies at halftimes, and worked with local pastors in outreach.

AMERICAN ASSOCIATION FOR JEWISH EVANGELISM

The American Association for Jewish Evangelism, born in 1943, was first headquartered in Chicago but was then moved to Winona Lake, where it occupied quarters in the administration building on Park Avenue. Its primary purpose was to evangelize Jews. It produced literature, sponsored missionaries, led tours of Israel, and conducted annual conferences in Winona Lake.

Leading figures in the organization included J. Palmer Muntz, Dr. William Culbertson of Moody Bible Institute, and Dr. Hyman Appleman, an attorney and a converted Jew. He was a guiding force in the ministry of the AAJE, serving as president for a number of years. Theologically, the tenor of the conferences had a dispensationalist premillennialist bent. A week-long prophecy conference with emphasis on Israel and its place in biblical prophecy continues to be held in Winona Lake each summer, though it is now sponsored by the Friends of Israel organization.

KEN ANDERSON FILMS

Shortly after moving to Winona Lake from Muskegon, Michigan, to work for S. Lambert Huffman's Christian publishing enterprise, a restless and brilliant young Ken Anderson began to dream of reaching millions for Christ through dramatic films. Anderson's son, Lane Anderson, provided much of the following background information and explanation of the growth and development of Ken Anderson Films in Winona Lake.

Ken Anderson never knew his mother—she died on the day of his birth. He was raised by his maternal grandmother, who took him for long walks on their Iowa farmland and instilled in him a love for nature and a Christian philosophy of life. It was during his freshman year at Wheaton College in Illinois in 1936 that he came, in his words, to "a vital assurance of my salvation."[36] A message by Dr. Harry Ironside challenged him to full-time Christian service, and Anderson enrolled in Trinity College the next year.

At Trinity Anderson met and married his wife, Doris, and shortly thereafter they moved to northern Minnesota where Ken served as a student pastor. Eventually they returned to Illinois and Anderson enrolled at Northwestern University's School of Journalism. While there he had success publishing in *Collier's* magazine, and began working with the fledgling Youth for Christ organization. He served as managing editor of *Youth for Christ* magazine from 1945 to 1953, when he was succeeded by Mel Larson.

In the early 1940s while living in Wheaton, Illinois, Anderson began writing novels, offering them to various publishers. Ted Engstrom was editor at the newly formed Zondervan Publishing House, and he invited Anderson to Grand Rapids, Michigan, to meet Pat and Bernie Zondervan. A friendship was established through which dozens of early Ken Anderson manuscripts made their way into print with selections for adults, teenagers, and children.

It was through Youth for Christ and Wheaton College contacts that Anderson's early career networked with so many individuals, including Billy Graham, who later became key figures in the Christian world. During Billy Graham's years at Wheaton, Anderson often ghost-wrote articles for him, based on concepts Graham would provide. Often this produced articles that appeared in *Youth for Christ* magazine, which Anderson edited.

Lane Anderson noted that also located in Wheaton, Illinois, was a Christian filmmaker named Charles O. Baptista. Christian films up to this time pretty much were documentary presentations or sermon-type material. In 1948, when Baptista decided he wanted to produce his first dramatic story, he went looking for someone who could develop such a script. Ken Anderson was recommended to

---

[36] Wiersbe, Warren. "His Typewriter Belongs to Teens." *Youth for Christ* magazine, July, 1961, p. 21.

him, and after writing his very first screen play, Anderson was invited by Baptista to direct the film, as well.

With no previous experience, Anderson did direct the film, working with a cinematographer who, up until this time, had only operated a still camera. The challenges were huge, but were overcome. Having developed a few projects with Baptista and also sensing that a much greater opportunity existed, Ken Anderson was encouraged by his Youth for Christ friends to begin his own Christian film ministry. Many of these leaders were looking for high-quality youth films to use in their Youth for Christ rallies.

One such man, Morry Carlson, who operated Muskegon, Michigan, Youth for Christ, invited Anderson to move into the area and even gave him a piece of land upon which he could build a home. On property immediately adjacent, land also was given for the first Gospel Films studio office and production facility. "Uncle Morry" Carlson, who died in 1994, also served for a time as director of the Winona Lake Bible Conference.

Over the next ten years, 12-15 films were produced, and distribution began, including a couple of international productions which garnered tremendous results for the sake of the Gospel in English-speaking corners of the world.

In 1948, Bob Pierce, who later founded World Vision, invited Anderson to travel to China with him to speak to rallies of young people. They flew to virtually every major city in China, and tens of thousands of young people gave their lives to Christ prior to the closing of China and the takeover by Mao Tse-tung.

Upon his return, Anderson was invited to share his experiences at the Youth for Christ Convention held annually at Winona Lake. It was at this rally in the summer of 1949 that a man by the name of Sidenham Lambert Huffman was present, and he thereafter approached Anderson about assisting his ministry. Huffman's publishing offices at that time were located in Killarney Castle on the island in Winona Lake. The Anderson/Huffman relationship was maintained during the Gospel Films years of the 1950s.

Many years, Gospel Films held screen tests which were shot during the Youth for Christ Convention in the Rainbow Room of the

Westminster Hotel. Some of the company's finest amateur talent came from those summers. A few of the people became frequent lead players in films for years to come.

By 1960, it became apparent that Anderson and the board of directors for Gospel Films were heading in different directions. Setting out a fleece, Anderson received God's answer that he needed to leave. One of the opportunities to earn an income and re-establish himself in Christian films was the open invitation from Lambert Huffman to come full-time and work for him. This was attractive because at that time, the beginning of the 1960s, Winona Lake was a robust center of the evangelical Christian world.

Part of the arrangement in coming to Winona Lake was the establishment of a partnership between Ken Anderson and Lambert Huffman in a new venture to be called Ken Anderson Films. Ken and Doris Anderson would own 51 percent of the stock, and Lambert Huffman 49 percent. The business was to be a Christian tax-paying entity. In the late '60s, Lambert Huffman's portion was bought out, and the ministry was a family-owned organization from that point forward.

The very first Ken Anderson Film, produced in 1961, was *The Family That Changed the World.* Featured in that film was Knute Larson, a Grace Theological Seminary student. Knute Larson also became a proofreader, then an editor, and ultimately he took over all of Anderson's responsibilities with the commentary and Sunday school materials development.

Local news media noted that the first showing of a movie filmed in Warsaw, *The Family That Changed the World,* was set for Saturday, October 21, at a Kosciusko County Youth for Christ rally in the Lincoln School building. Norma Jean Weckler, a 1961 Warsaw High School graduate, and Knute Larson, a senior at Grace College, would be present at the premiere showing. Both Weckler and Larson appeared in the film along with professional actors from the Chicago area.

Over the years, Ken Anderson Films became very well-known all over the world. Employees used to call themselves the best kept secret in the evangelical world, because it seemed people didn't know them nearly as well in the USA as did Christians around the world. Many productions occurred in other countries and continents, including Africa, India, and Asia.

More than 70 manuscripts were published through the years, the first 41 of which were by Zondervan. Other publishers included Word, Inc., Victor Books, Creation House, Thomas Nelson, New Leaf Press, Pacific Garden Mission, Tyndale House, and some lesser names.

Through the era of Ken Anderson Films, more than 200 Christian films were produced with selections for children, young people, and adults. Probably the best-known film was *Pilgrim's Progress,* which was produced in 1978 and introduced an unknown stage actor, Liam Neeson, to the screen. Other popular titles, often using local acting talent, included *Senior Year, Hobo and the Runaway, Kidnapped, Toby's Treehouse,* and others.

During the years of the Winona Lake Christian Assembly, Ken Anderson served at different times on the board of the association. He also served on the President's Council of Grace College under the leadership of Dr. John Davis and he taught magazine writing at Grace College.

In 1962, Ken Anderson Films was hired by John Haggai, an aspiring USA arena evangelist, to produce a film that would promote his ministry of city-wide evangelism. It was through this contact that Ken Anderson was invited in 1975 to become a visiting instructor in Journalism and Audiovisual Evangelism at the Haggai Institute, originally begun in Singapore and later expanded to a second campus in Maui, Hawaii. Over a period of 25 years he often taught three to four times a year, connecting with thousands of Christian leaders from every corner of the globe. It was through these contacts that ultimately another ministry was born.

In 1991 InterComm, which initially was deemed to be the international communication ministry of Ken Anderson Films, was initiated to carry on relationships with leaders met through the Haggai Institute. A 501(c)(3) fund-raising venue, a mission organization, was needed to assist in securing the finances to pay for audiovisual tools that Third World leaders could not afford or could not import.

Though Ken Anderson died in 2006, this legacy continues. InterComm has developed lip sync dubbed versions of many films, such as *Pilgrim's Progress*, to be used for evangelism in countries around the world. It is through InterComm, now directed by several of Ken Anderson's sons, that the greatest impact for eternity has been noted. Anderson's legacy lives on through the lives of those impacted by his scripts and films.

WIN-SOME WOMEN

Win-Some Women, Inc., a women's bi-annual retreat ministry which ministered to more than 30,000 women over 36 years, began in the spring of 1966. Throughout its history, the ministry used Philippians 1:6 as its theme verse, "being confident of this, that he who began a good work in you will carry it on to completion until the day of Christ Jesus."

A group of eight women from the Winona Lake/Warsaw area attended a Christian retreat in Canada. When they were unable to obtain reservations for the following year, they birthed the idea of beginning a local ministry of interdenominational retreats.

A formation meeting attended by ten women was held in the home of Ethel Anderson on March 22, 1968, followed by a meeting at the Winona Hotel in April at which "Win-Some Women" was officially born as an organization. The first retreat was held at the Winona Hotel in the fall of 1968. Kay Grove was co-founder and co-chairman with Ethel Anderson for several years and, even after having moved away, she returned to the retreats to help with leadership.

Speakers for the earliest retreats included Millie Dienert and Corrie ten Boom, with pianist/composer Beatrice Bush Bixler directing the music. A retreat at the Winona Hotel in March of 1971 featured Vonette (Mrs. Bill) Bright as speaker. The next year Jill Briscoe was the feature. By 1974, when Beverly LaHaye was the featured speaker for the March retreat, about 1,000 women were attending.

In 1977, with more than 1,400 registered, several hundred registrations had to be returned because all facilities were at capacity in Winona Lake. By 1980 the group was offering the option of both mid-week and weekend retreats to accommodate all who wished to attend.

Musician Beatrice Bush Bixler continued to compose a new theme song for each season, and housing accommodations were expanded to include the International Friendship House (Westminster), the Holiday Inn in Warsaw, and other available lodging options.

Headline speakers for the 1984 conference were "Speak Up With Confidence" director Carol Kent and actress/playwright Jeannette Clift George. In addition to the nationally-known speakers, there were always local women leading sessions and workshops on specific topics. Some local speakers included Char Binkley, Miriam Uphouse, Carin Roy, Frances Haslam, Barbara Woodring, Maryon Titus, Judy and Bill Reneker, Ethel Anderson, and more. Daisy Hepburn, author of the *Life With Spice* Bible study series, joined the speaker's roster in 1987.

In 1990, the venue for the local retreat was moved from Rodeheaver Auditorium to the Wagon Wheel Theatre on Center Street in Warsaw, Indiana. The 25th anniversary retreat was held in October of 1993 at the Wagon Wheel with Jeannette Clift George and Dorie Van Stone ("The Girl Nobody Loved") as speakers.

Other speakers of note throughout its history included Kay Arthur, Peg Rankin, Liz Curtis Higgs, Margaret Jensen, Anna Mow, Evelyn Christenson, and Maria Anne Hirschmann ("Hansi"). For many years the musicians for the events were the Fort Wayne, Indiana, team of "Sharon and Robin." Fran Dickinson of Fort Wayne was an integral part of the staff, as well.

After 36 years, Win-Some Women held its final retreat at the Wagon Wheel Theatre October 8 and 9, 2004. The featured speakers were Jill Briscoe and Margaret Jensen, who fashioned their messages around 2 Tim. 4:7, "...we have finished the course; we have kept the faith." The musician was Carla Karst.

Ethel Anderson had chaired the organization all through its 36 years. Staff members at the end included Anderson, Pam Valentine, Bambi Wilson, Carin Roy, and Treleen Cox. Throughout its existence, the ministry had a faithful auxiliary and "people helper" group, formed by Dorothy Toirac, that was the envy of many other retreat organizations.

The program for the final retreat carried this note of celebration:

The Win-Some Women staff thanks you for your faithful support of this ministry during the last 36 years. We were called to provide Christian teaching and fellowship and to model spiritually inspiring retreats. We are unanimous in believing we have fulfilled our mission. Therefore, the fall retreat will be our last one as we publicly thank our Lord Jesus Christ for His faithfulness in beginning this work and carrying it to completion in this celebration finale!

Win-Some Women spawned a number of retreat organizations in other locations. Among them are the Victorious Women in Kentucky, the Women of the Rock in Illinois, and Reaching Women in Ohio.

MEN FOLLOWING CHRIST

Men Following Christ began in 1999 as Men For Christ in Winona Lake, following the pattern of Youth For Christ, which was started in Winona Lake more than 55 years earlier. Founders Rod Mayer and Don Clemens both served on YFC's local board. Their foundational verse for the men's ministry was and is 1 John 2:5b-6 "This is how we know we are in Him. Whoever claims to live in him must walk as Jesus did."

Clemens and Mayer sought to establish a 2 Timothy 2:2 ministry, helping local pastors form men's groups in their churches. They used 5 E's: Evangelism, Establishing, Equipping, Encouraging, and Extending as the goal for men.

Today, some 125-150 men meet the last Saturday of every month (except December) for breakfast, fellowship, worship, and a message. More than 40 local churches usually are represented at each Men Following Christ meeting.

SPANISH WORLD MINISTRIES

Tucked into the woods at the corner of Pierceton Road and County Road 250E in Winona Lake is the headquarters for a ministry that for years has had a major impact on the Spanish-speaking countries of the world.

After 28 years as a missionary to Cuba, Haiti, France, and Spain, Florent Toirac, a Cuban national well aware of the difficulties of reaching the masses in remote areas, and convinced that radio was a way to reach them, established Spanish World Gospel Broadcasting with the radio program, *El Camino de la Vida* ("The Way of Life"). Toirac lived in Winona Lake and his wife, Dorothy, headed the foreign language programs at Grace College.

Initially the program was broadcast from Tangier (North Africa) into Spain, and later into Latin America where an expansion of the transmissions began to take place. To accomplish the discipleship process, national missionaries were added. They were supported through ministry partners in the USA, and were periodically supplied with literature, New Testaments, and Bibles to assist them in their evangelistic efforts. With expansion of nationals and literature, the ministry's name was then changed to *Spanish World Gospel Mission*.

Toirac died in 1989 and Cornelius Rivera became executive director in 1991, serving until the end of 2010. During his time as director he provided vision to the ministry, expanding the radio outreach by assigning to the national missionaries the responsibility of finding the radio stations for airing the broadcasts, duplicating the programs, distributing them, and monitoring their transmission in their countries.

Rivera continues with the production of two radio programs for distribution by missionaries. He also teaches at the Seminary for Expository Teaching in Honduras. In summer of 2010 he published a commentary in Spanish on three of the minor prophets because there are very few exegetical commentaries in Spanish.

After serving as a pastor in a church in the northern part of Mexico, Daniel Sandoval joined Spanish World Ministries as the Ministry Coordinator in 2002. For eight years he was in charge of coordinating, training, and overseeing the work of national missionaries. In January of 2011 he was appointed as director of the ministry.

A hurricane that devastated Honduras in 1998 became the opportunity for a humanitarian work which has resulted in establishing a small community, a church, a medical clinic, and a missionary training center. In addition three other congregations have been established in Honduras and a congregation has been planted in Argentina. The mission is now known as Spanish World Ministries, reflecting its multi-faceted global outreach (spanishworld.org/).

The missionary team has grown to 19 missionaries, ministering in 15 countries. The radio outreach is present in every Spanish-speaking country, heard over approximately 1,600 stations.

WORLD MISSIONARY PRESS

World Missionary Press began in the hearts of Watson and Rose Goodman while they were missionaries in South Africa. On their wedding day in Plymouth, Indiana, in August, 1943, they dedicated themselves to missions and then enjoyed a one-day honeymoon in Winona Lake. They began their 16-year ministry in South Africa in 1945. While they were at sea en route to Mozambique on a Portuguese vessel, the first atomic bomb was dropped on Japan, signaling the close of World War II.

In 1951, they established Gospel Centre Work, a faith ministry, concentrating their efforts mainly on evangelizing the children and youth in neglected black areas of South Africa. The Goodmans would clear off their dining room table, place a mimeograph machine on it, and run pages with Scriptures and pictures to color for the 2,000 black children they taught weekly in the five townships surrounding Germiston, South Africa.

Watson and Rose's printing progressed to a small printing press in their garage. They began printing the 48-page Scripture booklet *Help From Above* in the Zulu language, stapling the booklets by hand.

Watson's vision for reaching the world through Scripture booklets distributed free of charge grew in intensity. In 1961, God led them to return to the U.S. to establish World Missionary Press in Winona Lake, Indiana. At their farewell service, Watson and Rose sang as their last duet in Africa *Beyond the Sunset*, written by Virgil Brock of Winona Lake. To their surprise, they later found Dr. Brock still living at Winona Lake. In fact, Brock was the very first person to contribute a gift annuity to their fledgling ministry.

World Missionary Press was incorporated in the state of Indiana on July 7, 1961. Dr. Myron Boyd, speaker for the Free Methodist's

Light and Life Hour, was made chairman, and Dr. Woodrow Goodman, president of Marion College, became secretary, a position he held for 40 years. Watson Goodman was named president and general manager and Rose Goodman, vice-president and treasurer.

Local builder/developer Bill Bibler (1926-2012) sold them land on Wooster Road and constructed their first building, 40 x 50 feet, for just a $300 down payment. The new building at 907 Wooster Road was dedicated the afternoon of November 11, 1961.

The ministry expanded rapidly, and construction began in April of 1966 for a 40 x 60 foot addition, which was dedicated debt-free on June 25, 1966. At the ministry's annual dinner in November of 1969 the couple's daughter, Vicky, was moved to join the work and shortly thereafter she became the publications manager.

Vicky and her husband, Jay Benson, had been married in the Winona Lake Free Methodist Church in October of 1967 after both had completed their master's degrees in journalism at Syracuse University in New York. Both were employed at the Free Methodist Church World Headquarters in Winona Lake, where Jay was managing editor of *Light and Life*, the Free Methodist denominational magazine.

Jay's father, John Benson, was plant manager of the Free Methodist Publishing House and a member of the Winona Lake town board. Later, upon his retirement, John Benson worked at World Missionary Press for nine years, developing their pre-press department. John's wife, Mary, was manager of the Light and Life Bookstore in Winona for a number of years and later taught English and journalism at Warsaw High School.

The late Jay Benson was one of the two Benson brothers rescued by N. Bruce Howe from a house fire in 1956. The Bensons' father, John, served on the town board when they approved the purchase of expensive airpacks which, having been unpacked the very morning of his house fire, saved the lives of his two sons.

World Missionary Press's Winona Lake building was soon outgrown for adequate and efficient work, but zoning restrictions would not permit another expansion to the existing building. Plotting on a map the locations from which volunteer workers were coming,

Goodman identified New Paris-Nappanee, Indiana, as the central focus point. A plot of 3.75 acres of land, already properly zoned for a printing operation, was found near New Paris, about 20 miles north of Winona Lake.

A couple from New Paris who had been driving to Winona Lake to volunteer at World Missionary Press had been impressed by God not to sell their land in New Paris just yet. When Watson and Rose Goodman approached them about buying the land for WMP's new headquarters, the couple offered the land at one-fourth of its value because it was to be used for the Lord's work.

A modern, all-steel building, 100 x 120 feet with a loading dock, was designed, built, and was dedicated on Sunday, November 7, 1970. Although operations moved to New Paris, World Missionary Press retained its post office box 276 in Winona Lake for the next 25 years because mail continued to arrive from around the world in response to Scripture booklets still in circulation that carried that address on the back.

Grace College later purchased the Wooster Road building, added the brick façade and wing, and it became Byers Hall, then East Hall, which housed the college's music department until the building was occupied by Trine University in a joint engineering program agreement with Grace College in 2011.

Watson Goodman's initial three goals for World Missionary Press were:

1. To believe God eventually for a million dollars a year.
2. To send out one million Scripture booklets a month free of charge.
3. To print in 300 languages.

The organization's website says, "God's provision has far surpassed Watson's first two goals. Income has risen to about $3 million a year. WMP currently prints 6 million Scripture booklets per month for free distribution in 210 countries and islands. The third goal was reached in January 2000 with the production of language number 300--Hmong Daw for Laos, Thailand, and Vietnam. We are currently printing in 337 languages."

Rose Goodman always remembered the black children in South Africa whom she tearfully had left behind. So in 1991, when given the opportunity, she wrote the illustrated children's booklet, *The Way to God*. WMP now prints 19 publications, including topical Scripture booklets, Bible studies, and New Testaments.

Watson and Rose Goodman passed the baton when they retired from WMP in 1987 to begin another work, Enterprises For Emmanuel, producing children's salvation coloring books including *He Is Risen!*. However, in January of 2000 EFE closed its doors and publication rights to the coloring books were given to World Missionary Press.

After a four-year stint in Indonesia with the Christian and Missionary Alliance publishing house there, Vicky and her husband Jay returned to Indiana and were involved with World Missionary Press after their return in the fall of 1976. Jay became president in 1988 and served until his death in January of 2013. Vicky Goodman Benson is now vice-president, having served as treasurer for 30 years and having compiled several Scripture booklets and Bible studies. Watson Goodman passed away in January 2002 at the age of 82. Rose Goodman passed away in February 2006 at the age of 86.

VICTORY SKY PILOTS

From the middle 1940s to the early 1950s Rev. Paul Hartford, dubbed "The Flying Preacher" or "The Flying Parson" by news media, operated a flying school out of Winona Lake to train potential aviator missionaries in the use of single-engine aircraft.

Descriptive material on a missionary aviation scholarship to Moody Bible Institute which was endowed by Hartford's daughter and grandchildren describes Hartford's life as "a life lived with great enthusiasm, talent and ability, and totally dedicated to spreading the gospel through use of the single-engine airplane." The material notes that Hartford was the founder of Victory Sky Pilots, Inc., "the first flight school in the U.S. dedicated to training missionaries to use the airplane on foreign fields."

The memoirs of the first woman pilot to graduate from the program, Helen Jean Moose Zwyghuizen, notes that Hartford's program was headquartered in the Garfield Hotel on Chestnut Street in Winona Lake.

Aviation columnist William Mollenhour, writing in the October 27, 1947, issue of the *Warsaw Daily Times*, noted that Hartford was the owner-operator of the smaller of three airports located in the Warsaw area. Named "Victory Field," the airport was described as 80 acres nestled on the west shore of Chapman Lake. The field at that time had three runways, and construction of facilities was continuing, with the Hartford family living in a country home next to the airport. Mollenhour noted that "Few local pilots fly at Victory Field, for it caters mostly to ministers and mission-folk on their way to foreign fields where the airplane is not only an asset, but a necessity."

Noting that there were currently 26 graduates of "Victory Sky Pilots, Inc.," Mollenhour indicated that 120 students have studied at the aviation school, utilizing seven planes. He also noted that Rev. L. L. Grubb, executive field secretary of the Grace Brethren Home Missions Council, based his own Cessna plane at Victory Field and he "hops off to all parts of the United States by air."

Hartford was also a representative of Youth for Christ, speaking frequently at YFC events and at other young people's meetings. An advertisement for one of his appearances in Florida indicated that the person bringing the most people to the YFC rally would be rewarded with a flight in Hartford's plane. Hartford, who had been a missionary, also was a skilled trumpeter and vocalist and often included music in his speaking engagements.

Mollenhour reported that Victory Sky Pilots was guided by a board of directors consisting of Mr. and Mrs. Hartford; Dr. Ralph Neighbor of the Fort Wayne Gospel Tabernacle; Dr. Sidney Correll, editor of the *Missionary Digest* in Dayton, Ohio; Dr. Torrey Johnson of Chicago, president of Youth for Christ International; Dr. J. G. Gay, Longview, Washington, president of the Grace Gospel Evangelistic Association; and Dr. John Huffman, dean of the Winona Lake School of Theology.

Hartford's aviation school received wide attention, including a write-up in *Newsweek* magazine. An article from the *Presbyterian Guardian*[37] described the schedule.

---

[37] *Presbyterian Guardian*, March 10, 1945. Volume 14, No. 5, p. 66

Devotions start the day. Ministry students get three home-cooked meals a day on the field, but are likely to be asked to "help with the dishes." To his students, Hartford stresses: "You can become a frontier messenger, take a new 'grasshopper' ship loaded with supplies and reach a new tribe which never has heard of Jesus Christ. Or you can become a ferry pilot, taking a plane to a missionary halfway around the world. Or you could become an explorer, taking a flight of a few thousand miles into remote regions and explore the terrain to discover the best type of aircraft suitable to the region.

The 1947 newsletter from the annual Winona Schools Reunion, which was held for a number of summers, noted that, "Paul Hartford, new owner of the Garfield, who has the Winona Flying School for Missionaries, delivered a missionary to his station in a jungle country, made a general survey of the air route through Central and South America, and dropped an airmail note for his friend, Robert E. Neighbor, a missionary near Daderba, Colombia."

The newsletter noted that "Winona seems to be air-minded," since the School of Theology now offered a ground school course in aviation and Fred Strauss Skyways was offering chartered flights anywhere in the U.S. Strauss said his planes, "are well equipped, seats wide and upholstered, has radio and loudspeaker and adjustable heat."

Unlimited Potential Incorporated

A unique ministry that focuses on the world of professional baseball is also based in Winona Lake. Unlimited Potential Incorporated (UPI), founded in 1980 by baseball player and coach Tom Roy, has chronicled its history and impact in a book by Roy entitled *Released: A Story of God's Power Released in Pro Baseball* published by BMH Books of Winona Lake in 2010.

Tom Roy is the president and founder of UPI. After a very brief time in the San Francisco Giants organization as a pitcher, Roy went on to a career in radio, taking his first job in West Virginia. Shortly after that he felt called to pursue a college degree and enrolled at Grace College in Winona Lake. Upon completion of that degree he coached high school baseball for three years and at the college level for nine years, including coaching at his alma mater, Grace College.

In 1978 plans for the organization began to form for Roy and his wife, Carin. In 1980 the ministry became a reality. Roy and his associates have now ministered to players through chapels, in camps and clinics, including speaking and conducting clinics in more than 60 countries around the globe.

In January of 2008 Roy assumed the role of President/Founder and he now works with the advancement of the ministry as well as staying in contact with UPI alumni and caring for ballplayers through counseling. There are also specific ministries to the military and through the format of hunting trips.

According to its website (upi.org), "The purpose of UPI has always been to share the greatest news ever told through the greatest game ever played." One of the major emphases of the ministry has been evangelistic baseball clinics both in USA cities and in cities throughout the world.

UPI's first clinic was held the summer of 1981 in Milwaukee, Wisconsin, with Faith Bible Church. Christian ballplayers from both the Oakland A's and the Milwaukee Brewers participated. As a result of the baseball strike the next summer, ministry opportunities were limited, but UPI was able to return to Milwaukee for a second citywide baseball clinic outreach with ten major leaguers participating, including seven from the Brewers and three from the visiting Detroit Tigers. Nearly 1,100 children and adults attended from the greater Milwaukee area and approximately 125 children and adults recognized their need to trust Christ through the testimonies of these ballplayers. The next clinic in 1982 was in Akron, Ohio, in conjunction with the Chapel in University Park with players from the Cleveland Indians and the New York Yankees participating. Even though it rained, nearly 1,800 gathered inside and the ministry was begun.

Since those first years, the clinic ministry in the USA has grown. Churches in many cities have begun hosting clinics on their own, with UPI turning the leadership over to the local churches. This gives the UPI staff opportunity to develop clinic ministries in new cities as the opportunities present themselves.

Since its inception, the overseas ministry of UPI has grown considerably and many more doors have been opened. The growing popularity of baseball throughout the world has opened doors in unprecedented ways to teach baseball fundamentals and to share the Christian message.

Every major league and minor league baseball team has a chapel program, which has given UPI staff members opportunity to train and disciple players within the Baseball Chapel program. Each Sunday, every baseball team holds a chapel service which gives the players, who are unable to attend traditional church services, the opportunity to hear and respond to the Word of God.

MASTERMEDIA INTERNATIONAL

Another high-visibility ministry that had its roots in Winona Lake is Mastermedia International, which now has offices in Los Angeles and New York. The ministry was founded and is directed by Larry Poland, who grew up in Winona Lake.

Poland, who moved with his family to Winona Lake in 1949 when he was 10, is the son of Frank and Alta Poland. Frank, who died in 2008, moved to Winona Lake to begin a long-term career as business administrator of the Brethren Home Missions Council, the Grace Brethren church-planting organization. Alta Poland died in 1982.

Larry Poland as a youth worked as a bellhop at all three Winona Lake hotels—the Inn, the Winona Hotel, and the Westminster. He recalls starting that job at age 12 and says he made about $6 a week lugging suitcases for the many conference-goers, speakers, and musicians who came to Winona in the summers.

His entrepreneurial streak showed itself early when, during the construction of McClain Hall in 1950 and 1951, the young Poland would load his bicycle basket with milk and juice at the Winona Dairy on Kings Highway and would then pedal to the construction site where he would sell the drinks—at a profit—to the construction workers.

Poland was elected student body president at Warsaw High School, was a national speech contest winner, and was an exchange student to Germany and France in 1956. He graduated from Warsaw High School in that year and entered Wheaton College in Illinois, graduating with a degree in social science.

Shortly after his marriage in 1962, Poland and his bride moved into a basement apartment on Chestnut Street in Winona Lake to begin studies at Grace Seminary. He took a summer job as captain of *The Virginia*, a long, slender, pencil-like tour boat that had survived a previous life at the Wisconsin Dells.

In addition to daytime cruises, Poland also took conference attendees on "Moonlight Cruises," which commenced from the entrance of the canal at about 10 p.m., when evening conference sessions were ended. Poland would narrate over the loudspeaker as the boat circled Winona Lake, spinning off stories about the history of the area. His spiels were, he admits, "mostly true," with "only minor embellishments."

One of his more memorable cruises ended abruptly when he ran the boat aground on a sandbar and his passengers alternately rushed from stern to bow as Poland rocked the boat vigorously and gunned the engine to free it from the sandbar.

Poland teamed up with Jerry Lelle, who ran the "Lelle Pad" pizza restaurant in the Eagle Arcade building, to sponsor all-the-pizza-you-can-eat cruises. However the hungry young Assembly staff members discovered the pizza bonanzas and ate so much the entrepreneurs were soon forced to discontinue the pizza-buffet cruises.

Poland's higher education continued with dual enrollment in Grace Theological Seminary for theological studies, and at Purdue University for a master's in educational administration. He completed a Ph.D. in educational administration with minors in sociology and political science at Purdue in 1967.

During this time he also served Grace College in several roles, including registrar, director of financial aid, director of admissions, teaching fellow, and in the area of institutional studies. One day he received a call from Lambert Huffman, who lived in the Killarney Castle on the island and was a board member of a struggling, small Bible college in Florida.

Huffman invited Poland to consider becoming president of the school. Poland accepted the role as president of Miami Christian College in 1967. For several years of his presidency, Lambert Huffman was chairman of the board of the Florida school. Poland was widely recognized as the country's youngest college president at age 27.

In 1973 he became director of the Agape Movement of Campus Crusade for Christ, International, which placed 800 short-term missionaries in 35 nations in eight and a half years. He later headed the World Thrust ministry for Campus Crusade.

In 1985, while pastoring an Evangelical Free Church in Redlands, California, he began the Mastermedia International organization, which he then joined full-time in 1991.

Mastermedia International (http://www.mastermediaintl.org/) provides consultation, research, and one-to-one counsel to media leaders to help create a deeper understanding of the Christian faith as well as the Christian community as a market for media products. Mastermedia's clients include decision-makers within ABC, CBS, NBC, Fox, Disney, DreamWorks, Sony, Paramount, Time Warner, AT&T, Hearst Corporation, MTV, HBO, AMC, Hallmark Channel, CNN, Fox News, and ESPN.

The organization also mobilizes prayer through the Media Leader Prayer Calendar, and provides spiritual support for media decision-makers as a platform for sharing the love of Jesus Christ. A primary focus has been building bridges of love and trust in place of the animosity which has often marked the relationship between Christian believers and media leaders over the content of their film and TV fare.

Poland has written eight books, travelled to 104 countries, and has started two Christian schools and a Christian radio station.

HEPHZIBAH HOUSE

Hephzibah House (hephzibahhouse.org/) is a private Christian boarding school for teenage girls, founded in 1971 and located in Winona Lake. For more than 40 years the ministry has sought to help teenage girls receive a Christian education as well as being taught how to improve their relationships with parents and pastors.

Hephzibah House operates under the authority of Believers Baptist Church, an independent, fundamental Baptist church, also located in Winona Lake, which is pastored by Don Williams, son of the founder, Ron Williams. The organization operates a Christian school for its students, promotes character development and a work ethic, and provides physical exercise opportunities for clients as part of its program.

Ronald E. Williams is the founder and director of Hephzibah House, Inc. Williams served in the United States Marine Corps Reserves from 1960 to 1966. He was educated at the State University of South Dakota at Vermillion and at Augustana College in Sioux Falls, South Dakota, earning the Bachelor of Arts in Political Science and History with a minor in Russian. He worked as a Public Health Advisor with the National Venereal Disease Control Program of the United States Public Health Service for seven years.

He studied at Grace Theological Seminary, earning the Certificate in Biblical Studies in May, 1977, and the Master of Divinity (cum laude) from Grace in 1979. While at Grace Seminary, he was awarded the annual Glenn Russell Fink Award in expository preaching (1978). Williams was honored by the Great Plains Baptist College, Sioux Falls, South Dakota, with the honorary Doctor of Divinity degree.

Williams is the speaker/teacher on the weekly 15-minute radio broadcast *The Voice of Hephzibah House.* He has written several booklets and tracts on home and family-related themes. He and his wife, Patti, were the biological parents of nine children (one deceased). Patti died in January of 2011.

Hephzibah house's ministry has been controversial, attracting public attention a number of times in its history. Complaints have been lodged about its strict policies, and there have been public accusations of child abuse. However, the facility and program have been scrutinized by officials, including the local state representative, and no legal actions have resulted from any of the accusations. In June of 2008 a spokesman for Kosciusko County Prosecutor Steve Hearn said his office was not investigating the allegations.

The school's original facility is on School Street in Winona, but its larger campus, which it occupied around 1984, is at 2277 E. Pierceton Road just west of Co. Rd. 250 E.

CHRISTIAN WRITERS GUILD

Norman B. Rohrer, a lanky, genteel young Wheaton College graduate from Pennsylvania Dutch country, matriculated at Grace Theological Seminary in the early 1950s. Always interested and involved in writing, Rohrer recalled, "I worked my way through seminary chiefly by writing articles—most of them sold to Vera Bethel and Helen Hull, who were on the staff of *The Evangel,* published by Light and Life Press of the Free Methodist Church, headquartered in Winona Lake at the time. Pursuing those articles took me all over northern Indiana, to Chicago and even to Michigan."

Rohrer graduated from Grace Seminary in 1956 and that same year married Virginia Page from southern California. Virginia's sister, Beverly, was also married to a Grace Seminary alumnus—Homer A. Kent, Jr.—who had received his M. Div. from the seminary in 1950 and was teaching in the collegiate division. Kent later taught New Testament and Greek in the seminary and served as president of the combined college and seminary for ten years.

After seminary graduation, Rohrer became editor of *World Vision Magazine* in Pasadena, California. He and Virginia were living in La Canada Flintridge nearby. A neighbor began selling a course for "Famous Artists' School" in 1963 and Rohrer began to wonder... *would fledgling writers enroll for a study course?*

Rohrer said,

> As a writing major at Wheaton College, I graduated with loads of stuff on writing and had nearly a decade of experience, so I began assembling a course. Providentially, Virginia invited to dinner in our house a Hollywood Christian writer named Dorothy C. Haskin. I learned that evening that Dorothy was ready to dump her course [which she had written and was operating] and concentrate on books. I bought her course that same evening by agreeing to give her 10 percent of all proceeds and began at once enlarging and expanding the "Personalized Writing Course." But we needed a new name for it and a fresh, scintillating ad.
>
> At about that time I read an article in a sales magazine that opened with this line: "Once upon a time there was a sales-

man who was fired...fired with enthusiasm for developing his sales team into a winning squad to take his company to the moon."

After pondering that thought for several days I wrote an ad for my new writing course that endured for three decades, enrolling thousands of students--all serviced from my office in La Canada Flintridge. The ad read:

I FIRE WRITERS...fire them with enthusiasm for developing God-given writing talent. Write for my FREE Starter Kit, Christian Writers Guild, PO Box 707, La Canada Flintridge CA 91011. (I included a photo of myself and wrote a jaunty package of promotional material for my "kit.")

Rohrer reported, "Names and addresses of inquirers and students grew. In one year, I dropped Dorothy Haskin's course and had my own ready. Virginia and I scheduled 'Write To Be Read' workshops all over the United States, in Australia, Philippines, Canada, and even in such remote places as Haiti."

In 1998, best-selling Christian author Jerry Jenkins visited the Rohrers at their home in Hume Lake, California, in the Sierras to speak to a writers' group at Hume Lake Christian Camps. Jenkins' blockbuster *Left Behind* series, which he wrote for Tim LaHaye, was three years into its 15-year run. Jenkins had long admired Rohrer and what he was doing to train writers.

Jenkins bought Norm Rohrer's Christian writing course in 2001, changed the name to The Jerry B. Jenkins Christian Writers Guild, kept Rohrer on as Dean of Instruction, and invested time and money in upgrading and enlarging the offerings and taking it digital. For many years Rohrer used the U.S. Postal Service to communicate with writers—now the internet is the primary carrier of course content between writers and experienced mentors. Rohrer remains on the board of the organization.

The Guild promotes its writing program through an annual *Writing for the Soul* conference in Colorado as well as internet correspondence courses entitled *Writing Essentials, Apprentice, Journeyman, Craftsman* and *Published,* using a staff of mentor authors and publishing professionals. The Guild also has *Page* and *Squire* programs to help develop young writers. Early in 2013 the organization announced the formation of *CWG Publishing*, a self-publishing arm that links a self-publishing author with a six-month mentored course.

Norman B. Rohrer has had a distinguished career in Christian journalism, serving as publications director for International Students, Inc.; editorial coordinator for *The King's Business*; editor of World Vision; executive secretary and News Service Director of the Evangelical Press Association; and as the founder and director of the Christian Writers Guild.

Rohrer has authored or co-authored more than 30 books, including the biography of Grace Seminary founder Alva J. McClain (*A Saint in Glory Stands*), and hundreds of news and magazine articles. He and Virginia have two adult children and now live in Franklin, Tennessee.

Association of Christian Schools International

When E. William Male joined the Grace College faculty in the early 1960s, he brought with him a passion for helping and encouraging Christian schools at the elementary and secondary level. The summer of 1961 he and several other Christian educators sponsored a "Christian School Seminar" in Winona Lake. Designed to attract Christian school administrators and pastors, the week included both instruction and recreation for the spouses and children of those attending. While it attracted several dozen participants, Male later described it as "too big and too soon."

Ten years later, the timing was right and the vision had matured. By then Male had more experience and a wider network of contacts. He hired an old friend and fellow classmate from Temple University, Roy Lowrie, to initiate a one-week summer institute for Christian school administrators. Lowrie, who directed the Delaware County (Pa.) Christian schools, utilized his networking ability to recruit qualified faculty and participants.

Each summer the institute grew. Attendance peaked in 1978 when 344 administrators enrolled. There were already networks of

Christian schools in Ohio, California, and several other locations. In 1978 a merger of several associations was conceived. At a meeting in McClain Hall on the Grace campus, paperwork was signed to initiate legal incorporation for the Association of Christian Schools International. The new organization used the mailing address of the western association; and its director, Paul Kienel, became the primary mover in the young organization's dedication to promoting and upgrading Christian elementary and secondary schools.

The merger included three associations: the National Christian School Education Association; the Ohio Association of Christian Schools; and the Western Association of Christian Schools. Soon after the new association formed, several other Christian school associations joined ACSI: the Southeast Association of Christian Schools; the Association of Teachers of Christian Schools (Midwest); the Great Plains Association of Christian Schools; and the Texas Association of Christian Schools.

First headquartered in La Habra, California, ACSI moved to an expanded facility on 5.6 acres in Colorado Springs, Colorado, in 1994. Today, ACSI serves nearly 24,000 schools in more than 100 countries. ACSI is a leader in strengthening Christian schools and equipping Christian educators worldwide, providing services through a network of 28 regional offices. The organization accredits Protestant pre-K-12 schools.

Meanwhile the vision for providing education and professional assistance for Christian schools continued to grow on the Grace campus, and eventually three different master's degrees in Christian school administration and curriculum were offered. These degree programs continued until the programs moved to Columbia International University in South Carolina in 1994.

The website of the Lowrie Center for Christian Education at Columbia contains the following information:

> Recognized as one of the fathers of the modern era of Christian schooling in America, Roy W. Lowrie, Jr. was the founding president of the Association of Christian Schools International (ACSI) and headmaster at Delaware County School in Newtown Square, Pennsylvania, for more than 25

years. Through a friendship and common interest in promoting Christian school education, Dr. William Male and Dr. Roy Lowrie began the Institute for Christian School Administration in 1971 on the campus of Grace College in Winona Lake, Indiana. This Institute became a gathering place for Christian school administrators during the rapid expansion of schools during the '70s and '80s.

Through this annual intensive week of instruction on the biblical basis for schooling, a strong networking relationship among leaders across America was established. These annual gatherings and deep friendships led to discussions that eventuated in the formation of ACSI in 1978.

In response to the growing interest in the Christian school movement, Grace Seminary began a master's degree program to train administrators not only to lead biblically but establish schools on the solid footing of a Christian philosophy of education. Both the master's degree and the Institute, now known as the International Institute for Christian School Educators (IICSE), were moved to the campus of Columbia International University (CIU) in 1994.

Today CIU's College of Education builds on the foundations laid by Dr. Male and Dr. Lowrie through its Master of Education degrees in Administration and Curriculum and Instruction in addition to a doctorate in Educational Leadership. The Lowrie Center hosts the annual Institute as a means to continue the tradition of preparing leaders and teachers to think and teach Christianly.

In 2010 Columbia International University created the Lowrie Center for Christian School Education at Columbia International University to honor Dr. Lowrie's legacy.

Lowrie was director of the National Institute of Christian School Administration in Winona Lake from 1971 to 1993 and director of Grace Seminary's M.A. program in Christian School Administration from 1986 until 1993. Lowrie died unexpectedly of a heart attack January 29, 1994, at age 66 at his home in South Carolina.

KEN TAYLOR AND TYNDALE HOUSE

Another towering Christian figure of the latter half of the 20th century, Dr. Ken Taylor (1917-2005), founder of Tyndale House Publishers and the originator of *The Living Bible*, also had early connections to Winona Lake.

According to the Tyndale House Publishers' website, Taylor's life's passion was to make Scripture accessible for all people. Concerned that his ten children were having a hard time understanding the King James Bible, Taylor began paraphrasing the Scriptures so they could better understand their nightly Bible readings.

In 1954, as he rode the commuter train to his job in Chicago, Taylor started rephrasing the New Testament into modern English. After seven years of writing and rewriting, he submitted the manuscript to several publishing houses, but it was rejected by all of them. Convinced that there was value in the work for more than just their children, Taylor and his wife Margaret, decided to use their limited savings to publish *Living Letters*.

In 1962, Taylor exhibited his self-published *Living Letters* at the Christian Booksellers Association convention. The following spring Billy Graham saw a copy of *Living Letters* and asked if he could print a special edition and offer it on the telecasts of his crusades. Half a million copies were given away through the Graham crusades. Ken Taylor's dream had become a reality and more—a publishing entity had been born. Tyndale House Publishers grew from a modest start into a major publishing entity that reaches every continent in the world.

Taylor, who spent 65 years in the publishing industry, began his career as editor of *HIS* magazine and later served as director of Moody Press in Chicago. He was the author of many children's books, including *The Bible in Pictures for Little Eyes* and *My First Bible in Pictures.* But Ken Taylor is probably best known as the man who wrote *The Living Bible,* a paraphrase of Scripture that has sold more than 40 million copies.

Mark D. Taylor, Ken's son, who succeeded him as president and CEO of Tyndale House Publishers, Inc., in Carol Stream, Illinois, verified that his parents Ken and Margaret Taylor and their four small children lived in Winona during the winter of 1947-48.

Mark Taylor recalled, "Dad worked in Chicago, but in that post-war era they couldn't find affordable housing any closer than Winona Lake!"

"It was actually a very difficult period for my parents," Mark Taylor said. "They had four little children, and they lived in an otherwise closed hotel. They did not have a car, so my mom and the kids were stuck in two poorly heated rooms of the hotel. Dad took the train to Chicago on Monday mornings and stayed in Chicago all during the workweek, returning to Winona Lake on Friday evening."

Mrs. Ken Taylor later identified the hotel as the Garfield (on Chestnut Street, no longer standing), which she described as "strictly a summer hotel that was used by people attending Bible conferences in Winona Lake."[38] With more than 15 rooms and an eclectic architecture that made it stand out from the many boarding houses in Winona Lake, The Garfield could accommodate small groups and was located directly above the Auditorium. At that time it was owned and managed by the Leo Polman family—Polman himself was an itinerant evangelist and Bible teacher.

Margaret Taylor recalled, "Ken would leave at 4 a.m. each Monday to walk to Warsaw to catch the . . . train, and he returned on Friday night after the children were in bed. He stayed with a fellow employee, Ray Hill, during the week. I cried every Monday morning as I crawled back into bed after Ken left. Just the mechanics of living with four young children—then five—kept me busy during the day, but the evenings were pretty awful."[39]

This was six years before Ken Taylor had begun his work on *Living Letters* and *The Living Bible,* so the time in Winona Lake did not directly relate to those writing projects. More of the story is told in Ken Taylor's autobiography, *My Life: A Guided Tour,* and the privately published autobiography of his wife, Margaret Taylor, *The Way I Remember It.*

---

[38] Taylor, p. 165

[39] Taylor, p.167

WINONA SCHOOL OF PROFESSIONAL PHOTOGRAPHY

One of the notable organizations which drew top national and international photographic talent each summer was the Winona School of Professional Photography, which was completely independent of the Winona Christian Assembly.

The school originated in 1912 as the Indiana School of Photography and was operated by the Professional Photographers of America (PPA) until its move to a Chicago suburb in the mid-1980s. Famous photographers from around the world taught at Winona during summer-only classes.

Three facilities were used by the school. The first was the Daguerre Building, located at the corner of 13th and College. Local media reported on April 7, 1904, that the Indiana Association of Photographers, which held a convention in Winona Lake each year, had made arrangements for the construction of a building that would house the Daguerre Memorial Institute. Construction of the building was to start "at once," and was to include an instruction room, a permanent exhibition hall, dining room, and chapel. Estimated cost of the building was between $6,000 and $8,000.

It was named for Louis-Jacques-Mandé Daguerre (1787-1851), a French artist and physicist recognized for his invention of the daguerreotype process of photography. He became known as one of the fathers of photography. Though he was most famous for his contributions to photography, he was also an accomplished painter and a developer of the diorama theatre.

In 1921, the Daguerre Club of Indiana donated the building to the Professional Photographers of America for the purpose of establishing a photography school. The Daguerre Building was enlarged in 1937. The Winona School of Professional Photography held classes each summer until 1984, when the school relocated to Mount Prospect, Illinois, where it operated until 1994 when it moved to Atlanta, Georgia.

In 1984 Winona Lake Grace Brethren Church bought the facility and used it for administrative offices and classrooms. The building also housed the Winona Lake town offices for a short period. The building was abandoned in the mid-1990s due to safety issues. On Tuesday, April 1, 2008, the Daguerre Building was razed and its former site is now lawn/playground for Winona Lake Grace Brethren Church.

A second facility used by the photography school was the auditorium, built in 1956 (now The Hub). Darkroom facilities were located in the old Winona Dairy building on Kings Highway, now part of the Grace College physical facilities plant.

An early advertisement for the photography school said, "Since 1922 the Photographer's Association of America has conducted a school better known to the profession as 'The Winona School.' It is not a school for beginners but is primarily intended to give studio owners a chance to 'brush up' their knowledge of photography and to afford employees with some experience an opportunity to become capable photographers. Winona School differs from all others, not being conducted for profit. The tuition fees are fixed each year by the Trustees at a figure which will cover the expenses for the staff and upkeep of the building and equipment, no more."

The photographers' professional association was first organized in 1869. Present at early conventions were many American daguerreotype pioneers, including John H. Fitzgibbon, who began making daguerreotypes as far back as 1841. The daguerreotype was the first practical and profitable photographic process, introduced in 1839-40. It was at the 1888 convention that George Eastman introduced his Kodak camera and film processing service, winning a first prize medallion and special certificate of honor.

In its early years, the association established a tradition of continuing education for members by providing annual forums for noted photographers, including Alfred Stieglitz, Edward Weston, Dr. C. E. Kenneth Mees, and Edward Steichen.

By the beginning of the 20th century, photographers began to recognize the importance of sharing information, a contrast from the usual business methods of that day. At that time business was very competitive, and trade secrets were guarded out of fear of losing customers. As photography became a profitable business, its professional association provided programs to deal with management and financial problems.

A newspaper report from July 16, 1912, noted that the Daguerre Institute for Photographs wrapped up its annual convention at Winona Lake with about 300 photographers from throughout the nation in attendance. By 1913, the association had grown to 725 members, expanding to 2,272 members in 1916.

Thousands of photographers from all parts of the world attended Winona classes over the years to update their skills or to develop abilities in other fields of photographic application under the guidance of some of the nation's outstanding professional image makers.

Moving the school from Winona Lake to the organization's headquarters in Illinois was approved by the photographers' national council at its July 11, 1982, convention meeting in Las Vegas.

Ed Purrington (1918-2012), who was director of education for the Winona school, said, "The style of teaching will continue, but it will broaden with the move to Chicago."

Among the reasons for moving, Purrington said, were easier air transportation (the new school would be eight minutes from O'Hare), easier access by interstates for those driving, increased coordination by being closer to the Chicago headquarters, more teaching and personnel resources in the greater Chicago area, and "unlimited subject matter for architectural photography in downtown Chicago, environmental possibilities in the surrounding forest preserve system, and opportunities to visit major commercial photography studios."

Purrington concluded, "We'll be incorporating into the new facility changes for today and for the future."

FLYING FARMERS

An unusual event took place on Sunday, June 11, 1950, when the "Flying Farmers" of Michigan, Indiana, Illinois, and Wisconsin converged on Winona Lake for a worship service. All told, they landed 307 airplanes at Warsaw's municipal airport and Smith Field, in craft ranging from J3Cubs to a Lockheed Lodestar. Two hundred additional Flying Farmer families arrived by automobile and were joined by thousands of local citizens at the Billy Sunday Tabernacle, nearly filling it to capacity.

Arthur McKee, executive manager of the Winona Lake Christian Assembly, estimated that 6,000 persons saw and heard such nationally-known personalities as Homer Rodeheaver, Mrs. Billy (Ma) Sunday, and R. G. LeTourneau.

Once safely on the ground, visitors were greeted with Flying Farmers and Junior Chamber of Commerce personnel, who handed each a cup of coffee, wafers, and a glass of iced orange juice. Transportation from the airports to the Tabernacle was by bus, with many vehicles provided by William Kinsey, Clifford Loser, and Gerald Horrick.

At the Tabernacle, McKee introduced "Ma" Sunday, widow of Billy Sunday. Homer Rodeheaver, who had returned from Florida especially for the occasion, led a 30-minute song service and played his trombone. R. G. LeTourneau told of his partnership with God, which had earned for LeTourneau and his religious charities millions of dollars. The departing farmers were given an added surprise at the Warsaw city park when Mr. Rodeheaver suddenly appeared and chatted with various picnicking groups for nearly an hour.

Prohibition Party

The Prohibition Party made Winona Lake its national headquarters in 1947.

On September 6, 1955, the Prohibition Party, at its national convention held at Camp Mack on Waubee Lake near Milford, Indiana, scrapped its old name Prohibition Party in favor of the new name Pioneer Party. The announcement was made by Dr. Lowell H. Coate, national chairman of the Prohibition Party, who said the old name was scrapped in an effort to broaden, modernize, and streamline its appeal.

The party nominated prominent Free Methodist educator and politician Enoch Arden Holtwick, (1881–1972) as the party's candidate for president in 1956 and voted to establish its new national headquarters in Chicago and also open a special Washington office. The party's presidential candidate in the previous election (1952) was California-based Christian cowboy songwriter Stuart Hamblen.

Founded in 1869, the Prohibition Party is a political party in the United States best known for its historic opposition to the sale or consumption of alcoholic beverages. It is the oldest existing third party in the US. The party was an integral part of the temperance movement.

The Prohibition Party's proudest moment came in 1919, with the passage of the 18th Amendment to the United States Constitution, which outlawed the production, sale, transportation, import and export of alcohol. The era during which alcohol was illegal in the United States is known as "Prohibition."

Although never one of the leading political parties in the United States, it was an important force in the politics of the United States during the late 19th century and the early years of the 20th century. It has declined dramatically since the repeal of Prohibition in 1933. Its 1948 and 1960 conventions were held in Winona Lake, the latter in the Westminster Hotel.

The alcohol issue surfaced more recently in January of 1979 when a delegation representing the Women's Christian Temperance Union and concerned residents appeared at the Winona Lake town board meeting to discuss the news sweeping the lakefront about a liquor license application submitted to the Indiana Alcoholic Beverage Commission in November.

Twenty-one residents, all vehemently opposed to opening a liquor store inside the town's corporate limits, questioned the constitutionality of the license application submitted to the state ABC by Sonny Nellans, of Rt. 7, Warsaw.

James Walmer, the town's attorney, said he believed state ABC members could grant one package liquor license per 5,000 population in a town. Walmer said he would research the law. If that point were accurate, the attorney questioned whether Winona Lake would be eligible for a package liquor store license since the town's population was 2,811 when the 1970 census was taken.

On February 15, 1979, Kosciusko County Alcoholic Beverage Board members set a precedent by voting 2-1 in favor of a liquor, beer and wine dealer license for Sonny Jay Nellans. He proposed to open Nellans Wholesale Liquors, a package store, in a building on the east side of the Lakeview Shopping Center. The proposed location was 100 feet inside the corporate limits of Winona Lake—a town that had been "dry" since it was founded. The following April, however, three members of the Indiana Alcoholic Beverage Commission members voted to disapprove a license application for Nellans' proposed store.

More recently, the town's two leading restaurants, BoatHouse and Cerulean, were granted three-way liquor licenses and the issue seems to have disappeared as a point of public controversy.

MERGER TALKS, MAIL SERVICE, AND A BANK

In 1955, some talk took place between Winona Lake and Warsaw officials of merging the two towns. News reports on July 27, 1955, said that, "No one in an official capacity wished to be quoted. However, one member of the Winona Lake town board said there had been some talk among board members on this subject and that he thought it would be a good idea."

On August 3, the Winona Lake town board members issued a statement in which they termed as "false impressions" reports that they had considered a possible merger between Winona Lake and Warsaw, and in which they stated they were opposed to such a suggestion.

House-to-house city mail service began in Winona Lake on May 16, 1959. The postmaster was Phil Laurien and delivery serviced 520 homes and business establishments in Winona.

Winona Lake's first modern banking facility began when Bruce Wright, executive vice president of Lake City Bank, announced on August 10, 1965, that contracts had been signed for construction of a $75,000 branch bank at Winona. Wright said construction would start within two weeks and the new bank would be in operation by mid-November. The location bridged between Chestnut Street and Kings Highway, just to the north of the Winona Hotel.

In 1995, the annexation of a tournament-quality golf course, Stonehenge, and surrounding housing stretched the boundaries of the town and placed a major tourist draw within Winona Lake's town borders.

CHAPTER 12

Youth for Christ

*"Youth for Christ continues to communicate the life
changing message of Jesus Christ to our youth before it's too
late. We have been fortunate through the years to touch
millions of lives and today, more than ever, we need to
continue our quest to reach the lost youth around the world."*
Billy Graham

DURING WORLD WAR II, PASTORS IN WIDELY SEPARATED CITIES IN
the United States and Canada began holding huge evangelistic rallies especially aimed at young people, including those in the armed
forces. These rallies had been inspired by the youth work of men like
Paul Guiness and Jack Wyrtzen, and included entertainment, singing, and vigorous preaching. These formerly unaffiliated activities
became collectively known as "Youth for Christ" campaigns

Wyrtzen was a young ex-insurance salesman who had also played
the trombone in a cavalry band. The Youth for Christ campaign idea
spread to Washington, D.C., Detroit, Indianapolis, and St. Louis.
In 1944 Torrey Johnson, a Baptist minister and pastor of Chicago's
Midwest Bible Church, staged "Chicagoland for Christ" and became
the most successful advocate of this type of campaign.

Torrey Maynard Johnson (1918-1995) was a Chicago Protestant evangelist who is best remembered as the founder of Chicagoland Youth for Christ and Youth for Christ International. For a time
Johnson had his own local radio program called *Songs in the Night*
which he later turned over to Billy Graham.

Formation of Youth for Christ International

The Youth for Christ organization began at a meeting in Winona Lake in July of 1944. The initial national conference was held at Winona in 1945 featuring Rev. Billy Graham. YFC International conventions continued to be held in Winona for more than 35 years.

In addition to Johnson and Wyrtzen, other important leaders of the movement were Walter Smyth from Philadelphia, Roger Malsbary from Indianapolis, Richard Harvey from St. Louis, George Wilson from Minneapolis, and Edward Darling from Detroit.

In August of 1944, most of these men and others, including J. Palmer Muntz, Arthur McKee, and V. Raymond Edman, met at Winona Lake, Indiana, to form a temporary organization to serve as a channel for the various rallies to render mutual assistance to each other.

Ted W. Engstrom, in his autobiography entitled *Reflections on a Pilgrimage*, recalled this meeting, "In 1944 Torrey Johnson, then pastor of the Midwest Bible Church in Chicago, and director of the Chicagoland Youth for Christ program, called together those individuals who were leading these rallies to meet at the Christian conference grounds in Winona Lake, Indiana, as the guests of the conference director, Dr. Arthur McKee. At this week long conference, a charter was drafted and a constitution developed, officially organizing what became Youth for Christ International" (p. 33).

Another meeting was held in Detroit in November. Torrey Johnson was elected the chairman of a temporary committee. Johnson soon recruited Billy Graham, who had worked on the Chicago rallies, to become the organization's first full-time evangelist. A magazine also was begun. It was an expanded version of the periodical put out by the Indianapolis rally.

Less than a year later, 42 delegates from the various rallies, including Charles Templeton of Toronto, Canada, met again at Winona Lake to make Youth for Christ International (YFCI) into a permanent organization. Torrey Johnson was elected president, Richard Harvey vice president, George Wilson secretary, and Walter Block treasurer.

By 1946 (*Time Magazine,* February 4, 1946), Youth for Christ International had approximately 300 units in the United States and possibly 200 or more overseas. The average attendance at rallies in 1946 was 350. The largest attendance at that time was 70,000 at Soldier Field in Chicago.

The organization originally called Youth for Christ International was essentially based in the United States, although clubs started in other countries at an early date. Over the years, autonomous national organizations started in other countries and a national coordinating office, also called Youth for Christ International, was started. About 1980, the United States branch was officially renamed Youth for Christ/USA.

Organizationally, YFC-USA became more centralized in the late 1940s. Its headquarters were moved to Wheaton, a Chicago suburb, in 1953. Although local clubs retained a degree of autonomy, their staff went through the YFC training program, used YFC materials, and agreed to abide by YFC policies and statement of faith.

The annual business meeting was shifted from the summer Winona convention to a midwinter convention, usually held at the beginning of the year in different cities around the nation. Eventually the Winona convention was discontinued altogether as a national gathering. In August 1990 YFC moved from Wheaton to Denver, Colorado, which became the headquarters for both YFC-USA and YFC International's United States office.

An astounding number of major Christian leaders were or are members of the "YFC alumni club," having been part of the YFC movement at one time. The most famous YFC alumnus is undoubtedly Billy Graham, the first full-time employee of Youth for Christ in the 1940s. He conducted evangelistic campaigns for YFC in the United States and the United Kingdom prior to his becoming a world-renowned evangelist following his 1949 crusade in Los Angeles.

Billy Graham said of his experience, "After 50 years, YFC continues to communicate the life-changing message of Jesus Christ to our youth. We all know that the problems confronting today's youth are staggering. I can think of no greater cause than to reach our youth for Christ."

Cliff Barrows, long-time associate of Billy Graham, also came up through Youth for Christ. An internationally recognized alumnus of Youth for Christ, Bob Pierce, was the founder of World Vision, the world's largest international Christian relief agency, now active in almost 100 countries. Perhaps Pierce's best-known quote is, "Let my heart be broken by the things that break the heart of God." Bob Pierce also founded Samaritan's Purse, which later would be directed by Billy Graham's son, Franklin Graham.

Other YFC alumni who were leaders of Christian international relief organizations include Merv Rosell of Global Concern, Roy McKeown of Global Concern and World Opportunities, Wendell Amstutz of National Counseling Resource Center, and Keith Phillips of World Impact.

Ravi Zacharias, world-renowned Christian apologist and founder of Ravi Zacharias International Ministries, is an alumnus of Youth for Christ.

Another YFC alum is the Christian composer Ralph Carmichael. He founded Carmichael Enterprises, Lexicon Music, and LIGHT. His songs include *He's Everything to Me, Beyond All Time, All My Life, The Restless Ones, Tell It Like It Is, Love Is Surrender, Brother, Let Me Take Your Hand, My Little World,* and *The Savior Is Waiting,* according to the website ralphCarmichael.com.

Top Christian author Philip Yancey also got his start in Youth for Christ. One of his best-known books is *What's So Amazing About Grace?* Some of Yancey's other books include *Prayer: Does it make Any Difference? Where Is God When it Hurts? Rumors of Another World, Disappointment with God, Finding God in all the Wrong Places* and *The Jesus I Never Knew.*

Other writers who began their ministries in YFC include devotional writer Warren Wiersbe; *Left Behind* series co-author Jerry Jenkins; current CEO and editor-in-chief of *Christianity Today* Harold Smith; chairman of Christianity Today International Harold Myra and CT senior writer Tim Stafford.

Another YFC alum is Dick Snavely, founder of Family Life Ministries. Now located in Bath, New York, Snavely started Area Youth for Christ in 1957 in the Finger Lakes region of western New York.

Over the years Area YFC expanded to include adult programs, family and marriage counseling, and a network of FM radio stations. In 1964 the ministry changed its name to Family Life Ministries to reflect its expanded ministry offerings.

The Family Life Network began in 1983 and is a listener-supported Christian radio network that broadcasts in many areas of New York and Pennsylvania. It reaches a potential listenership of 3.5 million.

Another YFC alum is Larry Kreider, founder of The Gathering, an organization that presents major outreach events for men, showcasing well-known personalities who have had their lives transformed by a living Christ.

Not surprisingly, many Youth for Christ alumni went on to start or lead youth ministries. These include Dick Weidner, co-founder of Teen Discovery; Loren Soft of Yellowstone Boys and Girls Ranch; Bob Simpson of Strategic Kingdom Youth (SKY) Ministries; Joe Schultz, founder of Campus Living Assoc.; Al Metsker (deceased) of Youth Evangelism Assoc.; Rick Little of International Youth Foundation; James M. Leckie, founder of Family Ministries and Youth Guidance; Ray Clendenan of Teen Ranch; Victor Eliason, Voice of Christian Youth (Milwaukee); Joe Ellis, Jr., co-founder of Teen Discovery; Don Landis of Jackson Hole Bible College; Jerry Landrum of Youth Outreach; Chris Clark, founder of Children of the Nations; Mel Johnson (deceased) of Tips for Teens and Young World Radio; Wes Arum of Living Waters Circle Ranch; and Youth Specialties co-founders Mike Yaconelli (deceased) and Tic Long.

Other YFC alumni who are founders and co-founders of Christian organizations include:

Ken Anderson (deceased), *Ken Anderson Films and Gospel Films*
Floyd Ankerberg (deceased), *Ankerberg Evangelistic Association*
John Ankerberg, *Ankerberg Theological Research*
Art Brown, *Editora Vida Nova (New Life Publishers)*
Ken Davis, *Dynamic Communications International*
Fred Carpenter, *Mars Hill Productions*
Ralph Cavanaugh, *Outreach of Delaware*

Chris Clark, *Children of the Nations*
Warren Bolthouse, *Family Life Radio Network*
Randy L. Carlson, *Family Life Radio Network*
Ray W. Carpenter, *Encouragement Resources*
Wayne Coombs, *Adam Children's Fund International*
Jack Cox, *Ankerberg Evangelistic Association*
Alan Davis, *The ProSource Group and the National Council on Child Abuse and Family Violence*
Paul E. Freed, *Trans World Radio*
Bob Evans, *Greater Europe Mission*
Bob Finley, *Christian Aid Mission and International Students*
Marv Hollenbeck, *ARC Ministries*
Jim Hullihan, *Motivational Media Assemblies and Camfel Productions*
Bob Neff, Sr., *Bob Neff Tours, Inc.*
Jack Larson, *World Servants*

BILLY GRAHAM'S EVANGELISTIC BEGINNINGS

Evangelist Billy Graham took over Torrey Johnson's local radio program called *Songs in the Night* which was broadcast over a local station in Illinois and predated YFCI. Later still, Graham left YFCI to form his own evangelistic association and to begin *The Hour of Decision* broadcast.

Success for Graham came from the promotional publicity in the newspapers and magazines owned or influenced by William Randolph Hearst. Due to the publicity by Hearst during his 1949 Los Angeles campaign, Billy Graham suddenly became a media star.

In his autobiography, *Just As I Am*, Billy Graham recounted the story to President Harry Truman, during his first meeting with the president in 1950:

> I told him about Los Angeles the previous fall, where we preached in a huge tent but initially attracted virtually no mention in the press. Then newspaper tycoon William Randolph Hearst, for no apparent reason, had directed his editors to focus on what was going on inside the tent. Almost overnight we became nationally known. During the fifty days of meetings there, attendance snowballed to a total of

350,000, an unheard-of crowd for an evangelistic gathering in those days (p. xx).

Billy Graham later recalled, "Youth for Christ came into being as a result of a conversation that Torrey Johnson and I had while fishing off the coast of Florida in late 1944. He had the vision and the plans in his mind of what could be done, and he asked if I could join with him and become the first associate and evangelist. It was my privilege to be the first full-time employee of Youth for Christ.

"The goal in those days was to reach not only young people, but also our servicemen who were on leave from wars. It grew rapidly, and thousands of young people came to Christ. After 60+ years, Youth for Christ continues to communicate the life-changing message of Jesus Christ to our youth before it's too late."

A little-known aspect of Winona Lake's connection with Billy Graham's ministry came to light in March of 1973 when Sherwood Wirt, the editor of *Decision*, the magazine of the Billy Graham Evangelistic Association, published an article entitled "The Lost Prayer Meeting."[40]

In that article he detailed a meeting in the Rainbow Room of Winona Lake's Westminster Hotel that had 40-50 in attendance during the fifth annual convention of Youth for Christ. The newly elected president of YFC, Robert A. Cook, had told the young rally directors from all over the U.S. and Canada that "The price of leadership is prayer."

This led Armin Gesswein, a Lutheran evangelist from southern California, to initiate an all-night prayer meeting that consisted of prayers, praises, verses of Scripture, and requests for more prayer.

At about 3 a.m. Gesswein stood to his feet, Wirt reports, and said, "You know, our brother Billy Graham is coming out to Los Angeles for a crusade this fall. Why don't we just gather around this man and lay our hands on him and really pray for him? Let's ask God for a fresh touch to anoint him for this work."

Graham was at that time vice president of YFC. He got up from his seat, walked to the front of the room and knelt on the oak floor.

---

[40] Wirt, Sherwood E. "The Lost Prayer Meeting." *Decision Magazine*, March, 1973, p. 4

After hands were laid on him and his ministry was prayed for, he opened his Bible to Joel 3:13 and read, "Put ye in the sickle, for the harvest is ripe: come, get you down; for the press is full, the vats overflow."

"Fellows," he said, "I'm taking that verse with me to the West Coast. I believe if we will put in the sickle, we shall reap an unprecedented harvest of souls for Christ."

Two months later, at the corner of Washington Boulevard and Hill Street in Los Angeles, Graham's tent crusade began. It was extended to an unprecedented eight weeks. Crowds began to flock to the tent, dramatic conversions were reported, and there was sudden nationwide interest following a feature story in the Los Angeles newspaper on the emergence of Billy Graham's ministry as a religious phenomenon of the 20th century.

Billy Graham tells the story of the Los Angeles crusade in his autobiography, *Just As I Am*.[41] The early days of the crusade had not drawn particularly large crowds. With some trepidation, the crusade team had decided to extend it beyond the projected closing date and Graham recalls being stunned one evening when he arrived at the crusade tent and it was crawling with newspaper reporters and photographers.

When he asked one of the journalists what was happening, the reply was, "You've just been kissed by William Randolph Hearst."

Though Graham didn't know what that meant, he soon discovered that his crusade had attracted the attention of Hearst, the great newspaper owner, who publicized the crusade in the *Los Angeles Examiner* and the *Los Angeles Herald Express*, both owned by Hearst. The story was soon picked up by Hearst papers in New York, Chicago, Detroit, and San Francisco, and then by all their competitors. Graham said, "Until then, I doubt if any newspaper editor outside the area had heard of our Los Angeles campaign."

Dr. Robert A. Cook, president of The King's College in New York, said, "I remember that night [of the prayer meeting] clearly. We prayed in faith and felt that we had got through to God. . . I am grateful to have had some share in those beginning days."

---

[41] Graham, p. 149

Dr. Ted W. Engstrom of World Vision International said, "No one who was at that prayer meeting in Winona Lake in 1949 could possibly have forgotten it. It was one of the greatest nights that those of us present could ever remember."

Armin Gesswein, who led the meeting and who was the founder of Revival Prayer Fellowship of Los Angeles, recalled, "It was probably the greatest of the many nights of prayer we had in those days. . . We had a very special burden of prayer for Billy, and we were really asking God to do a new thing on the evangelistic front."

As his reputation grew, Graham occasionally returned to speak at Winona.

On July 10, 1950, a newspaper account says Graham spoke to an estimated 23,000 people in Winona Lake. It was at the sixth annual convention of Youth for Christ, and some 11,000 people crowded into the Tabernacle, and an estimated 2,000 sat in a lighted outdoor amphitheatre, and at least 1,500 stood inside, four-and-five deep along the outside, looking in the windows. Local resident Jesse Deloe, a boy at the time, vividly remembers crawling on the roof of the Tabernacle with his buddies to hear Graham speak.

The paper reports that following Graham's gospel message on "The Cross as the Center of All Things," more than 150 people professed faith in Jesus Christ or reconsecrated their lives for Christian service. Graham was 31.

Converted Los Angeles gangster wiretapper Jim Vaus told the crowd, "Being a Christian so far exceeds any thrills I had working for Mickey Cohen that there simply is no comparison." At the service, Ma Sunday announced, "I told these Youth for Christ leaders two years ago that when they filled this great tabernacle I would give them $5,000 for their great job of evangelizing the world in this generation. Now, they've done it, and I'm stuck for $5,000. And I'm going to give it to them this coming year."

Arthur McKee, executive director of the Winona Lake Christian Assembly, said, "The crowds Sunday were the largest we have experienced since the days of Billy Sunday. Our population of 1,400 was swelled to 25,000 and at least 4,000 cars were on the grounds all day."

This may be the meeting Graham later referred to in his autobiography, *Just As I Am*, where he recounted his first meeting with President Harry Truman in July, 1950, and said, "The invitation to the White House was for me alone, but I corralled my colleagues Grady Wilson, Cliff Barrows, and Jerry Beavan into flying with me to Washington from the Winona Lake, Indiana, Bible conference at which I had been preaching" (p. xix).

A newspaper account from two years later, July 21, 1952, notes that, "Carrying on a schedule that would leave many a businessman thoroughly exhausted, Billy Graham flew into Winona Lake during the weekend for a two-day appearance at the world's largest Bible conference grounds."

The article noted that, "Graham himself appears to be a rather quiet, unassuming chap, but nevertheless manages to give the impression of bubbling enthusiasm for his own two-fold purpose in life which he states is 'to carry forth the advancement of the Kingdom of God and to build his church. Secondly, to see a nation-wide spiritual and moral reanimation.'"

Accompanying Graham on this trip were his associate evangelist Grady Wilson, pianist Tedd Smith, organist Paul Mickelson, soloist George Beverly Shea, song leader Cliff Barrows, and executive secretary and public relations director Jerry Beavan.

Noting that "God doesn't necessarily intend Christians to wear dull, gloomy dark colors," Graham appeared in a "pistachio green suit with brightly colored ties."

Graham last spoke at Winona at the opening night of Youth for Christ's 25th anniversary convention on June 30, 1969, in the Billy Sunday Tabernacle. The press said that the two-week YFC conference annually attracts more than 5,000 teenagers from across the U.S. and Canada. Prior to preaching Graham visited with guests of Jim and Ruth Rodeheaver Thomas at Rainbow Point.

THIRD WAVE RISING

*A Cultural Rebirth
(1969-Present)*

CHAPTER 13
Changes in Ownership

*"As the financial situation worsened, it became evident that the
Assembly was not going to survive without massive aid."*
Mark Sidwell

GRACE ASSUMES THE CHRISTIAN ASSEMBLY

IN THE SUMMER OF 1968, THE EXECUTIVE COMMITTEE OF THE WI-
nona Lake Christian Assembly initiated action to give control of the
Assembly and all of its facilities to Grace College and Seminary.[42]
Limited use of the conference facilities during the off-season and the
decline of interest in Bible conferences by an aging population had
once again created significant financial problems for the Assembly.

The directors offered ownership of all the grounds, buildings,
and facilities of the Christian Assembly together with the assumption of obligations that were in excess of $500,000. The arrangement
also included the direction of the annual Bible conference, which
was approaching its 78th year of operation.

Recognizing an opportunity that probably would never come
again, the Grace trustees on July 9, 1968, accepted the proposal and
created a new board of directors comprised of 16 members, four of
which were former Christian Assembly board members with the remainder from the board of Grace College and Seminary.

Final approval of the Assembly board was given at its annual
meeting in the Winona Hotel on August 23, 1968. An organization-

---

[42] Plaster, p. 156

al meeting was held the last day of September, 1968, and Dr. Herman A. Hoyt, president of Grace College and Seminary, was elected president of the Winona Christian Assembly Corp. and was named chairman of its board of directors.

Grace took over operation of the facilities on September 30, 1968, and utilization began immediately, including the use of Rodeheaver Auditorium for combined chapel services and concerts. Rental facilities, including the Winona Hotel, were transformed into dormitory housing. The Eskimo Inn was remodeled into a student center and was renamed The Lamp.

One of the first uses of Rodeheaver Auditorium under Grace's management was the memorial service for Grace founder and former president Alva J. McClain, 80, who had died on November 11, 1968, in Waterloo, Iowa, after a prolonged illness.

THE FREE METHODISTS

The departure of the Free Methodist denominational headquarters and publishing house from Winona Lake in 1990 had a huge impact on the town.

The Free Methodist Church was organized in 1860 at Pekin, New York, with Benjamin T. Roberts as the first general superintendent. In 1868 the first issue of *The Free Methodist* was published, with Levi Wood as editor and publisher (now called *Light and Life* Magazine). The Free Methodist Publishing House was founded in 1886 at 104-106 Franklin Street, Chicago, Illinois.

For years there had been discussion in favor of moving the publishing house out of Chicago, but the opposition had been too great. However in March of 1933, B. H. Gaddis, who took office as publishing agent in April, 1933, was passing near Winona Lake and stopped to see the Mount Memorial Building which had been built as the administration building for a college and which was the property of the Winona Lake Christian Assembly.

An examination of the building revealed its possibilities and in April, 1934, the Free Methodist board, after considering four other sites, decided to purchase the Winona Lake property. An agreement was reached with James Heaton, who represented the Winona institutions, for the transfer of the property for $22,500. It included fifteen acres of land and the building, which had been little used and was in a state of disrepair. Its original cost of $130,000, however, had produced a structure of great durability and permanent beauty.

The move from Chicago to Winona Lake, after extensive remodeling and equipping of the building, took place in February, 1935, under the trade name Light and Life Press. The one-story gray granite office building (23,000 sq. ft.) was added to the south in 1960, and was connected to the Mount Memorial building via an enclosed walkway. When Grace Brethren International Missions (now Encompass World Partners) purchased the smaller building in 1997, the buildings were once again disconnected and the walkway dismantled.

The Free Methodists purchased the Westminster Hotel in 1970 and re-named it "The International Friendship House." A news media report from May 1, 1970, announced that "In a quarter-million dollar transaction, Mr. and Mrs. James E. Thomas have transferred their Westminster Hotel property, Winona Lake, to the Free Methodist Church of North America."

In 1990 Free Methodist headquarters moved to Indianapolis and was re-named Free Methodist World Ministries Center.

When the Free Methodist headquarters left town, that left the future of their entire properties (Mount Memorial building, Light and Life Press building, the Friendship House, ABC/Word warehouse, and considerable open acreage) in question.

The properties were in the name of the Free Methodist Foundation and the local operative, Joe Beeson, had entered into an agreement with an auctioneer to auction off the properties either as a unit, or in parcels.

MOUNT MEMORIAL PROPERTIES

Greg Weimer, who at the time was working with Grace Brethren International Missions (GBIM), inquired of Beeson on September 4, 1995, whether the auction might be forestalled if GBIM had serious interest in purchasing the Light and Life Press Building. Stuart Hake joined GBIM's financial management team in January of 1996 and quickly became involved in working toward GBIM's purchasing the property.

A key meeting was held on October 24, 1996, to begin creation of a coordinated proposal to secure the entire Free Methodist property, not just the Light and Life Press building. Key figures in that meeting were Tom Julien, Greg Weimer, and Stuart Hake (all of GBIM) and Brent Wilcoxson (Winona Restoration). Later, Steve Popenfoose (Grace College and Seminary) entered discussions as well, because Grace had an interest in the Mount Memorial building. Winona Restoration was interested in restoring Mount Memorial to its original historical state.

The coordinated closing was completed on May 6, 1997. Tom Julien, who was executive director of GBIM, commented later that the decision to purchase the entire property, rather than to let it be auctioned in parcels, "saved Grace College campus from being split in two—maybe separated by strip malls."

GBIM moved into the renovated Light and Life Press Building the second week of December, 1997, and an open house was held on February 8, 1998.

FREE METHODIST CHURCH

The local Free Methodist Church, located directly across from the front entrance of the Westminster Hotel, was built on the site of the former Otterbein building, which had been a women's dormitory. The Otterbein Hall, built in 1903, at Ninth and Chestnut Streets, was a girls dormitory for one of the several schools in existence during the Spring Fountain Park days.

Dr. Harold C. Mason, former president of Huntington College and professor of Christian education at Asbury Theological Seminary, was pastor of the Winona Lake Free Methodist church at the time the church building was built in 1940-41.

CHAPTER 14

Winona Restoration Partners –
The Park Avenue Revival

"Don't call it an obligation.
That takes all the joy of giving away from you!"
Dane Miller

A *CHICAGO TRIBUNE* ARTICLE (OCTOBER 14, 2011) PUT IT LIKE THIS: "It was the Assembly's money that built much of what modern-day visitors experience in Winona Lake. But following the departure of a number of religious groups in the 1970s and '80s, the cottages and businesses were abandoned; the tranquil town became a slum."

A shift in consumer tastes, a lack of vision, and deteriorating facilities led to another reorganization in 1968. Grace Schools took over operating control of the Assembly as well as assuming the accumulated debt. The school continued to operate conferences in the summer while utilizing the facilities for dormitories and other school uses in the remaining months.

By the late 1980s a continued lack of investment in the facilities and declining numbers of attendees led to the termination of all summer conferences and programming. The '70s and '80s also saw a severe decline in much of the housing stock and infrastructure in the rest of the community. By the late 1980s, Winona Lake was headquarters only for the Grace Brethren Church and some smaller organizations, and the town was heavily populated with sub-standard buildings and slum housing.

The earliest versions of a master plan for a restored downtown Winona Lake emerged in a paper Brent Wilcoxson wrote for a marketing class at Grace College taught by Prof. Bill Gordon.

In a September 22, 1997, article from *The Indianapolis Star*, "Restoring the Glory," Wilcoxson laid out some of his history with Winona Lake and his plans for the future. Indicating that Wilcoxson's family roots in the community went back five generations, the article noted that, although he grew up in Fowler, Indiana, he returned to Winona Lake to go to school at Grace College, where he majored in history and met his wife, Debra. They settled in Winona Lake and began raising a family of four children.

In 1991 Brent Wilcoxson was working on his master's degree in business administration when he decided to focus on transforming the derelict village into a tourist attraction. In his thesis, Wilcoxson suggested that the renaissance be based on a European model, transforming renovated cottages along a quaint canal into boutiques as well as residences for the shopkeepers.

Wilcoxson worked as a financial planner for a local financial management company when he bought a beautiful old house (the Felsenheim, a decorative concrete block home built by William Fluegel in 1910) and began fixing it up. Moving in small steps, he started buying properties and restoring them, using money from his investment business.

A partnership, entitled Winona Restoration Partners LP, was formed in 1990. The partners were Jack and Retha Hicks, Jim and Lisa LeMasters, Gary and Alberta Longworth, and Brent and Debra Wilcoxson. These couples all contributed funds and sweat equity to purchase a home at 100 Fourth Street with the intention of converting it back to a single family residence (Wilcoxson called it a "five-unit slum").

This was accomplished, and the property was sold to Steve and Lauren Wishart as their personal residence.

Realizing the need for more capital, Wilcoxson connected with Dr. Dane Miller, the founder, president, and chief executive officer of Biomet. Miller and Wilcoxson bought out the other partners and operated the limited partnership until converting it to an LLC in 1996. Miller, in agreeing to become Wilcoxson's partner, noted, "Brent has a real soft spot in his heart for Winona Lake's history. And, as I got to know him, I realized he had a real vision for bringing the community back."

Dane Miller's self-published biography records it this way: "In 1989 the Winona Lake Historical Society was trying to raise funds to keep the Westminster Hotel from being torn down. The Millers responded with a promise of $20,000—the largest commitment the Historical Society had yet received. As things turned out, the building was bought and restored by Grace College, so the gift was not needed. But this situation brought about the meeting of Dane Miller and Brent Wilcoxson, who had a vision to restore Winona Lake to its former glory."[43]

Eventually, Wilcoxson quit his financial planner job so he could devote full time to restoring Winona Lake. The initial step was to buy and restore formerly stately homes that had been divided into multi-unit rentals. They began work on Terrace Avenue, where 39 apartments were converted to six single-family homes. They were renovated to become beautiful one-family owner-occupied properties, inspiring others in the community to invest in and restore their properties, as well.

In 1996 an opportunity emerged for further revitalization when Grace College representatives made an offer to sell its properties near the lake. Miller and Wilcoxson decided to turn this area into a collection of artisan shops and related businesses to bring outsiders to town. Instead of mowing down the old houses as many developers might have done, they restored the homes for retail use and sought businesses that would appeal to customers looking for something special.

The purchase of the original Assembly grounds from Grace in 1997 and the restoration of nearly thirty properties into a historic summer resort led to an economic resurgence of the community. The creation of commercial and residential areas, using restored original structures, has brought recognition to Winona Lake as a prime location for visitors and residents alike.

---

[43] Kavanaugh, p. 109

A White Paper update on the restoration written by Kosciusko Leadership Academy (KLA) participants Steve Barrett and Dan Gehrke in April of 1998 noted that "changes are taking place right now that are preserving the past while restoring the future for the area." The report noted that not only would some 70 new permanent jobs be added when the Village at Winona project was complete, but taking the assembly property off tax-exempt status and adding it to the town's taxable area would bring an estimated annual $75,000 increase in tax revenue, as well.

In 1999, the first ten retailers opened in the area bordered by Canal Street and Park Avenue in homes that were restored and, in some cases, moved into the old Chautauqua Assembly grounds from other spots in the village.

Wilcoxson and Miller called the collection of stores the Village at Winona, essentially a smaller town within the larger town of Winona Lake. Most of the shops today have large wooden porches and matching vintage-looking mailboxes. Many also have original flooring and architectural elements such as built-in cabinets, ornate archways, and stairwells.

Miller estimates that their total investment has now reached $35 million in renovations to the lake community and bringing the Village at Winona to life.

In 2002, The Indiana Association of Cities and Towns awarded Dane Miller the 2001 IACT annual award for civic service and his contributions to the town of Winona Lake.

In 2003 the Historic Landmarks Foundation of Indiana bestowed its top award on Winona Restoration Partners LLC for efforts toward "inspiring an entire community to become engaged in revitalization based on historic preservation."[44]

A *Chicago Tribune* story by Jay Jones, "A Sojourn in Temperance Country" published on October 14, 2011, says that Winona Lake is once again a charming community that invites guests to come for a day or a weekend to learn about its history, explore the shops and

---

[44] Much of this material was taken from an article "Committed to the Community" by Ann C. Smith in the *Symphony of the Lakes Magazine*, published in Fall, 2007 by Michiana Business Publications Inc.

eateries, and to enjoy the many summertime festivals. The town has one man—and his graduate thesis—to thank for its rebirth, according to the *Tribune* article.

"Probably 80 percent of what you see in Winona Lake now was in my original business plan," Wilcoxson told the *Tribune.*

A high point in the celebration of the town's history and heritage was reached in May of 1996 when the Winona Lake Historical Society and the Ma Sunday Secret Society Players presented "Sunday! A Centennial Trip with Billy 'Down the Sawdust Trail'" at the Hillside Amphitheater.

The event, which celebrated the 100th anniversary of Billy Sunday's start as a crusade evangelist, was billed as "a glimpse of the staging and drama that made Billy Sunday a household word." The event was part historical preservation and part fundraiser, as guests were asked to assist the Winona Lake Historical Society in raising $100,000 to establish a Billy Sunday museum.

In the presentation, Billy Sunday was portrayed by Steve Grill and Helen "Ma" Sunday by Kathleen Allison. Brent Wilcoxson was Homer Rodeheaver and Mindi Jentes was Virginia Asher. B. D. Ackley was portrayed by Dave Rank.

Jonathan Saylor was narrator and Randy Maxson directed a large crusade choir comprised of area church musicians. The songs performed were numbers made famous by Rodeheaver and the Sunday crusades, including *Brighten the Corner Where You Are* by Charles H. Gabriel, *Master, the Tempest is Raging* by H. R. Palmer, *My Anchor Holds* by D. B. Towner, *De Brewer's Big Hosses* by J. B. Herbert, *The Old Rugged Cross* by Rev. George Bennard, and *In the Garden* by C. Austin Miles.

The Miller/Wilcoxson partnership ended acrimoniously in 2012, but the deed was done. The town of Winona Lake had been rescued from further deterioration, there was new momentum for the arts and shopping, and the "Park Avenue Revival" had worked a miracle on the streets of this historic little town.

HISTORY OF BIOMET

Dane and Mary Louise Miller's ability to make such a heavy financial contribution to the town's rebirth can be traced directly to the success of Biomet, the orthopaedic firm Miller co-founded. Biomet, Inc., was founded in 1977 by four young men infused with a bold entrepreneurial spirit. Dane A. Miller, Ph.D., Niles L. Noblitt, Jerry L. Ferguson, and M. Ray Harroff, all experienced in the orthopaedic industry, shared a vision shaped by a desire to be highly responsive to the changing needs of orthopaedic surgeons and a belief that their company could set a new standard for quality and clinical durability.

To finance their venture, they pooled their own money and obtained a loan from the Small Business Administration. Despite their confidence in the orthopaedic industry and the company they envisioned, the path to success was anything but easy. With just eight team members at the time of its incorporation—the four founders and their wives—Biomet began to establish the foundation that would shape the company's future and allow it to emerge as a worldwide leader in the medical devices industry.

Dane Miller, born to schoolteacher parents in Springfield, Ohio, on February 7, 1946, early showed a deep love for math and science. He married Mary Louise Schilke, the daughter of a Springfield physician, in 1966 and went on to formal education through the General Motors Institute (GMI) and the University of Cincinnati, completing the Ph.D. degree in biomedical engineering. He began his career in orthopaedics in December of 1972, when he joined Zimmer Orthopaedics in Warsaw, Indiana, as a 25-year-old in charge of the Wear Testing Lab in the research and development department.

Dane Miller's story, including some time working in California before founding Biomet, is told in his self-published autobiography, *The Maverick CEO,* written by Patrick Kavanaugh and published in 2008.

During its first year of operation, Biomet recorded sales of only $17,000 with a net loss of $63,000. From its beginning, Biomet pioneered major technological advances. In 1978, Dane Miller's grandmother received Biomet's first hip implant, further demonstrating the founders' firm belief in their new company and its products. By 1980, Biomet had reached the $1.1 million mark in net sales and had broken ground for its current facility.

Biomet's initial public offering (IPO) was in 1982; public stock was also issued in 1983 and 1986. In 1984 Biomet acquired Orthopedic Equipment Company (OEC), thereby establishing an international presence, increasing manufacturing operations in Europe, and bolstering its distribution network in the United States. The company's net sales in 1984 totaled $10.6 million, and Dane Miller, Biomet's president and CEO, was named Indiana's Small Business Person of the Year.

By the end of its first decade, Biomet had gained state and national recognition for its unique corporate philosophy, which focused on customer responsiveness, teamwork, and innovation. The founders attributed much of the company's success and rapid growth to its ability to quickly introduce innovations to the market.

Much more of Biomet's history may be obtained from its website. Dane Miller retired as president and CEO in 2006, and Biomet was purchased in 2007 by a consortium of private equity firms.

Now a global industry leader with an unmatched reputation for innovation, responsiveness, and clinical success, Biomet distributes its products in approximately 90 countries and generates annual sales of more than $2.5 billion.

FINANCIAL ADJUSTMENTS AGAIN NECESSARY

The Billy Sunday Museum was built in 2000 at 1101 Park Avenue in the style of the temporary "tabernacles" that Sunday had erected of wood after his revivals became so popular that tents were inadequate. The structures were usually dismantled after the revivals and the wood sold to offset the costs. They were called "Glory Barns" by the public. The museum enjoyed several years of expansive "Billy Sunday Festivals."

On June 12, 2004, for example, the festival began at 10 a.m. with a "Billy and Ma Sunday Look-A-Like Contest," then a Billy Sunday postcard and memorabilia trader exhibition, a "Ma Is in Da House" free open tour of the Billy Sunday home staffed with volunteers and Kathleen Allison portraying "Ma" Sunday.

At noon, *Sunday in Manhattan* was presented, a one-man musical by Brent Grosvenor containing eight scenes in Act 1 and five scenes in Act 2 featuring vignettes and songs to tell the story of Sunday's life and ministry.

The festival continued with live bluegrass music in the afternoon and autograph signing by several authors of books on Billy Sunday. A Vintage Base Ball Tourney, featuring a round robin style tournament, was played on Tabernacle Field where the Billy Sunday Tabernacle once stood. The players wore 1860s authentic uniforms and used 1860s rules. Teams included the Village at Winona Blue Laws, the Warsaw Fleetfoots Vintage Base Ball Club Nine, and the Elkhart Bonneyville Millers.

Following more than a decade of growth, re-development, and favorable publicity for the town's re-birth, the Winona Lake Town Council in November of 2008 heard that the Billy Sunday Museum may have to close because of its deficits.

A proposal was approved that the town, in cooperation with Grace College, the Village at Winona, and other potential individuals and entities, investigate transitioning the Billy Sunday Home and Museum into a visitors center.

Winona Lake Clerk-Treasurer Retha Hicks warned that the Village at Winona would be suspending operations of the facility December 31 unless a break-even financial structure could be achieved.

Hicks said current deficits of the center were $60,000 per year against income of approximately $10,000 per year. Expenses of labor, utilities, repair and maintenance, and cost of goods was approximately $70,000 per year.

The proposal sought to have Winona Lake, Grace schools, and the Village at Winona combine financial resources and employ Museumcroft as an independent contractor to manage the Billy Sunday facility as well as the Reneker Museum of Winona History in Westminster Hall.

Bill Firstenberger, curator of the museum, was the owner of Museumcroft. Firstenberger began working with the Village at Winona in 1998, serving as curator of the museum and hosting tours of the Billy Sunday home. He also compiled a master listing of all the Billy Sunday crusades. A graduate of Notre Dame, he had previously worked with several museums in South Bend.

Brent Wilcoxson, managing director for the Village at Winona, said the center hosted 7,000 to 8,000 visitors a year, and local elementary school students visit the center as well. He said busloads of people from Chicago also visit the center.

"The museum has limited marketing ability, but the Billy Sunday home is in the top 1 percent of art and craft bungalows in the United States," Wilcoxson said. Built in 1911, the Billy Sunday home was restored according to Interior Department guidelines in 2000.

The visitors center contained two offices of approximately 200 square feet each, a 20-seat video viewing room, women's and men's restrooms with 13 total fixtures, and mechanical space. The remainder of the structure was dedicated to exhibit space related to Billy Sunday and his work.

The buildings and grounds were owned by Grace, with the Village at Winona providing all repairs and maintenance for the facility including lawn/landscaping and snow plowing. The Village at Winona managed the building.

Although this arrangement worked for a short while, it was a temporary solution. Ultimately, Firstenberger was released, most of the museum contents were moved to the Reneker Museum of Winona History in Westminster Hall, and the Park Avenue building was thoroughly renovated to accommodate a new tenant, The Remnant Trust, Inc.

CHICAGO AREA RE-ENACTMENTS

A Chicago-area pastor, author, and speaker, Ray Pritchard, also contributed significantly to the preservation and interpretation of Billy Sunday's story with his annual portrayal of Sunday during an annual commemoration called *Tale of the Tombstones*.

About 1992 or 1993 Pritchard read a newspaper article that advertised a "Cemetery Walk" sponsored by the historical society, and when he read that Billy Sunday was buried in the Forest Home Cemetery (described as the premier non-sectarian burial ground of Chicago's west suburban area), he began to research the evangelist.

Pritchard, who was then pastoring a church in Oak Park, Illinois, portrayed Sunday over a period of about ten years under the sponsorship of the Historical Society of Oak Park and River Forest.

Pritchard would outfit himself with a wooden bat, a scuffed-up baseball, and a weather-beaten glove and, in period dress, would tell the story of Sunday's life in the first person. His minister of music impersonated Homer Rodeheaver and had choir members from the church playing and singing gospel songs, including Sunday's theme song, *Brighten the Corner Where You Are.* Pritchard recalls, "It was always a highlight of the year for me."

He would perform an eight-minute presentation numerous times (16-20 repetitions were not unusual with one day's attendance estimated at around 600). At the end of each presentation, Pritchard invited people to come forward and shake his hand as a sign they were accepting Christ, which is the way Sunday did it in his crusades. He closed with a classic Sunday question: "When the Great Umpire of the Universe makes the Final Call, will he find you 'Safe at Home' or 'Out for all Eternity?'"

Pritchard gave his final presentation in October of 2003 and since has left the church and moved from the Chicago area to lead his own ministry, entitled *Keep Believing.*

THE REMNANT TRUST

Grace College and Theological Seminary announced in January of 2010 that the Billy Sunday Visitors Center collection would move to a new home in the Reneker Museum of Winona History, located in Westminster Hall.

The building that previously housed the visitors center was shortly to be occupied by The Remnant Trust, a public educational foundation that archives and preserves rare historical documents. This priceless collection of antiquities is loaned to colleges, universities, and other institutions for display and research by students, faculty, scholars, and the general public.

These archives include significant works, including some of the first copies of the Magna Carta, early printings of the United States Constitution and the Declaration of Independence, and one of only two existing copies of the ancient Book of Enoch. Some pieces date as early as 1250. The collections are on public display at select times in Winona Lake, and will tour other locations around the country.

Dr. Ron Manahan, speaking as the president of Grace College and Theological Seminary, said, "We're thrilled to welcome The

Remnant Trust to our community. This organization continues to protect original and first-edition historical documents while making them accessible for research and review. Grace is also proud to continue honoring Billy Sunday's memory by giving the visitors center collection a new home within the Reneker Museum, one that will allow the museum to provide a more complete picture of Winona history."

Dr. Dane A. Miller, founder and board member of Biomet Inc., served on the board of directors for The Remnant Trust and echoed Dr. Manahan's comments. "I am delighted to bring our archives to Winona Lake and look forward to making a significant contribution to the community and the college with our presence," he said.

The Remnant Trust relocated to Winona Lake in 2010 from its headquarters in southern Indiana. Part of the cost of modifying the Sunday Museum building for use by the Trust was funded through a $50,000 grant from the Kosciusko County Community Foundation. Issues involved outfitting the collection with temperature, humidity, light, fire suppression, and security monitoring controls.

Russ Pulliam, previously editorial page editor for *The Indianapolis News* and director of the Pulliam Fellowship since 1992, commented in June, 2010, on The Remnant Trust's move to Winona Lake. He said:

> Winona Lake, Indiana, already has staked a strong claim as a historic site. But Warsaw-based civic leader Dane Miller wants to add more history: original copies of the Constitution and the Federalist Papers. The Remnant Trust, which preserves such original documents, will relocate from Louisville to Winona Lake this year.

> Evangelist Billy Sunday lived and preached in Winona Lake about 90 years ago, and his home is a historic spot. Three-time Democratic presidential nominee William Jennings Bryan spoke often at Winona Lake, helping the Northern Indiana town to become a Chautauqua meeting spot. Thousands would gather to hear orators like Bryan or Will Rogers. Crime figures such as Al Capone and John Dill-

inger also stopped by, but presumably not for cultural or spiritual renewal.

Now Miller wants to add the trust as one more jewel in Winona Lake's crown. Founder of Biomet in nearby Warsaw, Miller has helped make the lakeshore a destination that features Billy Sunday history sites, artisan shops, and the MasterWorks Music Festival.

Grace College is up the hill from the lake, with a new home court and athletic facility, the Orthopaedic Capital Center. The new arena is a tribute to the civic responsibility of nearby Warsaw's big three bio-medical companies, Zimmer, DePuy, and Biomet. Miller worked for Zimmer and then worked in San Diego before returning to Indiana to launch Biomet, where he still serves on the board. Combined revenue for the three companies runs more than $10 billion a year, creating major employment options in the region.

Miller, who has a doctorate in biomedical engineering, is an entrepreneur. Why would a visionary from the lab worry about the preservation and display of original documents like the Constitution or the Federalist Papers?

"This was a project of passion and not necessarily economic sense," he says. "I guess it's a hobby."

After reading the Federalist Papers and other classics, he realized the value of first editions. "The second or third editions are not precisely the same as the original," he said. "You want to make sure you are dealing with the original version. We tend to make things politically correct and meddle with history."

Remnant Trust founder Brian Bex of Hagerstown, Ind., said college and university faculty love original documents.

"These works for centuries have been hidden in private collections or locked up in vaults," he said. The trust preserves them and sends them out for a semester or two to colleges and universities.

"When we take them to places such as DePauw University or Hanover College, the reaction is unbelievable," Bex said.

The trust's oldest manuscript dates to AD 1258, when Pope Innocent III explained the value of indulgences.

Winona Lake already has much charm for music lovers, history buffs and sports fans. Now the scholars may want to come, too.

More information is available at *www.theremnanttrust.com.*

CHAPTER 15

The Lakes Are Alive with the Sound of Music

"God's purpose in creating these natural tools certainly must include the gift of joy that music has brought to every culture. But it also may have a higher calling, as we use music to communicate directly with God Himself, expressing our gratitude to Him for creating such 'music of the spheres.'"
Patrick Kavanaugh

THE GRACE COLLEGE CAMPUS IN WINONA LAKE ANNUALLY HOSTS the MasterWorks Festival, a month-long intensive summer training program that focuses on instruction in the performing arts from a Christian worldview. It was co-founded in 1997 by Dr. Patrick and Barbara Kavanaugh and Dr. James and Mary Jeane Kraft.

Originally the festival took place at Houghton College in New York. After five successful years there, it moved to Winona Lake, where several businessmen were working together to restore the town's economic vitality. The event, together with the new Village at Winona, became the perfect catalyst to revive a small town that had once been the home of evangelist Billy Sunday and various other ministries. In 2004, the town became the official headquarters of the festival, and the Grace campus eventually came to serve as the offices and classrooms that participants needed for the event.

Fifty-five students attended the first year in 1997, but both students and faculty in attendance each year are now in the hundreds. Moreover, the event has gone international as it has now been offered in London, England, and in Zhengzhou, China.

Christian Performing Artists' Fellowship (http://www.christian-performingart.org/), the non-profit umbrella organization for the MasterWorks Festival, had its start in the Washington, D. C. area with local musicians Patrick and Barbara Kavanaugh and Jim and Mary Jeane Kraft. Jim Kraft played trombone with the National Symphony Orchestra. Barbara Kavanaugh and Mary Jeane Kraft were both cellists who played with local orchestras and ensembles, and Patrick Kavanaugh was minister of music at a local church, Christian Assembly.

The Krafts and Kavanaughs, along with dancers Bob and Robin Sturm, formed a collaboration and performed Patrick's opera *The Last Supper* at Washington's Folger Theatre in the spring of 1984. This first performance proved to be the genesis of CPAF.

The first official performance of CPAF took place on November 20, 1984, at Christian Assembly. Joined by opera singers and Juilliard graduates Steve and Linda Schnurman, the two dancers, four singers and a handful of musicians took the stage for their debut performance of the Bach *Cantata No. 140*. As it developed, the group took the name Asaph Ensemble, and it continued with performances of Mozart's *Requiem*, Bach's *Magnificat*, Stravinsky's *Symphony of Psalms,* and, in 1987, a performance at the Kennedy Center of movements from the Bach *Mass in B Minor.*

In the summer of 1988 the Kavanaughs went into the CPAF ministry full-time. A connection with Metropolitan Opera singer Jerome Hines (1921-2003) led to several collaborations, including a 1992 performance of Boito's *Mefistofele* at the Kennedy Center and, in July of 1993, a two-week tour of Russia with 191 people, highlighted by a performance of Hines' opera *I Am the Way* at the Bolshoi Theater in Moscow. In 1996 the Asaph Ensemble performed on Christmas Eve in Bethlehem's Manger Square at the invitation of the Israeli government.

Although CPAF's ministry was expanding and was well-received, the leadership felt a growing need to form some kind of vehicle to pass their vision on to the next generation of Christian performing artists. Gradually the concept of a summer festival was formed, one which would train young performers both artistically and spiritually for one month, then send them back to their secular schools to make an impact for Christ. The first MasterWorks Festival took place in Houghton, New York, on June 21, 1997.

The festival doubled in attendance, and then doubled again. In the spring of 2001 an article about MasterWorks in the *Power for Living* Sunday school take-home paper was brought to the attention of Brent Wilcoxson, whose brother, Jeff, had picked up the paper at a Fort Wayne church.

Wilcoxson and his partner, Dr. Dane Miller, had taken on a project to restore the small town to its former glory and in 2002 Wilcoxson invited the MasterWorks Festival to take place on the Grace College campus. In 2004, after two successful summers in Indiana, the MasterWorks Festival and its CPAF headquarters relocated to Winona Lake with the Village at Winona and Grace College providing offices and living space for CPAF staff.

CPAF established an arts administration intern program which enables talented young artists to train for an entire year. During the school year, performances are held each second Sunday, with interns and faculty members performing, usually followed by a short community hymn sing.

SYMPHONY OF THE LAKES

Since the earliest days of Winona, choral and instrumental musical ensembles have enriched the programming at Winona. With the founding of Grace College in 1948, however, it became common for joint college-community groups to form and perform.

Some of the earliest choral performances, including Handel's *Messiah,* were directed by Donald Ogden, James Lynn, Tammie Huntington, Ardis Faber, and others.

In 1959, an area instrumental ensemble directed by Willard Snapp was featured in the summer program of the Rodeheaver School of Music in Winona Lake. In the 1960s a joint college-community wind ensemble was directed by Terry White. For many years Jerry Franks, virtuoso trumpeter, clinician for Elkhart-based instrument manufacturers, and Grace College artist-in-residence maintained a popular college-community band and produced several recordings.

That tradition has continued under the baton of longtime community band director Martin Becker. Pit orchestras were formed as needed to accompany performances such as Handel's *Messiah*.

A concert orchestra was organized by Ethel Anderson, again comprised of Grace family and community players, along with hired professionals. This organization continued under the direction of Ardis Faber. Local musicians Richard and Ethel Anderson promoted local performances and several groups were formed, including an occasional orchestra called the Warsaw Symphony.

The natural successor to the Warsaw Symphony was Symphony of the Lakes, a professional orchestra founded in 2004 and directed by CPAF director Patrick Kavanaugh, dedicated to bringing music of the highest quality to the people of Kosciusko County.

This year-round orchestra was directed by Kavanaugh until he retired after the first concert of the 2012-2013 season to concentrate on MasterWorks Festival and Christian Performing Artists' Fellowship, which he also directed. To guarantee that quality performances are available to everyone, the concerts of the Symphony of the Lakes are free of charge.

In 2005 the orchestra chose to change its name for two reasons, according to Kavanaugh. First, there was already a Warsaw Symphony Orchestra in Poland, and Kavanaugh said, "They make a lot of recordings so it is well-known."

Second, symphonies are generally named for the largest town in the area. Warsaw is the largest city of Kosciusko County, but Kavanaugh said the orchestra's support base was bigger than the name implied. "We have a broad constituency throughout the area, including people who reside on Tippecanoe and Wawasee lakes," Kavanaugh said.

The mission of Symphony of the Lakes is to enhance the cultural climate of the community and to encourage the appreciation and enjoyment of symphonic music through inspiring performances of the highest quality to an ever-growing audience.

Prior to the Symphony of the Lakes, the Lakeland Community Concert Association was founded in the winter of 1959, and still continues, bringing world-class artists to the community for relatively inexpensive ticket prices.

For example, a *Warsaw Times-Union* article from April 13, 1961, announces that an LCCA membership drive, headed by Prof. Donald Ogden of Grace College, was underway, with more than 600 memberships already secured. The schedule of programs for 1962 included the St. Louis Symphony Orchestra on March 16, Metropolitan Opera bass-baritone Jerome Hines on February 13, duo-pianists Stecher and Horowitz (they bring their own Steinway concert grands) in November, and Aliani and Diard, soprano and tenor, in January.

Yet another community cultural opportunity was made available beginning in 1990 through the generosity of the Rodeheaver family. The Rodeheaver Series for the Performing Arts is funded by a bequest to the First United Methodist Church of Warsaw from Ruthella Feaster (Mrs. J. N.) Rodeheaver, who was the last surviving family member in the area. Her husband, Joseph Newton (Dr. J. N.) was a brother to Homer Rodeheaver and helped found the family publishing business with Homer and their brother Yumbert of South Bend.

The series is named for the Rodeheaver family, legendary for their development and support of Christian music and long-time members of First United Methodist Church. The first performance in the series was by organist Jesse Eschbach, a Warsaw native of national acclaim.

CHAPTER 16
Churches of Winona Lake

*"Church attendance is as vital to a disciple as
a transfusion of rich, healthy blood to a sick man."*
Dwight L. Moody

THE WINONA FEDERATED CHURCH/PRESBYTERIAN/CHURCH OF THE GOOD SHEPHERD

THIS FIRST CHURCH IN TOWN WAS AN OUTGROWTH OF THE WINONA Assembly, and especially of the schools which made the establishment of a church a necessity for the community. Accordingly, the Winona Federated Church was founded in 1905.

Dr. Sol C. Dickey and Dr. J. Wilbur Chapman were to supply the pulpit during the summer, and Dr. Frank N. Palmer, Dr. J. C. Breckenridge and Dr. E. S. Scott, who were connected with the Winona schools, were to discharge the pastoral duties during the year.

Services were held at the Daguerre Building until construction of the Westminster Hotel in 1905. Services were then moved to the Westminster where they were maintained each year from September until the opening of the Old Auditorium in June. In September of 1911, Dr. Joseph W. Clokey became pastor, and he retired two years later.

The congregation felt the need of becoming affiliated with one of the established denominations, and so by majority vote it was decided to reorganize as a Presbyterian church. The organization was effected on June 27, 1913, with 44 charter members. An invitation was extended to Dr. James A. Gordon, who had been pastor of the Presbyterian church in Van Wert, Ohio, for 22 years. He was installed at the Winona Lake church on January 23, 1914.

Gordon was born into a Scotch-Irish family that immigrated from Ireland and settled in the Cumberland Valley of Pennsylvania. His father was a pastor, and James attended Wooster College in Ohio, graduating in 1882 at the top of his class, and then matriculated at Princeton Seminary in New Jersey for three years. He was ordained June 9, 1885, into the Presbyterian ministry.

Gordon served churches in Michigan, took a post-graduate fellowship at Harvard Divinity School, served a church in Van Wert, Ohio, and in 1902 received the honorary Doctor of Divinity degree from the College of Wooster.

He was given a leave of absence from his congregation and traveled throughout Europe, Palestine and Egypt. He resigned the Van Wert church and left in October of 1912, spending most of the next year with his wife traveling along the Pacific Coast from San Diego to Alaska. On his return, he accepted a call to pastor the reorganized church at Winona Lake, where he had been a frequent summer visitor.

For nearly all of his 16 years as pastor, he was a member of the board of directors of the Winona Lake institutions, and served a decade as recording secretary of the board and secretary of the executive committee. He was active in local organizations including the Kiwanis Club and the Warsaw Chamber of Commerce.

Realizing it would need a permanent location, the church bid on four lots when the bankrupt Bible Conference had a sale of lots on November 4, 1915. After meeting for a decade in the Westminster Hotel, the congregation purchased the land where the current church building sits (Chestnut and 7th St.) for $576 with a loan from Mrs. Billy ("Ma") Sunday, which was reimbursed to her over the next several years from funds raised by the Ladies Aid Society.

On October 20, 1921, a congregational meeting was called to consider construction of a church building. The building at 7th and Chestnut was constructed for a total cost of $55,000. The cornerstone was laid June 24, 1923, the building was dedicated on August 3, 1924, and regular services in the building began on November 9, 1924.

The Gothic Revival structure was designed by Dr. O. H. Newlin. Typical of this architectural style are the square tower and arched windows. Interior features include the vaulted ceiling and folding oak doors in the sanctuary. Numerous stained-glass windows surround the building and fill it with color.

The pulpit and pews came from a disbanded church in Waterloo, Indiana. The bell was one that hung for years on the lakefront and was used as the fire bell and for curfew. The window of the Good Shepherd was a gift from Homer Rodeheaver in memory of his brother, Jack, who died in an airplane accident. The Gethsemane window in the main sanctuary was given by the Men's Bible Class.

The communion table was given to the church by Katherine Carmichael in remembrance of her mother. The original organ was installed in 1951 and the present organ was donated by the family of Dr. J. R. Baum. The flags and stands for the chancel area were presented to the church by Mabel Robinson in 1961 in memory of her son, Capt. Richard C. Robinson, who died in a plane crash in Europe.

A bequest from Harriet Gawthrop in the 1990s made it possible to expand the church building, including the addition of a modern elevator. That annex was dedicated on November 15, 1998.

In August, 2009, the congregation voted to change the name to Church of the Good Shepherd "to better express our fundamental focus on following Christ in mission in Winona Lake, Warsaw, Kosciusko County, and wherever the servants of God whose work we support may minister around the world." The church to-date has had 15 senior pastors.

WINONA LAKE FREE METHODIST CHURCH

Work began in the fall of 1934 to remodel the Mount Memorial building, which would become the world headquarters of the Free Methodist Church and the Free Methodist Publishing House. A few families had moved to Winona Lake in advance of the relocation of the publishing house from Chicago, and this group held cottage prayer meetings during the fall and winter of 1934-35. The group included Rev. and Mrs. Carl L. Howland, Mr. and Mrs. B. H. Gaddis, Mr. and Mrs. H. E. Timbers, Mr. and Mrs. Don Endicott, Mr. and Mrs. Edgar Nerby, and their families.

The first Sunday service was held in the newly completed publishing house chapel (second floor, north wing) on April 28, 1935. The Rev. Mr. Howland, editor of the Free Methodist magazine, preached.

A Free Methodist society was organized on May 14, 1935, by the Rev. E. A. Cutler, superintendent of the Winona Lake district of the North Indiana conference. Lively growth occurred and a property known as the Otterbein, at the corner of Ninth and Chestnut streets, was purchased at a tax sale. Plans were drawn for remodeling and work started in the early spring of 1940.

B. H. Gaddis, publisher, and H. C. Mason, pastor, shared an interest in colonial architecture. As a result, the Otterbein was remodeled into a building patterned after the beautiful Martha and Mary Chapel in Henry Ford's Greenfield Village in Michigan. Don Endicott designed the sanctuary and Richard Siefken designed and installed the recessed lighting. The building was completed in 1942.

The narthex of the present building on that location was the sanctuary of the original building. A parsonage and Sunday school rooms occupied the remainder of the original building. The first service held in the new building, while the interior was still incomplete, was the funeral of missionary secretary Harry L. Johnson, in August of 1942.

In 1958 an attractive brick parsonage was built and in 1964 plans were drawn for additional space to be provided in two new wings— the present sanctuary and the educational unit. Groundbreaking followed the morning worship service on February 21, 1965. During construction the congregation worshiped in the facilities of Light and Life Press. The congregation met for the first time in the new sanctuary on August 21, 1966.

In November of 1978, the new educational wing was added to complete the building's current footprint. In the years that followed, additional interior changes were made on the upper level to provide office space for the senior pastor, an associate pastor, and support staff.

The story of the Don Endicott family is inextricably linked to the Free Methodist period in Winona's history. Endicott moved to Winona Lake from Evanston, Illinois, in 1934 to oversee the refurbishing of the Winona College (Mount Memorial) building, which had closed after World War I, and to prepare it for use as the world headquarters of the Free Methodist Church of North America.

Upon completion of that project, a minister requested that Endicott, a carpenter, make a pulpit. After completing that task, he began receiving requests for pews, altars, and other church furniture. Soon after, in the mid-1930s, the Endicott Church Furniture Company was founded and grew rapidly with a reputation for innovation and quality.

Don Endicott designed the first attached upholstered pew which has become a popular item in church construction and remodeling. In 1959, Endicott sold his church furniture business to Dalton Foundries of Warsaw. It became a division of Dalton, headed by Jesse Eschbach (1920-2005) who later went on to forge a notable career as a federal judge for the United States District Court for the Northern District of Indiana and the United States Court of Appeals for the Seventh Circuit.

Dalton Foundries, Inc., founded in 1911 by Donald J. Dalton, began with 25 employees. The only product they produced in the beginning was a home shoe repair kit. In 1974 the Dalton division of Endicott Church Furniture was sold to a group consisting of Charles H. Ker, Charles A. Ker, and James Lauwerens and it became known as Endicott Industries.

Don Endicott was first married to Frances Butts, who died in 1977. The following year he married Florence Hartford, who moved to Cleveland, Ohio, following Don's death in 1978. Don Endicott had two daughters by his first marriage, Ruth Helen "Peaches," who married Harold French of Warsaw; and Carolyn Ann "Pony," who married Louis Driskell of Orlando, Florida.

During the Depression in the 1930s Endicott brought to Winona Lake two of his sisters. Loverna Clare was married to William

Edwin Barber, who is the grandfather of Craig W. Tidball, local financial advisor. The other sister, Dorcas, married Vernon Gast, who later was employed as a regional salesman with Endicott Church Furniture.

WINONA LAKE GRACE BRETHREN CHURCH

The Winona Lake Grace Brethren Church, now meeting at 1200 Kings Highway, began with a small group of people meeting in each others' homes for prayer shortly after Grace Theological Seminary moved to Winona Lake from Akron, Ohio, in 1939. On June 23, 1943, the small group, meeting in Don Bartlett's home on 7th Street, decided to move ahead and start a church. The first officers were Leo Polman, chairman; Isobel Fraser, secretary; and Marvin Goodman, treasurer.

On September 5, 1943, the group began meeting in the Grace Seminary chapel, then located in the Free Methodist Publishing House (Mount Memorial building). Foy Miller became the first Sunday school superintendent, and when charter membership was officially closed 53 people were on the list. The church was known as the Winona Lake Brethren Church. Local residents who were charter members include the late Elaine Brenneman, Rev. Jesse Deloe, and Mrs. Joyce Griffith.

Grace Seminary faculty member Dr. Homer Kent, Sr., became the first pastor in 1946. Herman Koontz was installed as the church's first full-time pastor in September of 1949.

The congregation soon outgrew the chapel and moved in 1951 to the lower auditorium of the newly constructed McClain Hall. Don Ogden was engaged as the church's first music and youth director in 1953 and the first vacation Bible school was held in 1954.

That same year the church voted to purchase property at the corner of 13th Street and Kings Highway for an eventual all-church facility. A branch church was begun in the Herscher Addition in 1956, and that congregation is now Community Grace Brethren Church of Warsaw, Indiana. Later another daughter church was founded—called New Horizon—which for a time occupied the former Lakeland Christian Academy facilities on Wooster Road before moving to holding worship services in McClain Auditorium.

Richard DeArmey was installed as pastor in 1957. Charles Ashman became pastor in 1962. A building program was begun in 1966, plans were finished in early 1968, and ground was broken on April 21, 1968, for a facility.

Led by Pastor Charles H. Ashman, the congregation moved into their facility which was dedicated on January 25, 1970. In 1978 "Grace" was added to the name, making it Winona Lake Grace Brethren Church. In 1983 the adjoining piece of property was purchased from the Winona School of Photography. The school's Daguerre Building was renamed The Learning Center, and it housed most of the children's and youth ministries as well as the church office complex.

A brick house on the church property was the parsonage at first but later became the focal point of youth activities and was renamed The Turning Point. Eventually it was purchased by a private party and moved several hundred yards down Kings Highway where it again became a private residence.

In November of 1989 Pastor John Teevan came from Ashland, Ohio, and he pastored the church for 16 years until August 1, 2006, when he accepted a position with Grace College, overseeing and expanding the school's prison education program. The church restructured into a team leadership concept shortly thereafter, with associate pastor Bruce Barlow becoming the lead pastor of the team and Kip Cone heading up the Proclamation Team (preaching).

In 2011 the Daguerre Building (Learning Center) was razed and a $1.2 million renovation project enlarged and updated the old School of Photography auditorium building. Named The Hub, the facility houses the church's student ministries, a more contemporary worship service, and other activities of the church. The Hub is also available for community use, and is widely used.

CHRIST'S COVENANT CHURCH (REFORMED BAPTIST)

During the summer of 1977 several families who were of Reformed theological convictions decided to join together in a home on Chestnut Street in Winona Lake for corporate worship, Bible study, and mutual encouragement. More families joined them, and James Stewart was chosen as the first pastor, assisted by Rollin Jump and Ken Smith, who served as elders.

Originally oriented more toward a conservative Presbyterian denomination than the Reformed Baptists, the group experienced a peaceful, gradual theological change, and by the spring of 1981 Pastor Stewart stepped down and the church transitioned from a Presbyterian to a Baptist confession and constitution.

Under the direction of Rollin Jump, the church continued to function and grow, and in April 1981, the church contacted Larry McCall, a former attendee then doing a pastoral internship in Pennsylvania, about returning to the area to pastor the church. Pastor McCall and his family arrived in October of that year.

The group began meeting in the dining commons at the Cardinal Center, then moved to the Lakeview Shopping Center, renting additional space in the plaza as the church grew from about 25 to 130. By August of 1987 Christ's Covenant Church was able to move to its own recently constructed facilities on County Road 175 East, just a few blocks north of US 30.

By the fall of 2000 the congregation had outgrown their church building and moved into the newly constructed Lakeland Christian Academy building on County Road 250E in Winona Lake. There it experienced an influx of new attendees, leading the elders to add a second and third worship service each Sunday morning during the years at LCA.

In 2004, 19 acres were purchased at 2090 Pierceton Road, just a mile from the church's birthplace in Winona Lake. A new building was constructed, and Christ's Covenant Church moved into its current home in October, 2005.

Pastor Larry McCall now shares the leadership and care of the church with a team of elders, deacons, staff, and trained volunteers. Currently, 800 to 900 people gather on Sundays for worship, prayer, teaching, and fellowship. Other ministries to church members and to others in the community take place at various times throughout the week.

CELEBRATION UNITED METHODIST CHURCH

Situated in the middle of a spacious property on County Road 250 East, across from the main entrance to the Heritage Lakes subdivision, is a T-shaped building that houses the congregation of Celebration United Methodist Church.

Celebration has gained a reputation over the years for its help and outreach to all, with a strong ministry to "the hurting, the lost, and others who weren't comfortable within the structure of the more traditional churches in the area."

The church was conceived in the spring of 1989 when Steven Conger was appointed to start a traditional United Methodist Church that would attract and retain younger adults. The first service was held November 12, 1989, at the YMCA in Warsaw, Indiana. The congregation relocated to Edgewood School in January of 1990.

In December of 1991, with help from the Northern United Methodist Conference and gifts from local United Methodist churches, the group acquired a 30-acre site on County Road 250 East and moved the church office into a farmhouse situated on the property.

In August of 1993 the congregation began worshiping in a former motorcycle shop at County Road 325S and US 30. Celebration Church was chartered as an official United Methodist Church on March 5, 1995.

Pastor Steve Conger was reappointed elsewhere, and the next pastor, Scott Pattison, began in June of 1995. In July of 1995 the church's property became debt-free and the acreage on 250 East was used for many events, including cookouts, bonfires, Easter egg hunts, and many committee meetings.

In 1999 Pastor Pattison was reassigned, and Roy and Nancy Lee joined Celebration Church as interim pastors. The church was plagued by financial issues, and so it sold 12.5 acres of the original land and was again debt-free. The congregation moved into the building previously occupied by Christ's Covenant Church on County Road 175 East in June, 2001. Cindy Gackenheimer was named the new pastor on September 1, 2001.

Negotiations to purchase the Christ's Covenant building eventually fell through, and so the United Methodist congregation launched a prayer effort that led to a decision to build on the 250E property. Groundbreaking was held May 29, 2002. The first worship service in the new facility was September 29, 2002 and the building was dedicated October 27, 2002. The new permanent address for Celebration Church had become 1289 S County Road 250E in Winona Lake.

In the years since its relocation, Celebration Church's ministry has been distinguished by its relationship to Teen Challenge, by its annual "Blessing of the Bikes" service, and by short-term mission trips it has sponsored to Guatemala, Mississippi, and Liberia.

There have always been a number of smaller, younger churches, usually not having their own facilities, meeting in Winona Lake, as well. Currently such groups are using McClain Hall, Lakeland Christian Academy, and other suitable meeting places in Winona for worship services.

CHAPTER 17
Winona Lake and the Grace Brethren

*"Twenty-five years ago, when I was called to the presidency
of this school, it became my privilege to formulate the central
purpose embodied in our charter: 'To know Christ and to
make Him known as the only Savior and Lord of life.' Now
the time has come for me to address you at this final chapel
service as your president. And I feel that I can do nothing
better than to point your eyes and minds once more to Him
who is 'able to keep you from falling and to present you
faultless before the presence of his glory with exceeding joy.'"*
Alva J. McClain, May, 1962

BRETHREN CHURCH GROUPS HAVE HAD A SPECIAL AFFINITY FOR WINONA
Lake since 1892 and 1893 when the first Brethren General Conferences were held at Eagle Lake.[45] Attracted by the excellent lodging,
recreation and transportation facilities, and the growing reputation
of the interdenominational Bible conference, the Brethren continued to meet at Winona Lake.

Until 1939, nearly all Brethren Church General Conferences
and, until 1973 (with five exceptions), all Grace Brethren National
Conferences were held in Winona Lake. The 1925 annual Brethren
conference was marred by an outbreak of typhoid fever that caused
several deaths. Members of the Church of the Brethren also contributed $10,000 for the construction of the Billy Sunday Tabernacle in
1921-1922.

---

[45] *Brethren Encyclopedia* –Vol. 2, p. 1351

The modern Brethren movement had begun in Schwarzenau, Germany, when the Radical Pietist and Anabaptist Alexander Mack and his seven followers baptized each other by immersion in the Eder River, in response to what they understood Scripture to teach about baptism being for believers. That baptism occurred in August of 1708, and the group found a German nobleman who was tolerant enough of their religious beliefs to permit them to settle in the valley. What followed was a familiar search for a political environment in which tightly held religious convictions could be believed and practiced in freedom. As a result, the movement relocated to the United States in 1719 to the Germantown area of Philadelphia, Pennsylvania.

The movement grew and developed across the U.S. By the 1850s, however, a progressive spirit on the part of some was sending tremors throughout the group. The conflicts came to a head at the annual meetings in 1880 and 1881, with an elder named Henry R. Holsinger becoming the lightning-rod figure.

Brethren historian David Plaster[46] quotes an article that describes the contentious annual meeting which convened at Arnold's Grove, near Milford, Indiana, at the present junction of Indiana State Highway 15 and U.S. Highway 6. The grove is now gone, but an eyewitness at the time estimated the attendance at that meeting to be about 10,000 with some 35 acres of ground used in handling the conference. A large tent with a seating capacity of 5,000 was erected, and the Baltimore and Ohio Railroad built one and one-half miles of new track from their main line so they could deliver passengers to the meeting ground.

At this meeting the so-called Progressives, who aligned with Holsinger, were expelled from the main body. They remained throughout 1882 as an unorganized group, but by June 6, 1883, at a meeting in Dayton, Ohio, they had re-birthed as The Brethren Church. The group which expelled them is now the Church of the Brethren.

---

[46] Plaster, pp. 64-65

FOUNDING OF THE FOREIGN MISSION SOCIETY

The new, young group of churches began to grow rapidly, with annual meetings held each year, often (but not always) in Warsaw, Indiana. At the tenth general conference in 1900, however, which was held in Winona Lake, a very significant event occurred. A group of visionaries wanted to enter some foreign missionary fields, but met with resistance. At the 1900 conference, Jacob C. Cassel, a prominent elder in the church, presented a controversial paper on the subject, "Are We Ready to Enter the Foreign Missionary Field?" When the issue of organizing a mission society was brought to the conference, it met with no enthusiasm. The missionary enthusiasts were informed that there was plenty of room "out under the trees," where they could go to begin their organization, and that is exactly what they did.

The group retired to a small knoll just north of the auditorium building where the conference was being held. On this spot 53 men and women formed the Foreign Missionary Society of the Brethren Church. That knoll is marked today by a concrete pylon to which a permanent metal plaque commemorating the event is affixed. It is at the foot of the Ninth Street hill which comes down from the Westminster, and is located in the grass adjacent to the picnic pavilion and the swan pond. The plaque inscription reads "On this knoll, September 4, 1900, the Foreign Missionary Society of the Brethren Church was organized 'To testify the gospel of the grace of God.'"

From that founding came a worldwide missionary movement that by 2013 was active in approximately 35 nations of the world, with particularly strong works in Argentina, the Central African Republic, Brazil, and a number of countries in Europe and Asia.

For many years the motivating force and the functioning administrator of the Brethren foreign missions efforts was Pastor Louis S. Bauman of Long Beach, California. He oversaw communication with the missionaries, selection of new missionary candidates, and much more. He functioned in that role from 1906 until 1945, when Russell Barnard, who pastored a leading church in Dayton, Ohio, was tapped to become the first full-time secretary of the foreign missions program. He relocated to Winona Lake and served in that position for 20 years—until 1966.

The next leader for the organization was John "Jack" Zielasko, who had been a missionary in Brazil. He led the organization from 1966 until 1986. Tom Julien, veteran missionary to France who developed the Chateau de St. Albain ministry and pioneered new ways of engaging the French in spiritual discussions, led Grace Brethren International Missions from 1986 until 1990. Upon his retirement from the position, David Guiles, a missionary to Argentina, was named director in 1990 and he has steered the organization through its years of greatest change. This included moving the headquarters to Atlanta but retaining a small Winona Lake office staff in the former missionary residence building off Kings Highway adjacent to Jefferson Elementary School.

The first offices for the Society were on the top floor of Grace Seminary's McClain Hall. Later they moved to the Herald Building (BMH) and then "the Missions Building," now Kingsway Suites south of Grace College's physical plant building. More recently, the organization was headquartered in the former Light and Life building just south of Mount Memorial building until the organization changed its name to Encompass World Partners in 2011 and relocated its headquarters to Atlanta, Georgia.

FOUNDING OF GRACE SEMINARY

The Brethren Church, centered largely around Ashland College in Ashland, Ohio, experienced moderate growth and development through the first three decades of the 20th century. However, in Plaster's words, "A Brethren version of the Modernist-Fundamentalist controversy was on the horizon."[47] Led by Alva J. McClain, a former pastor from Philadelphia who had joined the faculty of the seminary division of Ashland College in 1925,[48] and Louis S. Bauman, pastor of the influential First Brethren Church of Long Beach, California, Ashland Theological Seminary opened in September of 1930.

After a contentious controversy involving disagreements over a statement of faith and lifestyle standards, Ashland Seminary request-

---

[47] Plaster, p. 90
[48] Scoles, p. 183

ed the resignations of McClain and Prof. Herman Hoyt from the seminary faculty because of "incompatibility." Ultimately, a "Brethren Biblical Seminary Association" was formed, and a group of officers met in Philadelphia and decided that the name of the school would be Grace Theological Seminary and that its temporary location would be in the Ellet Brethren Church of Akron, Ohio.

By the 1939 General Conference there was a clear division, with both groups claiming to be the Brethren Church. They held separate annual conferences, with the Grace group meeting in Winona Lake, Indiana, and the Ashland group in Ashland, Ohio. The late Brethren historian Todd Scoles noted, "Each developed its own foreign and domestic mission agencies, publications, women's organizations, and ministerial associations, and each supported its own school."[49] Although the division was functional, it was not formalized until 1986 when the Grace group incorporated as the Fellowship of Grace Brethren Churches.

At the founding of Grace Theological Seminary in 1937, Dr. Alva J. McClain was invited to become president of the seminary and Prof. Herman A. Hoyt was invited to become a full-time member of the faculty. A third invitation was issued to Homer A. Kent, Sr., then pastor of the First Brethren Church of Washington, D.C., to become a part-time teacher in the institution. Provision was made whereby other teachers could be invited as needed.

Plaster noted that there was great enthusiasm in the 1937 conference for the founding of the new seminary and, in fact, an unofficial rally was held in the Winona Lake Presbyterian Church with a capacity crowd of more than 500 present. There was singing, testimony, prayer, and the announcement concerning the plans for the opening of Grace Theological Seminary. Several financial gifts were given, including $1,000 from Miss Estella Myers, pioneer missionary to Africa. William E. Biederwolf, director of the Winona Lake Christian Assembly, was impressed with the proceedings and the spirit of the gathering and he invited Grace Seminary to make its home in Winona Lake, Indiana.[50]

---

[49] Scoles, p. 195

[50] Plaster, p. 114

Grace Theological Seminary opened in Akron, Ohio, on October 4, 1937, with a student body of 39. The next April the legal charter under the laws of Ohio was received and in June the first three graduates of the seminary were honored—Kenneth B. Ashman, Robert E. A. Miller, and Russell Williams.

The first permanent board of the seminary was elected at the first corporation meeting held in the Winona Lake Presbyterian Church on September 2, 1938. The school met in the Akron church for the first two years and after careful consideration of other places for a permanent location, and in response to Dr. Biederwolf's invitation, the seminary moved to Winona Lake to begin operation in the fall of 1939. Plaster noted, "The school occupied the upper floor of the three-story national headquarters building owned by the Free Methodist Church" [today named Mount Memorial building].

As the new Grace group began to develop, additional organizations were founded to support denominational functions. The Brethren Home Missions Council was created to assist with church planting and the designing and building of church facilities. Early leaders were Evangelist R. Paul Miller and L. L. Grubb. Dr. Lester Pifer led the ministry during most of its growth period. Grace Brethren North American Missions not only helped to start churches, but it also employed architects and building crews to erect church buildings around the country. For many years there was a vigorous and highly visible ministry with Navajo Native American children at a boarding school in Counselor, New Mexico, and in later years, development and maintenance of the military chaplain's ministry was directed by GBNAM's longtime leader, Dr. Larry Chamberlain.

As the 21st century began, GBNAM was disbanded, leading to the creation of a new church-planting entity, Go2 Ministries, headquartered in Telford, Pennsylvania, and headed by Dr. Tim Boal.

BRETHREN MISSIONARY HERALD COMPANY

The Brethren Missionary Herald Company (BMH) was formed in 1940 as the communications unit for Grace Brethren churches. BMH published a magazine and assisted the growing group of churches with communication functions. Leo Polman (1901-1979), a traveling evangelist and pastor who, though born into a Roman Catholic family, had been converted under the ministry of Billy Sunday, saw the need for a national magazine and a center for publishing. Polman founded the *Brethren Missionary Herald* magazine while pastoring in Fort Wayne.

The current BMH building at 1104 Kings Highway was built in 1956 under the administration of Arnold Kriegbaum, who was secretary and general manager. That building became a denominational headquarters with the foreign missions unit in one wing, the home missions unit in another, the publications and bookselling unit (Herald Bookstore) in the center, and the Sunday School/Christian Education functions downstairs. From 1969 until 1991 BMH also operated a job printing shop in the arcade building at the entrance to the town.

As the communication arm of the Fellowship, BMH had published a magazine from its founding in 1940 until 1996, when *The Brethren Missionary Herald* was discontinued. With the retirement of longtime publisher and general manager Charles Turner, the organization went into decline and essentially ceased functioning in the late 1990s. When the board sought a revival of mission and activity, former Grace College journalism professor Terry White was engaged in 2003 to revitalize and re-energize the company. He returned to Winona Lake from Washington, D.C. where he had been vice president of communications for Chuck Colson's Prison Fellowship Ministries.

A new publication (*FGBC World*) was founded, and blogs and websites were established. Non-mission-related radio stations and properties were sold. BMH books was re-energized as a publishing force in the religious book market. A long-term lease was secured with Tree of Life as a tenant bookstore to serve both the community and the textbook needs of Grace College and Seminary. After seven years as director, White semi-retired to focus on book publishing in January, 2010, and the board named Liz Cutler Gates executive director.

GRACE BRETHREN INVESTMENT FOUNDATION

Over time, both the foreign and home missions organizations moved into the building at 1401 Kings Highway, which is now Kingsway Suites. Ground was broken for that building on March 31, 1971.

Grace Brethren Investment Foundation had been founded in 1955 to provide investment accounts to Grace Brethren church members and to provide financing for church and school buildings within the Fellowship. The organization's website (www.gbif.com) says "Grace Brethren Investment Foundation was organized in 1955 to provide affordable mortgage financing for growing churches and ministry organizations affiliated with the Fellowship of Grace Brethren Churches." Additional ministries for women, chaplains, and internationals developed, as well.

Publicity produced for the 50-year anniversary of Grace Brethren Investment Foundation (GBIF) in 2005 pointed out that the founding year, 1955, was marked by several other significant achievements, including the opening of the first McDonald's restaurant in Illinois and the birth of Disneyland in Anaheim, California.

The announcement of the opening of GBIF promised "3% interest on investments of at least $1 and 5% for $500 or more." L. L. Grubb was the executive secretary of Brethren Home Missions Council at the time, which was the mother organization for GBIF. Frank Poland was business manager from 1955-1980, and Elmer Tamkin held the position of financial secretary from 1956 into the 1970s.

Walter Fretz directed GBIF from 1974-1988, followed by James W. Johnson (1989-1996) and Kenneth Seyfert, who has been Executive Director of Operations for GBIF since 1997. In late 2012, the GBIF board named Seyfert as the successor to President/CEO Larry Chamberlain upon Chamberlain's announced retirement in the spring of 2013.

The property upon which the GBIF building (Kingsway Suites at 1401 Kings Highway) was built has an interesting history. Originally owned by the VanFossen family, the property, which extended to the east and included the land where the Encompass building now stands, included a large Dutch Colonial home. Folk tales that it was a monastery or a convent are not true, but the attic of the house was once used to film a scene for a movie *My Son, My Son,* made by Ken Anderson Films.

The Brethren Architectural Service bought the property and the house, which dated from 1922, and remodeled the dwelling to include offices and drafting rooms on the lower level and an apartment on the upper level.

In 1972 William and Joan Darr purchased the house via a sealed bid for $527.32. As the Kingsway Suites building was nearing completion the two-story house was moved 1.1 miles down Kings Highway, around the bend, out Pierceton Road, and down into the Cherry Creek addition where it was situated on a new foundation and became the home of the Darrs. Area residents who watched the house-moving recall vividly the efforts to preserve trees, lift utility wires out of the way, and otherwise create a memorable spectacle as the house inched toward its final resting place on Cherry Creek. The cost of moving wires, as William Darr remembers it, far exceeded the charges of the actual house movers.

CE NATIONAL

One of the earliest Christian education efforts of the newly-formed Grace Brethren movement focused on youth. Leo Polman, who was then pastoring a church in Fort Wayne, saw the need during the summer Brethren conferences for the youth and teenagers of conference attendees to have productive and worthwhile programming.

He and his wife, Leila, conceived of a one-week summer youth camp that would utilize the Bethany Camp facilities on the waterfront at Winona Lake. They needed $200 to reserve the facility for the first year's camping in 1938, so they funded the reservation deposit with proceeds from the sale of their living room furniture following their most recent move

Anticipating that about 25-30 youth would attend the first year, they were surprised to have 106 young people enroll for the first year's Brethren National Youth Conference. Leila did the cooking and Leo cared for most of the programming. Today the successor to that youth conference—now named Momentum—often registers more than 2,000 youth at its annual one-week conference.

In 1980 the Christian education unit of the FGBC moved from rented facilities at BMH to the current CE National campus east of Grace College and Seminary off Presidential Drive. Previous leaders included Leo Polman, Harold "Pop" Etling (1954-1971), Ralph

Colburn, Dan Grabill (1964-1966), Ernie Bearinger, David Hocking, Knute Larson, and Howard Mayes. Under the leadership of executive director Ed Lewis, CE National developed a unified campus of facilities that includes the homes of former Grace administrators Arnold Kriegbaum, Herman Hoyt, and Grace professor Paul Fink.

The home built by Arnold Kriegbaum is now known as the Philemon Center and is used for the refreshment of pastors, elders, and church leaders. A beautiful new meeting facility, the Russell Center, dedicated in November of 2006, enjoys constant use not only for CE National functions but for the National Institute classes taught in conjunction with Grace College. The facilities are also used for community events such as weddings, banquets, and club meetings.

The Barnabas Center houses a number of offices and a conference room. This building was once the home of Dr. Herman Hoyt, president of Grace College and Seminary. The Leadership Center was a home built by Dr. James Boyer, which later became the residence of Dr. Paul Fink, who enlarged the facility when he and his wife adopted four children. The Leadership Center became the first of the four buildings that house the Life Application Center. The Leadership Center contains a number of offices and a free resource library of Christian materials

The Christian education organization changed its name to CE National—a Church Effectiveness ministry—in 1989. CE National acquired another facility in 1998 to serve as a laboratory for training students and church leaders in cross-cultural outreach. Named the Urban Hope Training Center, it is located in the Kensington area of Philadelphia, Pennsylvania, and it includes a church building, a youth center, and dormitories that house up to 70 people. It also includes eight apartments for interns and self-support volunteers for the inner-city ministry.

Groups from churches and colleges are trained in cross-cultural outreach at the inner-city location. The former Third Brethren Church turned over their facilities to CE National in 1998. CE acquired and renovated these facilities and a strategy was developed for planting a church in this Latino community starting with children and youth and growing into a church.

The current Urban Hope Community Church began with children's programs and later youth programs. It has evolved into a church with more than 150 in attendance weekly. Almost the entire congregation is made up of new believers. In 2011 nearly 1,000 people received training and lodging at Urban Hope. These visiting groups receive instruction and are then sent out into the city, equipped to love on people and to share their faith. The teams are lodged in the dormitories. Groups are sent back to their home churches with resources and tools and challenges to reach the over-looked in their communities and churches.

GRACE VILLAGE RETIREMENT COMMUNITY

In 1969, a committee established by the Fellowship recommended that an organization be created to establish a retirement home in Winona Lake. Articles of Incorporation were approved in 1970 for the organization that eventually became Grace Village Retirement Community, a sprawling campus on Wooster Road east of Grace College and Seminary.

Grace Village Retirement Community is the only not-for-prof-it continuing care retirement community (CCRC) in Kosciusko County. Grace Village is dedicated to preserving the richness of life for seniors in a comfortable and secure Christian setting. Grace Village is affiliated with the Fellowship of Grace Brethren Churches and seeks to do all in the spirit of Jesus Christ. Seniors of all denominations are welcomed at Grace Village.

Grace Village opened for occupancy in October of 1974. A health care facility was begun in September of 1981, and the chapel was completed in November of 1984. Construction began in 1986 on a number of independent living apartment homes on 10.5 acres east of the original facility.

The organization went through a very difficult time in 1994 and early 1995, culminating in a February 11, 1995, court judgment against 13 directors and the administrator of the facility. Financial judgments against the personal assets of directors caused great hard-ship to many, but in time, with a number of changes in personnel and policies, the organization regained its equilibrium and was able to continue with its mission.

Nearly 300 people from all walks of life call Grace Village home. There are 58 condo style homes called "Robin Hood Homes," 117 independent living apartments that include studios, efficiencies and one- to two- bedroom apartments. The licensed assisted living has 52 studios and suites. Health care offers both intermediate and skilled nursing care, and there is a beautiful rehabilitation center with 12 private suites. Grace Village is situated on a beautiful 43-acre campus.

Grace Village, currently headed by Jeff Carroll, is licensed by the Indiana State Department of Health and is certified by the federal government as a Medicare and Medicaid provider.

Growth of Grace College and Seminary

Grace Seminary, meanwhile, continued to grow and expand with the acquisition of acreage east of Kings Highway and south of Wooster Road. Plaster (p. 143) notes that the school first acquired "a beautiful tract of land comprising about three and one-half acres within the precincts of Winona Lake and adjacent to the Free Methodist building on the south."

Leadership soon realized the site would not be large enough for full-scale development of a school, so the Grace Seminary board purchased more than 30 acres east of Kings Highway, just outside the town limits, from Leo Polman.

Early school records (August, 1939) refer to "the Laura Busey estate recently bequeathed to the Seminary." Notes from some of the earliest board meetings refer to "final arrangements with the Winona Lake Summer School of Theology for a joint occupancy of the new building," and refer to a "120-acre estate given to the seminary by Mrs. Busey."

Recently correspondence has come to light that corrects an earlier assumption that the Busey farm might be the current school campus. The correspondence is written by Dr. Alva J. McClain to Dr. Homer Kent and the board of the school. The letters are from February and April, 1939, and the subject matter is the final decision about moving the school from Akron to Winona Lake.

A P.S. at the end of the April 13, 1939, letter says:

You will be interested to learn that a Mrs. Laura Busey of Champaign, Ill., who recently passed away, has bequeathed to Grace Seminary a fine 120-acre farm located fifteen miles straight south of Fort Wayne, Indiana, on a three-lane new concrete highway. The will specifies that we are to dispose of the property and invest the proceeds in a permanent fund to be known as the Laura Busey Memorial Trust Fund, the income to be used for the Seminary.

The will is to be filed for probate on May 15th, and we shall have an uncontestable title one year later. But the executor assures me that there is not the slightest possibility for any successful contest of the will. The income this coming year will be ours. The executor estimates the value at about one hundred dollars per acre, so we must have a property worth between ten and twelve thousand, even at present low prices.

This fine gift is surely an evidence of the blessing of God upon Grace Seminary. I had never met Mrs. Busey, but am informed that she was a member of the Church of the Brethren. I talked with the executor and also drove past the farm on a recent Bible Conference trip to Flora, Indiana.

Dr. McClain, writing in *The Brethren Missionary Herald* magazine toward the end of 1939, relates the following:

Just before Thanksgiving we reviewed the financial situation and found that there was ample provision for the month of November and for a small part of the month of December. Both students and faculty joined in special prayer that God would supply fully the December needs so that all expenses could be met until January when the first Christmas offerings of the churches begin to come in.

The answer to this prayer was very striking. With scarcely any delay a personal gift of one hundred dollars from one of the Seminary trustees was sent in. A few days later we learned from the tenant [later identified as Mr. Trenary] on the Busey farm that, contrary to all our expectations, our crop of soy beans had turned out a magnificent yield, and we were able to sell our half for the sum of $527.

It almost seems as if the Lord had bestowed some especial care on that particular piece of land. At any rate, an experienced farmer said the other day that he had a notion to get the Seminary to farm his land so that he could make some money! . . . This "bean" money added to the other gifts to date will carry the work nicely through the month of December.

Then McClain quoted Psalm 104:13-14, 35: "He watereth the hills from His chambers: the earth is satisfied with the fruit of Thy works. He causeth the grass to grow for the cattle, and herb for the service of man: that He may bring forth food out of the earth."

Additional land acquisitions to the campus are mentioned in school records, including an acre and a half purchased from the Free Methodist Publishing Company in 1944, three lots purchased from the School of Photography in 1945 and "five acres including a house and barn" referred to as "Kipker property" in 1949.

Shortly after Don Ogden began the college's music department in the fall of 1954, music classes were held in McClain Hall. Then Grace purchased an historic home on Kings Highway across from Jefferson Elementary School from Dr. Paul Bauman, and that became Rose S. Byers Hall (later the Omega Center), to honor the name of an early benefactor of the music department. It housed both the music and the art departments. Instrumental music was later moved to a now-demolished frame house, North Hall, at the corner of Wooster Road and Kings Highway.

Eventually, the college acquired the World Missionary Press building at the eastern border of the campus on Wooster Road. East Hall (later renamed Byers Hall) became the home of the music department after a brick façade and additional wing were added to the original building. The Visitors Center, behind the Omega/Byers building on Kings Highway was originally constructed as a retirement home for missionaries. Grace traded land with the Grace Brethren Foreign Mission Society to acquire that building, which was later demolished for the building of Indiana Hall.

Colonial Hall and Sands were formerly private residences along Kings Highway which were remodeled to house the classrooms, stu-

The Miniwanan Inn, originally built as a poultry and livestock exhibition building, was bought by the Winona Assembly in 1897 and was remodeled to become a 230-room hotel. It was the largest accommodations facility in Winona Lake. It was burned down intentionally on August 21, 1971, and the land on which it stood became a parking lot.

The Swiss Terrace – three interlocking rooming houses named Interlaken, Geneva, and Lucerne – were operated by Mrs. John Cooper and her daughter, Nelle. Constructed in a whimsical Swiss Chalet style around 1902, they were a prime lodging location for park visitors. Two of the buildings remain—the Geneva and the Interlaken.

Otterbein Hall, located on Ninth Street directly across from the Westminster, was built in 1903 as a women's dormitory for one of the Winona colleges. Parts of the original building are encapsulated in what today is the Winona Lake Free Methodist Church facility.

Park Avenue along the Winona Lake shore, was lined with vehicles once automobiles began to replace the railroad as the primary means of transportation to Winona Lake.

During the era of the world's largest Bible conference (second wave), the cafeteria sat on the lakefront at the entrance to the canal, approximately where the current BoatHouse Restaurant is now located.

Prior to the erection of the current Rodeheaver Auditorium in 1958, the Auditorium was the main conference venue in Winona Lake.

After the canal was dredged in 1902, creating McDonald Island, the annual Venetian Nights festival delighted audiences with its decorated flotilla of watercraft and its contest to name a queen and her court.

Three-time presidential candidate and former U.S. Secretary of State William Jennings Bryan (1860-1925) served many years on the board of the Winona Assembly, served as its president, and was a continual backer and popular speaker for Winona Lake events.

During Chautauqua days—and until the 1930s—all entrance to the town and attractions was through this gated entrance. Even those who lived in Winona Lake needed to purchase a pass. The Interurban Trolley dropped off passengers who arrived via the Warsaw railroad station.

Sightseeing cruises on Winona Lake have been part of the attraction of the area from the very first. A succession of watercraft were named *The Winona Queen.*

During the first wave of Winona's history, a trolley brought rail passengers and their luggage from the railroad station to the entrance building. Luggage was transferred to a narrow-gauge railroad which delivered it to many points along the lakefront, as far south as Kosciusko Lodge.

For many years, until the early 1990s, visitors to Winona Lake coming through the stoplight intersection entrance to town were first greeted with the sight of the Texaco gas station. The station not only cared for the mechanical and fuel needs of drivers, but was also a rental portal for bicycles, canoes, kayaks, and rowboats which visitors rented for recreation.

Chicago-area pastor Ray Pritchard for about 10 years performed a Billy Sunday impersonation near Sunday's grave in the southeast section of Forest Home Cemetery on the outskirts of Chicago. Outfitted with a wooden bat, scuffed-up baseball, and weather-beaten glove, Pritchard would tell the story of Sunday's life and preach a portion of a Sunday sermon, inviting "trailhitters" to commit their lives to Christ, as Sunday did. *(photo courtesy of Ray Pritchard)*

"Chautauqua Revived!" was performed in Winona Lake four days after the September 11, 2001 attacks as part of the Catherine Peachey Fund breast cancer research fund-raising event "Day at the Lake." Cast members included (front row, from left) Daren Maierle, Mark Soto, Alex Thio, Kathy Allison, Tim Yocum, Mike Yocum; (back row, from left) Brent Wilcoxson, Jake Wilkinson, Max Anders, Terry Julien.

MAP OF WINONA :: Winona Lake, Indiana

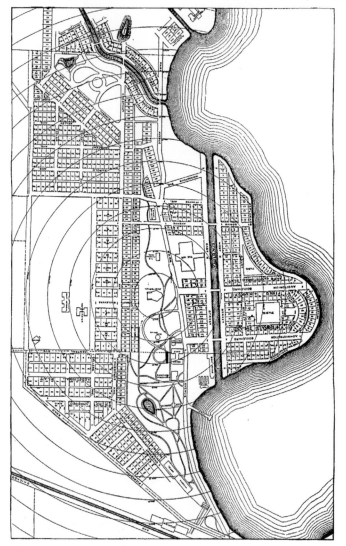

A Magnificent Park of 200 Acres : Unsurpassed Natural Attractions : World Famous Chautauqua : Greatest Bible Conference : Home of Conventions

This map of Winona Lake depicted the facilities and attractions of the height of the Chatauqua era—from about 1905 until about the 1930s.

dios and offices of the art department after it moved from North Hall. These buildings have now been razed and the art department moved to Mount Memorial in the fall of 1998.

The Lamp (formerly known as the Eskimo Inn) on Park Avenue served as a student union for many years. It was demolished in 1997. The Health Center, across Wooster Road from the library, was formerly a private residence which over the years housed counseling offices and counseling labs. It was razed for the construction of the Orthopaedic Capital Center.

The Physical Plant building at the corner of 13th Street and Kings Highway originally housed the Winona Dairy, which bottled milk and had an ice cream shop popular with visitors to Winona Lake. Later the building was used as darkrooms for the Winona School of Photography. Grace purchased the building from the School of Photography when the photography school moved to the Chicago area. Several expansion projects have enlarged the building.

The Winona Dairy, which processed milk from the early 1900s until the late 1950s, was owned by Irvin Van Dyke and, after he retired, by his nephew, Ralph Haney. The dairy's bottles carried a logo that featured a profile of the Winona princess.

Winona Dairy's first building was a barn that was converted into a milk processing plant, but it was replaced shortly after World War II with the current building. The bricks used for the building were "seconds" left over from the construction of the Eli Lilly pharmaceutical plant in Indianapolis. The yellowish-tan bricks were manufactured in Terre Haute and hauled to Winona Lake in an International Harvester truck that had been used during the war by the U.S. Navy.

The dairy's customers included all the hotels, boarding houses, and restaurants in Winona Lake, as well as the Chicago Boys Club. Many individual residences and stores were customers, as well, including a tea room operated by Virgil and Blanche Brock, composers of the popular gospel song *Beyond the Sunset*. Local resident Bob Haney remembers tea room patrons enjoying their milk while Virgil Brock sang and his wife, Blanche, played the piano. The dairy also had a small booth along the canal behind the Eskimo Inn where milk and juices could be purchased during the summer conference season.

Miller Field, named in honor of longtime Grace Brethren pastor and evangelist R. Paul Miller in 1978, is the home turf for Grace College athletes. It hosts men's and women's soccer matches, men's and women's tennis matches, and baseball and softball games. A new press box for the softball diamond was finished in 2010, along with a new scoreboard dedicated to the memory of the late Coach Phil Dick in 2009. The land for Miller Field was farmland originally obtained from Will "Bood" Bennett, former Wayne Township Trustee and Warsaw city parks superintendent. The widow of R. Paul Miller donated $17,000 toward the estimated $50,000 original construction cost of creating the diamonds and other facilities. The total campus is now about 180 acres.

The school began to build facilities beginning with McClain Hall in 1951. A two-year college division to feed the seminary was begun in 1948 and it was enlarged to a four-year college curriculum in 1954 necessitating the building of a classroom building, Philathea Hall, in 1958 (originally designed as a three-story structure, but only two floors were built) and the Lancer gymnasium in 1958 (razed in 2008). Alpha Hall, a women's residence and dining commons, was completed in 1964.

A local news story on February 5, 1964, noted that "Three floors of the new $819,000 women's dormitory at Grace College, Winona Lake, will be ready for occupancy on Saturday, February 8. On that day, 140 young women students will move from their present quarters at the Westminster Hotel to the ultra modern residence hall. The top floor will be ready for students next September."

Gamma A, Gamma B, and Gamma C at the corner of Maple Street and Kings Highway were purchased around 1966 from the Oriental Missionary Society, which had used the buildings for administrative use and housing for missionaries on furlough since 1942. Gamma B was demolished and a new residence hall was completed in June of 2007 replacing Gamma Hall, which was destroyed by fire on August 9, 2004. The new residence hall features a townhouse design with 10 bedrooms and 10 bathrooms (including two handicap-accessible baths). The building is divided into two sections, each with a kitchen and living room. The basement includes a large game room area and laundry facilities.

Other former Winona Lake Christian Assembly facilities used at one time by the college included Delta (Park Ave. and Administration Blvd.), Grace Courts, Lakeside (both on Park Ave. on opposite sides of the post office) and the Winona Hotel. Epsilon (Wooster Road) and Kappa (Kings Highway) were purchased and converted from private residences to dormitories. Shipley Dorm, also a former private residence located between Omega and Colonial, was demolished in about 1997. Lamp Post Manor on Wooster Road was purchased in the late '90s to be used for student housing, as well.

Beta Hall men's dormitory was built in 1967. The local paper reported on December 26, 1964, that Dr. Herman Hoyt, president of Grace College, announced that a $650,000 library (subsequently named the Morgan Library) would be constructed on the campus of the college at Winona Lake, beginning in March 1966.

On a wintry March day in 1969, the entire student body helped move the books from the second-floor library in McClain Hall to the new Morgan Library, forming a human chain and passing boxes of books along the line until all 40,000 books were moved. The entire process took about three hours. The library underwent several internal expansions in 1981 and 1998, when the remaining classrooms and faculty offices were moved from the library.

The library was named the Morgan Library as a tribute to Mrs. Betty (Zimmer) Morgan of Warsaw, Indiana, who in May of 1972 gave the largest gift ever received by the school at that time. She gave $100,000, pledged over four years. Betty Morgan was the daughter and only child of the founder of Zimmer Manufacturing Co., the late Justin Zimmer, who started the company in 1927.

In a letter of presentation, Morgan said she was making the gift, "because of the dynamic influence of Grace College in our community and because of the high caliber of students at Grace." Mrs. Morgan died at age 91 in May of 2006 in Warsaw, Indiana. After the Zimmer company was sold to Bristol-Myers Squibb in 1972, she focused on many philanthropic projects, including the Greenway Project, the Salvation Army, Baker Youth Clubs, and more.

When additional lodging and food service facilities were needed during its growth, the college housed both men and women at McKee

Courts Motel on the island in 1954, and later in the Westminster Hotel. Eventually McKee Courts became men-only and the Westminster became both a women's dormitory and the college's main dining facility.

Longtime Grace staff member Ron Henry, writing for the 50th anniversary edition of the school's magazine, recalled a wooden partition on the third floor of the Westminster that separated the men's dormitory on the right from the women's dormitory on the left. Henry recalled the messages shouted from one side to the other, various items being tossed to the other side, and the Grace renditions of "My Bonnie lies over the plywood." The Inn was also used for men's dorm space until it was demolished in 1971. McKee Courts were torn down in 1997.

Henry further recalled that Grace students shared the Westminster with the Rodeheaver Music Company. Bruce Howe, COO, lived on the second floor. Howe was known for his generosity toward students. In quiet moments, Henry noted, one might hear the strains of B. D. Ackley arranging music. On occasion, Jim and Ruth Rodeheaver Thomas would leave their Rainbow Point home and join the students for Sunday dinner, with Ruth sometimes singing. It was not uncommon for visiting Christian recording artists—affiliated with the Rodeheaver Company—to give short after-dinner concerts for Grace students in the Westminster dining room.

Herman A. Hoyt, president of Grace, announced on March 2, 1966, plans for a $1.5 million expansion program to include four new buildings, an athletic field, and an addition to the present classroom building. Hoyt anticipated that the expansion would enable the college to increase its enrollment over the following five years from 380 to 650. Subsequent campus additions included Kent Hall (dormitory), Indiana Hall (dormitory, student services, business office) and a science building.

The Cooley Science Center, dedicated in 1976, provided much-needed classroom and laboratories for the science department, as well as classroom space for the growing business department. The completion of this building was an important factor in Grace's accreditation by the North Central Association.

The building was named for Chester Cooley, a well-known local industrialist who, as president of the Da-Lite Screen company, moved that company from Chicago to Warsaw, Indiana. Da-Lite started building on Rt. 15 north of Warsaw in June 1956 and opened that facility with more than 100 employees—mostly women, as most men were farmers in Warsaw back in the 1950s. Cooley, who had been with the company since 1924, had succeeded his uncle, J. C. Heck, Da-Lite's first president, upon Heck's retirement in 1947. Cooley died in 1975 and his wife chaired the board of Da-Lite for a number of years thereafter.

Homer Kent, in an interview conducted for the 75th anniversary book of Grace Seminary, recalled that Cooley died shortly after having moved to Warsaw with Da-Lite from Chicago. "They didn't know very many people in town so they called up the president here, Dr. Hoyt, and asked him if he would conduct the funeral," Kent recalled. "That opened up a door and later on, Mrs. Cooley gave the largest gift we had received up to that time for the Cooley Science Center."

"This is an exciting and challenging day on campus," said Dr. Homer Kent, Jr., president of Grace College and Seminary, in accepting the keys to the college's new science center during the dedication convocation on March 15, 1978. The three-level science center encompasses 23,549 square feet and cost $1.125 million to build.

The Gordon Recreation Center has one of the most interesting histories of any of the Grace campus facilities.

The Rodeheaver Music Company, which had been managed for a number of years by James E. Thomas, brother-in-law of Homer Rodeheaver, was sold to Word, Inc., of Waco, Texas, in 1969. Thomas was replaced by Jarrell F. McCracken, president of Word, Inc., and plans were made to move the company into a new 35,000-square-foot building at the corner of College and Publisher's Drive in Winona Lake. That facility had been built by the Free Methodist denomination and it was leased to a succession of tenants until it was bought by Grace College and Seminary in 1999.

N. Bruce Howe, Jr., was executive vice president of the Winona operation when it was purchased by Word, Inc. He directed all functions at the new facility, through which Word distributed products to much of the United States.

In August of 1974 the acquisition of Word by American Broadcasting Companies, Inc. (ABC) was announced, in a deal worth about $6 million. At that time, the local managers were N. Bruce Howe, Jr., vice president, and Don A Smythe, plant manager. Word and its subsidiaries had consolidated revenues of about $14.5 million. Word had been founded in Waco, Texas, in 1952 by Jarrell McCracken, who continued through the acquisition as president of Word, Inc. Among Word's well-known recording artists were Burl Ives, Anita Bryant, Wayne Newton, and Danny Thomas.

ABC continued operating Word activities from Winona Lake until 1987, when it was announced that all warehousing and distribution functions of Word at Winona Lake would be closed by October 30, in order to consolidate functions at its main headquarters in Waco, Texas. About 25 local employees lost their jobs in this move.

Bruce Howe, who had retired as vice-president in December, 1986, but continued with the company as consultant, expressed his displeasure.

"I don't like it," Howe said. "But it's going to save the company money...consolidation is the name of the game these days. It's a company decision and everyone has to abide by it."

After ABC left town, the building's next tenant was Sofamor Danek. Sofamor Danek Group, Inc., prior to its acquisition by Medtronic in January of 1999, was engaged primarily in developing, manufacturing, and marketing devices, instruments, computer-assisted visualization products, and biomaterials used in the treatment of spinal and cranial disorders. The company was founded in 1983 and had been headquartered in Memphis, Tennessee.

The Fort Wayne *News-Sentinel* announced on November 3, 1998, that Sofamor Danek, a leader in spinal implants, had agreed to become part of Medtronic in a $3.6 billion deal. Medtronic was based in Fridley, Minnesota, and had been founded in 1949 as a medical equipment repair shop by Earl Bakken, who developed the pacemaker, and his brother-in-law, Palmer Hermundslie. Medtronic was No. 1 or No. 2 in most of its markets, and the Memphis-based Sofamor Danek was No. 1 in spinal products.

As Medtronic Sofamor Danek's business grew, company officials decided to relocate to newly-built facilities on the US 30 bypass west of Warsaw. Grace College and Seminary negotiated a deal with the Free Methodist owners to purchase the building, with tentative plans to make it into a student center and physical education and recreation facility.

One of its first uses under Grace's ownership, however, came as a result of a late-October tornado which tore through Warsaw in 2001. The Da-Lite Screen Company's headquarters on Indiana 15 North had been hit and Da-Lite was left with an estimated $10 million in damage.

The newest portion of the Da-Lite facility, located at the south end of the building, was destroyed, and at Grace's invitation, the company moved a portion of its warehouse (finished goods inventory and shipping) to the former Sofamor Danek building in Winona Lake. About 25 employees were based there until Da-Lite's reconstruction process could be completed.

Plans moved ahead rapidly for Grace to finance the purchase and renovation of the building to become a recreational center for the college. On February 21, 2003, local news media reported, "As student body president Ryan Egli heaved a sledge hammer into a sheet of dry wall, the dedication of the Robert and Frances Gordon Student Recreation Center was complete."

Ron Manahan, president of Grace, addressed the student body during the 10 a.m. chapel hour held in the building. He introduced local resident Robert Gordon who, along with his wife, Frances, provided funds to purchase the building in 1999, which has been named in their honor. Long-time supporters of the campus, the Gordons had given a $1.5 million donation toward the restoration of Westminster Hall and other campus projects.

Over the preceding three years, a total of $3 million had been raised to renovate and equip the 81,000-square-foot facility.

The building houses a collegiate basketball-volleyball court; two practice basketball-volleyball courts; a 160-meter jogging track with a separate 50-meter straightway and facilities for indoor tennis, badminton and other sports.

The 22,500-square-foot fitness area has a weight training area with $130,000 worth of new Cybex exercise equipment, an aerobics room, locker room facilities as well as physical education department offices and a classroom. The previous physical education facility was the 17,000-square-foot Lancer Gym, built in 1958.

A spacious new lobby replaced a maze of small rooms and manufacturing cubicles at the former Sofamor Danek facility on Kings Highway.

At the dedication, Ray Monteith, a board of trustees member, talked about the impact Grace College graduates have had on the community.

"As you leave today," he said, addressing the student body, "I hope you say to yourselves, 'I'd like to be like the Gordons and give back what God has given to me.'"

Robert Gordon offered the closing prayer.

Robert Gordon died November 16, 2004, at age 93. His wife, Frances V. Gordon, 95, died June 12, 2006, at Grace Village Assisted Living in Winona Lake. They were the parents of longtime Grace business professor William "Bill" Gordon.

ORTHOPAEDIC CAPITAL CENTER

The crown jewel of the Grace campus at this writing is the Orthopaedic Capital Center, a $9.4 million gleaming edifice of brick, steel, and glass which serves as a multipurpose facility, allowing gatherings for everything from chapel services to basketball and volleyball games. It is also a place for the business and orthopaedic community to hold conferences, trade shows, and business meetings.

The OCC features a movable stage and the latest in sports flooring, event seating, and energy-efficient arena lighting. The arena provides 1,800 seats for athletic events, 2,600 seats for concerts and trade shows and 650 seats for banquet events. The OCC also features three meeting rooms and houses the Grace College athletic and business departments. It was first occupied in May of 2007. The Architect of Record for the 63,287-square-foot facility was Design Collaborative Inc.

Grace College and Theological Seminary teamed with several community orthopaedic companies to fund and plan this unique facility. Prior to construction, it was necessary to remediate the site, a low-lying parcel across Wooster Road from the library and Alpha Hall, which had been a dump for hazardous materials.

The National Christian College Athletic Association (NCCAA) announced in December of 2010 in Greenville, South Carolina, that it had selected Grace College as the host for both the Division II Men's and Division I Women's Basketball Championships for 2012-2014. The championships were to be held on the Grace College campus in the Orthopaedic Capital Center. This was an extension of Grace's existing three-year hosting stint of the NCCAA Division I women's basketball championship with the addition of the men's championship.

Since its founding as the higher education affiliate of the Grace Brethren branch of the Brethren family tree, Grace College and Seminary have been led by five presidents. Alva J. McClain (1937-1962) was the founder and first president. During McClain's 25 years as president Grace Theological Seminary was established, and then moved to Winona Lake from Akron, Ohio. Grace College was founded in 1948 as a feeder to the seminary, and later was enlarged to a four-year liberal arts curriculum in 1953-54. During his presidency three buildings were built on the Winona Lake campus—McClain Hall (1951), Philathea Hall (1958) and Lancer Gym (1958). Highest enrollment reached during the McClain presidency was 490.

Herman A. Hoyt was president from 1962 to 1976. During his tenure Alpha Hall was built (1964) as the first residence hall and dining commons, as was Beta Hall (1966), the first men's residence hall. In 1968 Grace assumed operation of the Winona Lake Christian Assembly, and in 1969 the school's new library was dedicated. In 1969 the schools were re-incorporated in the State of Indiana. The highest enrollment during Hoyt's presidency was 1,168.

Homer A. Kent, Jr. was president from 1976 until 1986. During his ten-year presidency new graduate programs in missions were initiated (1977), the Chester E. Cooley Science Center was dedicated (1978), and new programs were begun including nursing and biblical counseling. The highest student enrollment during Kent's tenure was 1,378. The seminary enrollment reached a high of 451 credit students in 1984. After 20 years of effort, the college achieved regional accreditation in 1976.

John J. Davis was president from 1986 until 1993. On his watch the Doctor of Ministry program was added in 1990, there were renovations to Byers Music Hall, McClain Auditorium, Alpha Dining Commons, Philathea Little Theater, Morgan Library, and the Lancer Gym. The highest enrollment during this period was 1,066.

Ronald E. Manahan was named to the office in 1994. Manahan's term has been characterized by the strengthening of ties between Grace and the Warsaw/Winona Lake community, and especially with the major orthopaedic manufacturers in town. The most obvious symbol was Manahan's ability to bring together major philanthropy from DePuy, Zimmer, and Biomet to help build the Orthopaedic Capital Center on Wooster Road. At this writing, on the school's 75th anniversary in 2012-2013, enrollment is about 1,800 students with a college freshman class of just over 400.

In late March, 2013, Manahan announced his retirement from the president's office, effective at the next Commencement (May 11, 2013). Dr. Jim Custer, chair of the school's board of trustees, introduced Dr. Bill Katip as the new president-elect. Katip, a graduate and former employee of Grace, had nearly 40 years of experience in higher education administration and had been provost at Grace since 2007.

CHAPTER 18
Notable Locations, Organizations and People of Winona

"The charm and pull of Winona is something that cannot be explained, but which is felt far as well as near."
Jasper A. Huffman

EARLY LITERATURE DESCRIBED THE PARK AREA OF WINONA LAKE as, "gorgeous gardens, interesting statuary donated by the wealthy Heinz family, flocks of swans, and lots of interesting things to do for the entire family. The Good News Messenger statue can still be seen in the swan pond in Winona Lake today."

LANDMARKS
WINONA HOTEL
The Winona Hotel (now condominiums) has always been the premiere facility at the entrance to downtown Winona Lake. The hotel is the oldest building in the Village at Winona. It was constructed by the Beyer brothers in 1888 and it contained 40 rooms. In 1895, the hotel and property on the east side were sold to the fledgling Winona Assembly and Summer School Association.

The hotel was expanded several times between 1895 and 1910 to a total of 120 guest rooms, a large dining room, and a spa. Changes in tastes and financial problems over the years reduced the annual attendance at Winona from 250,000 in a summer to fewer than 50,000. In the late 1940s the hotel was altered by removing the porches, changing the windows, lowering the ceiling and cladding the structure in steel siding.

In 1968 Grace College and Seminary took over operating control of the Winona Assembly and the hotel served as a women's dormitory for the college until 1994. By 1990, Winona Lake was in serious decline. Maintenance efforts were lax, and the hotel had become a community eyesore.

Winona Restoration Partners purchased the building in the late 1990s and by 2005 it had completed a three-year multi-million dollar restoration project that transformed the hotel into a 24-unit condominium building. The effort restored the building to its turn-of-the-century appearance.

Originally 40 destination-style hotel rooms were planned, but according to Winona Restoration's Brent Wilcoxson, "as things changed and three hotels appeared on U.S. 30, a hotel here was more risk than we wanted to take."

So an alternate plan was devised to create spacious luxury condominiums on the hotel's first three floors, each named for one of the buildings or cottages that stood during Winona Lake's historical heyday. The first floor features broad porches, the second floor has a shared balcony, and each unit faces Winona Lake.

Because the building underwent several alterations in its history, the restoration project faced some unique problems. Balconies had been torn down and windows and doors of different sizes and configurations had been installed.

"When we tried to put the wooden siding back on, just 25 percent fit," Wilcoxson recalled. "Seventy-five percent is duplicate siding."

Crews discovered the porch on the southeast corner was almost totally underground, filled in and grassed over.

"No one knew it was there until we dug it out," Wilcoxson noted. "It was like an archeological excavation. We found the footers were shallow cement squares with three rows of brick. We shored up the entire building and poured new footers."

Mount Memorial Building

On March 19, 1903, the executive committee of the Winona Assembly approved the construction of the Mount Memorial building at a projected cost of $60,000. The building was to be the main location of the Winona Agricultural and Technical School.

Completed in 1905, the Mount Memorial building at 901 College Avenue was at that time the largest and most impressive building on the Winona grounds. The construction of Mount Memorial was regarded as one of the greatest achievements of the Winona Assembly.

Winona was created as an educational resort whose founders were committed to a system of education and philanthropy they called the "Winona Movement." Mount Memorial was a symbol of the educational priorities of the Winona Movement. Its commanding location, size, and decoration set it apart from other buildings in the resort.

Designed in the Neo-Classical style, Mount Memorial features elaborate carved limestone ornamentation. The building appears as it did originally with the exception of changes in the windows and a 1950s addition at the south façade.

Mount Memorial was built as the main building for the Winona Agricultural Institute, and as a classroom building for the courses offered by the Winona Assembly and Summer School Association. Later the building served as the main facility for the Winona Normal School. The area surrounding Mount Memorial was called "the campus."

In 2005 Grace College purchased Mount Memorial Hall from Brent Wilcoxson and Winona Restoration Partners for $1,940,897.19. Today it houses the college's art, education, and behavioral science departments. It is also home to the visitor's center and campus post office, along with community education offices.

THE BILLY SUNDAY TABERNACLE

A subscription invitation for the building of the Billy Sunday Tabernacle, dated January 19, 1920, described the projected building as "170 feet by 130 feet, seating 8,000, building of steel, brick, and glass." The building costs were projected to be $75,000, and Winona property owners were asked to subscribe "not less than $100—make it more if possible."

On the last weekend of April in 1920 construction began on the Tabernacle. It was completed in 1921, seated 7,500, and its total cost was $89,000. The first artist to appear on its stage after completion was the great coloratura soprano, Mme. Galli-Curci, who pronounced its acoustic properties "perfect."

The Billy Sunday Tabernacle was one of only two tabernacles built to be a permanent structure (the other was in Boston). Billy Sunday's New York City crusade tabernacle, named "The Glory Barn," was the largest Sunday tabernacle ever built. Located at Broadway and 168th Street in 1917, it required 400,000 feet of lumber and 250 barrels of nails. Its total square footage was 84,968 and seating capacity was 18,000. Cost to build was $68,000.

The Winona Lake tabernacle served as an auditorium for Bible conference lectures and Chautauqua gatherings, as a theater for dramatic plays and musical performances, and as an assembly hall for worship services and graduations.

Billy Sunday first encountered sawdust floors in crusades that he conducted in lumber country—the great Pacific Northwest. Sawdust's wonderful aroma, as well as the quietness it offered, convinced Billy to use sawdust for flooring in all of his later tabernacles. Eventually, "going forward" at a Sunday crusade became synonymous with "hitting the sawdust trail." Records showed nearly one million "trail hitters" over the course of Sunday's forty-year career.

On August 3, 1950, it was announced that J.C. Penney, founder of the large retail organization bearing his name, would speak at the Billy Sunday Tabernacle at Winona Lake. His subject was to be "The Golden Rule in Business and Industry."

A notable event of the world's largest Bible conference was scheduled for Sunday afternoon, August 10, 1950, in the Billy Sunday Tabernacle. George W. Sanville, associated for the previous 40 years as manager of the Rodeheaver Company, was given public recognition for 50 years of outstanding service in the realm of gospel songbook compilation.

Local newspapers reported on March 15 1992, that Winona's historic Billy Sunday Tabernacle was being demolished after 72 years of diversified use in the community. The cavernous tabernacle, now beset with leaking roof and deteriorating superstructure, sat on part of a 24-acre property of the Winona Lake Christian Assembly that was owned by Grace College and Seminary. Its site, now "Tabernacle Field," then became the home field of the Winona Blue Laws, an 1860s Vintage Base Ball team.

THE BOATHOUSE

One of the earliest buildings constructed by the Winona Assembly was the boathouse. The original boathouse, built in 1895, was used to store the nearly 300 watercraft the Assembly had available for rent. Located on the northern intersection of the canal and the lake, it was a center of activity for the hundreds of thousands who came to Winona.

In the 1940s, the boathouse was removed and a cafeteria was built in its place. The cafeteria served the revived Winona Lake Bible Conference until the 1960s when it was converted to a roller skating rink. The new BoatHouse Restaurant, established in 2000, is built on the same foundation as the old cafeteria and is designed as an architectural reminder of the original boathouse.

THE BEYER HOME

The Beyer Home (503 Chestnut) is a large hillside home built by two of the Beyer brothers, J. E. and C. C., in 1907. The living quarters for their families mirrored across a grand foyer where stained glass ceiling panels color light from a skylight. Described by the *Winona Assembly Review* as "the most imposing of the new winter cottages built at Winona," it is a massive cement block and stone building which dominates the Chestnut Street hillside.

In the Beyer brothers' handwritten diary, access to which was supplied by their granddaughters, J. E. Beyer wrote, "In the year 1906 we concluded to build the Beyer home at what was by this time Winona Lake. The house was a double one, the south side being occupied by Bro. C. C. Beyer and the north side by myself. I person-ally had charge of the construction . . . on completion in 1907, we moved into the north side half and Mrs. Beyer took great delight in this home and made it a pleasant place for us and her many friends and visitors to Winona."

The Beyer Home is a combination of styles popular at the turn of the century. It is predominantly Italian Renaissance Revival, but it also exhibits Romanesque characteristics such as the arched loggia at the entry.

The home's most distinctive feature is its interior layout. Completely symmetrical, each side housed one of the Beyer families and mimics the other in arrangement and decoration. The two separate "houses" are joined by a two-story central hall called the "Palm Court." Each of the three floors is decorated in a different style. The first is Colonial Revival, the second is French Rococo, and the third floor is done in the Arts and Crafts style. When constructed, the home was fitted with electric lighting and every modern electric appliance available.

"Electricity was the theme of this house," said Winona Restoration's Brent Wilcoxson, pointing out the six electric fireplaces and 250 light sockets in rafter tails under the eaves. The house included an "auto room" where the Beyer brothers' matching electric cars were stored and charged.

The great house was for a short time used as a Grace College dormitory where Brent Wilcoxson lived in a third-story turret room. Wilcoxson and his wife, Debra, later purchased the Beyer Home in 1986. During the summer of 1996 workers ripped drywall off beaded-board wooden walls, gutted an old kitchen that had been converted to a shower room, removed damaged plaster, and stopped leaks. The home was sold in 2012 to the owner of the BoatHouse Restaurant to again be used as a private residence.

BILLY SUNDAY HOME/*MOUNT HOOD*

Mount Hood was the home of Winona Lake's most famous residents, Billy Sunday and his wife Helen and their family. While first visiting Winona in 1899, the world-renowned evangelist and his family rented rooms in a boarding house on Park Avenue. Their stay in the newly developed resort was so enjoyable that they decided to purchase their own cottage.

For 11 years they summered in Winona and lived in a large cottage called the *Illinois,* located on the present site of *Mount Hood.* Deciding to make Winona their permanent home, Billy and "Ma" had the Illinois moved across the street and their *Mount Hood* bungalow constructed in 1911.

A visit to *Mount Hood* bungalow, the Billy Sunday home at 1111 Sunday Lane in Winona Lake, is a trip back in time. With its original furnishings and decorating, the home offers a glimpse not only of the Sundays' lives, but of what life was like in the early 1900s.

The house is a superb example of the Arts and Crafts bungalow style which is characterized by horizontal massing and simplified detailing. While the exterior has been altered with artificial siding, the interior remains intact. The home contains many artifacts of Billy's baseball and evangelistic crusade days, as well as beautiful examples of fine needlework done by "Ma."

In December of 1999 it was announced that, the following May 20, a newly constructed Billy Sunday Visitors Center would open its doors as the latest addition to the restoration of Winona Lake. The Center's design was reminiscent of the old tabernacle, and in it visitors would find a tribute to Sunday's life as a professional baseball player and a leading evangelist during the Prohibition movement.

The Visitors Center would later be reconfigured to house the Remnant Trust collection, with many of the Sunday artifacts relocated to the Reneker Museum of Winona History in Westminster Hall.

THE PRAYER CHAPEL

The "Little Chapel by the Lake" was designed, erected, and furnished by the Endicott Church Furniture Company. It was donated to the Winona Lake Christian Assembly on June 1, 1960, "as a place of meditation, prayer, and worship for all those who enter."

HILLSIDE AMPHITHEATER

For decades, guests enjoyed evening services while overlooking the lake at the Hillside Amphitheater. The amphitheater was constructed in 1910 with funds donated by a patron from Chicago.

SHERIDAN SPRING

A remnant of the well laid-out and formal gardens and sidewalks that added to Winona's beauty is the Sheridan Spring. Residents along the park's ridge still enjoy a colorful floral display each summer, thanks to the efforts of several local families.

GARFIELD PARK

Situated below the Billy Sunday Home, Garfield Park was named in the 1890s for the recently-assassinated U.S. President James Garfield. Soon after his death a hydraulic ram was purchased from his farm near Mentor, Ohio, and brought to the park where it harnessed a large, natural spring. The enterprising Beyer brothers were thus able to supply water to many cottages along the hillside while creating a tourist curiosity.

STUDEBAKER FOUNTAIN

The Studebaker Fountain was built near the Auditorium to harness one of the many natural springs in Garfield Park. The Studebaker Spring was donated by auto magnate J. M. Studebaker, original owner of the Tippecanoe Place mansion in South Bend and an early director of the Winona Assembly. Built in 1902, the fountain's dolphin spout is surrounded by granite and marble veneered walls.

WESTMINSTER HALL AND RENEKER MUSEUM OF WINONA HISTORY

Westminster Hall, built between 1905 and 1907, has a cornerstone which reads, "Presbyterian Building, May 19, 1905." Originally designed as a denominational boarding house for the Presbyterian Church, it was the last, largest, and most grand of Winona Lake's hotels. Later, during the winter months it served as a dormitory for the Winona College.

Local media reported on April 20, 1905, that work had begun on the "Presbyterian Building," which was to cost $40,000 and would have 40 rooms, a chapel, and a large dining room. The report said that in the summer the building would be used by Presbyterians attending conferences, and during the winter it would be used as a school for girls.

The lower level contained a laboratory and experimental dairy lab, while the upper level contained an auditorium and cafeteria. Described as "the finest and most modern hotel in Winona," it featured hot and cold running water, steam heat, health spa facilities, two large dining rooms, and an elevator operated manually with a pull rope.

During World War I, the Westminster was used as barracks for Camp Winona, a military training center where U.S. Army truck drivers and mechanics were trained. Local historian Bill Darr said, "Today, that doesn't seem like a big deal to us because about everyone drives. But back then most people traveled by horse."

One of the first radio broadcasts of a World Series game was featured at the Westminster on October 6, 1922. H. A. Dye of Winona Lake put a "wireless" in the Westminster, and it was able to pull in the Series game from New York City where the Yankees were playing the New York Giants.

The game was at the Polo Grounds with about 50,000 people in attendance. The radio reception in the Westminster was so good, according to news reports, that "when Babe Ruth was given a base on balls, the moan of the crowd could be heard in the Westminster." The Series was won by the Giants in five games.

Homer Rodeheaver, a pioneer of gospel music, purchased the building in 1932, according to local resident Bruce Howe, who began working for Rodeheaver in 1941. Howe said, "I worked for him for 15 years. It was a hotel at that time—I lived there for 26 years."

Rodeheaver's music publishing company utilized the Westminster for its offices and production facilities. Howe donated many of Rodeheaver's personal items which are now on display in the Reneker Museum of Winona History, which occupies one wing of the Westminster.

The 1942 newsletter for the reunion of the Winona Schools notes that "With his great interest in young people, Rodeheaver is equipping part of the basement with bowling alleys, shuffle board courts, ping pong tables, a ski ball alley, where people from near and far will have a place for clean entertainment." Rodeheaver, who was fond of bowling, often bowled with employees and guests on the bowling alley in the lower level. Winona Lake resident Jesse Deloe recalls being a manual pinsetter for the alley in the days before automatic pinsetters were common.

In the 1940s, the Westminster was the site of the all-night prayer meeting that launched the evangelistic career of Billy Graham, who was at that time a vice president with Youth for Christ (also founded in Winona Lake).

Grace College began using the Westminster for student housing and food service during the 1950s and 1960s. The Free Methodist Church of North America bought the hotel in 1970 to house missionaries and to use as a conference center. They renamed it the International Friendship House.

When the Free Methodist headquarters moved to Indianapolis in 1990, the International Friendship House was closed, and Grace College purchased the building in January of 1994 to respond to a growing need for student housing and to provide meeting space for community and corporate events.

The Westminster was the object of a wide-ranging renovation and fund-raising project in the late 1990s. During the Westminster Hall renovation project, Grace College saw the opportunity to realize a long-desired goal: the creation of a museum dedicated to preserving the remarkable spiritual and cultural heritage of Winona Lake.

Grace president Ron Manahan designated that the main floor west wing of the Westminster would be set aside for the museum. A generous gift from Mrs. Betty Reneker of Chicago funded the initial expenses of the project, and the museum was named to honor her son, Winona resident William "Bill" Reneker.

Prior to his death in 1993, William Reneker had been an energetic supporter of Winona's recent redevelopment. Reneker was named a Sagamore of the Wabash in December, 1993, and his widow, Judy, established an annual "Bill Reneker Memorial Community Service Award."

The Reneker Museum of Winona History has gallery areas that include the development of Eagle Lake prior to the initiation of the Winona Movement in 1895, displays that chronicle several distinct eras in Winona history, and special topics and office areas that highlight Chautauqua programs. It also houses the Homer Rodeheaver Collection, thanks to the generosity of Rodeheaver's longtime associate, Bruce Howe, and many Billy Sunday and Winona artifacts.

Hundreds of donors contributed funding for the Westminster restoration, many of whom are noted on engraved plaques in the building's grand lobby. The celebrated opening of the museum was in May, 2000, and it is now open to the public for regular visiting hours and by special appointment.

In recent years, the Town of Winona Lake has held an annual Winona Lake Community Appreciation Dinner at which updates from the town are given, individuals who have improved town properties are recognized, and the winner of the Bill Reneker Memorial Community Service Award is announced. Reneker award winners since it was initiated in 1994 include:

1994 – Brent Wilcoxson
1995 – R. Quentin Rupe
1996 – Dr. Stephen J. Peoples
1997 – Lisa LeMasters
1998 – Dr. Dane A. Miller
1999 – Lee Jenkins
2000 – Dr. Ronald Manahan
2001 – Al Disbro
2002 – Willa Henry
2003 – Dr. Stephen A. Grill
2004 – D. Blaine Mikesell
2005 – Dr. Patrick Kavanaugh
2006 – Dr. E. Michael Grill
2007 – Mary Louise Miller and Debra Wilcoxson
2008 – Jennifer S. Ortega
2009 – Bruce Howe
2010 – Mary Anne Cox
2011 – Denny Duncan

The late Grace Brethren pastor Gerald Polman (1922-2012), who served as a museum volunteer docent, was giving tours of the Reneker Museum of Winona History in the historic Westminster Hall in the summer of 2005.

"Do you recognize this young man at the pulpit?" he asked, pointing to a photo of a young Billy Graham preaching on the stage of the Billy Sunday Tabernacle in 1945 at the first international conference of Youth for Christ.

"Yes—he's my dad!" was the response.

To his surprise, Polman had been explaining Winona history to Ruth Graham, the third child of Ruth and Billy Graham. She was in Winona for the filming of some women's ministry activities with actress and model Jennifer O'Neill.

"She was quite interested and quite courteous," said Polman, who believed this was the first time Ruth Graham had visited the historic site. She knew many of her father's associates who were in the photographs of the founding of YFC at Winona Lake in 1944, and of other friends and associates of the world-famous evangelist.

"She was also interested in Homer Rodeheaver," recalled Polman, who would explain that Billy Sunday's song leader Homer Rodeheaver headed the world's largest Christian music publisher—Rodeheaver Hall-Mack—from these same rooms in the old Westminster Hotel.

Polman, who at that time lived at Grace Village Retirement Community with his wife, Phyllis, had been giving tours of the museum for about three years. Having graduated from Grace Seminary in 1946, he had first-hand acquaintance with some of the personalities and geographical features of the area. In fact, his family had once owned and operated the Garfield Hotel on Chestnut Street.

Polman would explain the Great Fire of 1914, the digging of the canal in 1902 to create McDonald Island, the building of the Billy Sunday Tabernacle in 1920, and the "Biggest Day in Winona," August 29, 1915, when there were 1,500 cars and 20,000 people in Winona Lake to hear Billy Sunday and William Jennings Bryan speak.

RAINBOW POINT

The essence of lakeside dwelling is embodied in Rainbow Point. This impressive home was owned by Homer Rodeheaver, music director for evangelist Billy Sunday. Many famous personalities visited him at this home. Among them were J. Edgar Hoover, Will Rogers, Billy Graham, and many popular gospel hymn writers. Large parties were often given by Rodeheaver with as many as 200 guests in attendance on the porches and lawn.

Rainbow Point began as a small two-story Gothic Revival cottage built around 1900. Purchased by "Rody" shortly thereafter, the home was added to frequently. Rodeheaver rebuilt the dwelling to look like a ship. Between 1939 and 1941 its distinctive "steamboat" style was achieved by flattening and surrounding the roof with iron railing. A recreational slide enabled swimmers to soar from the roof down to the lake below.

Spacious enclosed verandas surround Rainbow Point on three sides. French doors lead to the living and dining rooms, where a built-in window seat and corner cabinets are found. The central stairway features a custom-made "art deco" balustrade of oak. Upstairs are five bedrooms and a pine-paneled sunroom.

Homer Rodeheaver's business cards, dishes, glassware, living room rug, and bathroom towels featured rainbows, a reference to a line of a frequent theme song, "Every cloud will wear a rainbow/If your heart keeps right."

After the death of the last family member, most of the contents of Rainbow Point were sold at a highly-publicized public auction on June 25, 1980. Much of the furniture, including a unique bedroom suite which Homer Rodeheaver had built to his specifications as replicas of furniture he had seen in the film *Gone With the Wind*, were purchased by former Winona Lake police chief John Trier.

The former home of Katherine Carmichael, organist and colleague of Homer Rodeheaver, is located close to Rainbow Point at 1200 Court Street.

KILLARNEY CASTLE

Winona Lake's most eccentric structure, located on Esplanade Avenue at the tip of the island overlooking the lake, was built in 1902 by Dr. Solomon Dickey and was built of tin and shingle to the scale of a castle in Killarney, Ireland. Because it was built as a summer home, incorporation of outdoor space was important in the layout. Large porches on three sides of the house gave it a light and airy feeling and provided natural cooling from lake breezes.

Originally the Dickey family's cottage, it has since served as a rooming house, apartments, and publishing house complete with offices, auditorium, and puppet stage. Dr. Dickey owned the castle until his death in 1920 at which time ownership passed on to his wife. On Mrs. Dickey's death a few years later, their only son, Lincoln, became owner of the castle. Lincoln retained ownership for several years before selling it.

The castle has a total of 12 rooms (plus porches and baths). There are four bedrooms and three full baths. Over the years, alterations to the house included the enclosure of the once-open porches. Once described by the Fort Wayne *Journal Gazette* as a "shingle-and-tin fortress," the castle features a living room that looks up to an octagonal balcony. A bust of Dickey still sits in the living room, a gift to the current residents, who purchased the castle in 1985, from a garage sale scout. The castle's restoration was completed in July, 2005.

Lambert Huffman, one of the former owners of the castle, said he paid $8,000 for the "old shell" and he spent about $18,000 remodeling it in about 1957. He used the castle until about 1965.

During that time the castle was home to Lambert Huffman Publishers. Huffman said in private correspondence that the center room ceiling was closed when he took over the facility, and he made it into a little theater "to display my wares by 16 mm movie, the screen being on the south side and the projector on the north." According to Huffman, "30 theater seats from a Chicago theater gave it a very elegant and cozy atmosphere."

William Jennings Bryan, famous orator and one-time presidential candidate, would stay in the front turreted bedroom of the castle on his frequent trips to Winona.

When dredging created the canal in 1902, dirt from the canal was scattered over the island where trees were planted and homes were built. Al Cuffel helped with the construction of Sol Dickey's castle and Cuffel used to say it was the custom of Dr. Dickey to keep a telescope in his study high in the tower. Since all visitors had to cross one of two bridges to the island, Dickey would know who was approaching before the caller reached the castle. If the party was someone he wished to see, Dickey buzzed a signal to his wife downstairs.

OTHER HOTELS AND APARTMENTS
THE DORIC

Located at 608 Chestnut Avenue, the Doric is a large, impressive version of the cottage style that used a Greek temple form as an architectural theme. Following the classic lines of Greek architecture, it was designed and built by Rev. G. D. Adamson, with its interior divided into four quarters. Each quarter is a complete apartment unit. In recent years it has been renovated and is used as housing for Master-Works and Christian Performing Artists Fellowship personnel.

THE FRANCONIA HOTEL

This home, built in 1910, is at 907 Sunday Lane and was once known as the Franconia Hotel. It is unique because of its big porches, great view of the lake, and impressive restoration. At one time it was owned by Homer Rodeheaver and managed by his mother. It is now on the National Register of Historic Places.

CHESTNUT HOUSE BED AND BREAKFAST

The Chestnut House B&B, located at 806 Chestnut Street, is owned by the Village at Winona and is open to outside clientele. It was constructed in 1906 in the Princess Anne style. It has been renovated to include four beautiful guest suites, each with furniture in styles from the early 1900s.

Each suite features a different wood treatment (cherry, white oak, maple, chestnut) and each has a special feature such as a bay window, fireplace, or porch. Generations of Grace Seminary students knew the building as "Belle Dawson's Rooming House," named for the proprietor who always had rooms for rent to students.

Belle Dawson, who was forced to stop her formal education after the fifth grade to care for a family that had been decimated by smallpox, moved to Winona Lake from Mansfield, Ohio, in 1951 and shortly thereafter bought the large house on Chestnut Street. A hospitable, hard-working, pleasant woman, Mrs. Dawson filled the rooms of her house with seminary students during the winter and conference attendees during the summer. Her grandson, Larry Poland, recalls that one week, when programming packed Winona Lake with Youth for Christ teens and conference attendees, Mrs. Dawson had 60 temporary residents in her house at one time.

The residence was later called Chestnut Street Apartments. Mrs. Dawson died in March of 1975.

McKee Courts

The board of directors of the Winona Lake Christian Assembly built a 27-unit motel right in the middle of McDonald Island in 1952 and 1953. It was used by conference attendees for most of the 1953 season.

Upon the death of Dr. Arthur McKee on June 4, 1953, at age 62 after 13 years of directing the assembly's affairs, the board of directors voted to name the new motel "McKee Courts" in his memory. The board members voted to beautify the motel grounds with appropriate landscaping, to install a large neon sign "McKee Courts," and in other ways commemorate the memory of McKee. The motel was the last major building project which McKee undertook and supervised.

The motel was razed in 1997 and the land in the center of the island remains vacant.

OTHER NOTABLE RESIDENCES

THE FELSENHEIM (101 Fourth Street) is, translated from the German, "house of stone." Built in 1910, it is constructed of several types of decorative concrete block. Its asymmetrical composition, rounded turret, large wraparound porch, and use of color leaded glass are all characteristic of the Victorian Queen Anne style. Felsenheim, however, displays the popular mix of Classical Revival details including bracketed eaves, Palladian window openings, and paired columns.

The Fluegel family, originally from Nappanee, Indiana, occupied Felsenheim until 1943, when it was purchased by the Brethren Foreign Missionary Society and renamed "Bethany Missionary Residence." It housed many temporary and retired occupants in that capacity until it was sold to the Brent Wilcoxson family in 1986.

Immediately opposite The Felsenheim on Fourth Street is a nearly matching stone/block residence with a rounded room (music room) in the front. It was named The Hatfield for Victor Murray Hatfield (1859-1945) who had it built in 1909.

THE HATFIELD (100 Fourth Street) was constructed in 1909 as a residence for the Hatfield family. Later the building housed the Brethren Missionary Herald Company. L. S. Bauman advanced the funds to purchase the building, which housed the magazine and production offices in the basement, the Herald Bookstore on the first floor, and offices were placed on the second floor. The Leo Polman family moved into an apartment on the third floor, and rooms on the fourth floor were rented to Grace Seminary students.

The Hatfield was converted to apartments in the 1950s and was home to many college and seminary students. By 1990 the Hatfield was in deplorable condition, but a group of concerned neighbors purchased it with hopes of improving the neighborhood. It became a single-family home again in 1994 and restoration began, including opening up walls, rebuilding the oak grand staircase, and exposing the colorful art glass window from the living room.

Victor Hatfield, according to a letter from his son, George Hatfield, was involved in publicity, in real estate, in publications, and in a small office machine business in Winona Lake. He enjoyed writing poetry and published a small book of poems and often wrote a column for the *Warsaw Daily Times*. As a publisher, he published and sold *Winona Echoes*, which included sermons delivered at the Winona Lake Bible Conference.

His second wife, Susie E. Hatfield (Hatfield's first wife had died), was an excellent musician and piano teacher who taught music well into her 70s. Among her piano students were three of the Billy Sunday children, and according to her son, Homer Rodeheaver was a frequent guest at the house for parties and music events.

Susie Hatfield used innovative teaching techniques and invented a movable note chart, called "The Music Pilot." These innovations were featured in an article, "How One Woman Makes Piano Lessons a Pleasure for Children," in the June, 1914, issue of *The Piano Magazine*, published in Chicago. Hatfields also wrote and published a number of gospel songs under the name Park Publishing Company.

George Hatfield recalled that his parents sold the house "in the throes of the Depression" to the Oriental Missionary Society.

THE FAERHOLM, at 304 Chestnut, overlooks the once-lovely garden spot known as Dukes Fountain. It is the second home to stand on this location—an earlier structure was destroyed in the 1914 fire.

Faerholm was rebuilt on the remaining foundation between 1914 and 1917. It was inhabited until 1926 by evangelist Jilford H. Lyons and his family.

Faerholm exemplifies the Prairie style, which enjoyed a short-lived popularity during the early decades of the 20th century. It originated in the Chicago area with architect Frank Lloyd Wright, but vernacular forms like Faerholm spread throughout the Midwest. It is characterized by a low, hipped roof with widely overhanging eaves, a single-story front porch with massive porch supports, and the use of stucco on the exterior. The extensive use of woodwork lends an elegant richness to the interior, along with an impressive open staircase, crown moldings, plate rail in the dining room, and beveled French doors.

THE RODEHEAVER (102 Third Street) is a fine example of Craftsman architecture. This simple style is a result of the Arts and Crafts Movement espoused by Gustav Stickley in the early 1900s. It was a popular reaction to the excesses of the Victorian era and was considered appropriate as America entered the modern age.

It is characterized by original oak flooring, window seats in the foyer and dining room, glass enclosed bookcases alongside the fireplace, and an elaborate china cabinet gracing the dining room.

Bearing the name of one of Winona's most prominent families, the home was commissioned by Homer Rodeheaver in 1916. It served as a residence for his mother and sister and kept them near Homer's "home base" during his years of evangelistic touring with Billy Sunday. It, also, is listed on the historic home register.

THE INGLENOOK, 506 Chestnut Avenue, is a one-story example of the cottage style. It retains its original wide, overhanging eaves and decorative brackets.

SWISS TERRACE

The most impressive of Winona's guest cottages was an ensemble of three structures on Terrace Drive. They included the now-demolished Lucerne, the centerpiece Interlaken, and the Geneva to the north. All were constructed around 1902 in a whimsical Swiss Chalet architectural style.

The Interlaken in the Swiss Terrace has been turned into two condominiums instead of eight apartments, and the Geneva is a single-family home again.

The 1904 summer program indicated that for the 1904 season, Mrs. John Cooper announced her ninth season in Winona Park and the third season at her picturesque summer cottages, Geneva, Interlaken, and Lucerne. Together, the cottages constituted the "Swiss Terrace," with the guests limited only to "dining room seatings."

According to an advertisement in the 1904 Winona Year Book, a stay at the Interlaken put its guests "in the midst of the activity of the Park." Unfortunately, the years were not kind to the Interlaken. The structure housed several stores, an ice-cream shop, and numerous rental units. It suffered an unsightly addition and had much of its detailing hidden by artificial siding. In 1993, however, a major restoration began and it now appears as it did originally. Divided down the center, both sides are identical in design, with the north unit featuring the original fireplace.

THE HILLSIDE (701 Terrace Drive), built circa 1902, served as one of the earliest summer boarding houses for thousands of visitors who attended Winona's programs and conferences. Virgil Brock, composer of the popular hymn *Beyond the Sunset,* owned Hillside for a time, as did Homer Rodeheaver. Virgil and Blanche Brock used part of the residence as a tea house open to the public for a time. The badly-deteriorated Hillside underwent a transformation and is again a single-family dwelling which retains its original wood siding, windows, and expansive porches with a magnificent lake view.

THE BALDWIN

Built overlooking the site of the original auditorium, the Baldwin cottage at 909 Sunday Lane is an example of the Chautauqua cottage style. While only one story is visible from the street side, it has a unique two-story porch that extends out toward the lake to form a circular tower with a conical roof. The Baldwin was built around 1900.

"Heirloom" and "Yesterday"

These residences at 1200 W. Canal St. have been transplanted to the island. They were built in 1843 and were moved to their present location on the canal in 1933.

Brookside

Just steps away from the Rodeheaver Auditorium and across the street from where the Inn once stood, is the distinctive Brookside with its charming twin turrets on its wraparound porch. Built in 1903, the Brookside at 904 Park Avenue is an example of Victorian Queen Anne architecture.

Although much of the original detailing has been removed, the front-gabled roof with corner tower, "fish scale" wood shingles, and Palladian window are original. Inside, the living room fireplace is a treasure, decorated with tile and a carved mantle of oak. A second fireplace was discovered in the dining room. Several rooms are octagonal, adding to the uniqueness of this home.

Once occupied by James and Ann Wharton, who in the 1970s were among the early purchasers and remodelers of decrepit homes in Winona Lake, the structure now houses an ice cream confectionary.

THEN AND NOW
Texaco Gas Station

For a number of years the first sight visitors to Winona encountered at the stoplight was a Texaco gas and service station, located between the Eagle Arcade and the railroad underpass. It had already been a gas station when John Trier took over its operation in 1967, and the old brick building was upgraded with Texaco's white, green, and red branding.

Trier, who later became a Winona Lake policeman and eventually police chief for four years (1982-1986), operated the gas station and wrecker service until 1972. The station was also the rental portal for kayaks, canoes, boats, and bicycles.

Trier also established and operated, for a time, a marina and recreational rental service on the canal near the present BoatHouse restaurant. Winona Restoration demolished the Texaco station in the late 1990s.

THE EAGLE ARCADE

The very first building town visitors encounter, after passing under the railroad tracks and through the stoplight, is the Eagle Arcade building on Kings Highway. The arched gate building was constructed as an entrance to the park from the Pennsylvania Railroad station and it was erected by J. E. Beyer.

Originally it contained a ticket office and souvenir shop. Over the years it housed many businesses, including a sub shop, "Oggies," operated by Richard Ogden, and a pizza shop called the "Lelle Pad" operated by Jerry Lelle. F. B. Miller operated a print shop in the Arcade, and it also housed James Heaton's real estate office for many years.

It housed a job printing shop run by the Brethren Missionary Herald Company from 1969 until 1991. An abandoned set of concrete steps leading to the railroad tracks can still be seen today behind the arcade building. Today it houses a carpet store and a nail salon.

THE GOLF LINKS

For many years one of the most magnetic attractions at Winona was a 65-acre tract of land, lying across the Pennsylvania Railroad, where Argonne Road now runs. It was a nine-hole golf course, and the 1917 publicity for Winona described it like this:

> The game of golf attracts a great many persons to this place, and it is an interesting sight to see preachers, businessmen, college students, and visitors from all over the country, including both men and women, playing this fascinating and invigorating game. The grounds are always well kept, and players of national reputation are here to enter the lists with new found rivals. The course is laid out with nine holes, covering 2,850 yards. The manager of the links gives lessons to amateurs, and every possible provision is made to secure the utmost pleasure and benefit from this greatest of all outdoor games. . . Visitors should bring their own clubs and balls, although players' outfits may be rented to those who come without their equipment.

ABC INDUSTRIES

ABC Industries, Inc., (formerly American Brattice Cloth Corporation) is located at 301 Kings Highway in Winona Lake and was founded in 1926 by Daniel B. Mikesell.

Originally located at the corner of Cleveland and Jefferson Streets in Warsaw, the company began with just one product—jute brattice cloth—which was used to direct fresh air to the working areas of coal mines. In 1940 D. Blaine Mikesell, son of the founder, was named president of ABC at age 25 when his father died suddenly, and the company entered a stage of growth and expansion. Blaine Mikesell was the president of ABC for 32 years.

In the early 1960s a new plant was constructed on Kings Highway in Winona Lake. In 1972 American Brattice Cloth Corporation merged with Peabody International Corporation and in 1973 Robert M. Ellison was elected president, followed by Stephen Rufenbarger in 1984.

ABC is a manufacturer of ventilation products for the underground mining and tunneling markets as well as for industrial applications. Additionally, ABC manufactures vinyl-reinforced laminated fabrics for the industrial textile fabric marketplace.

ABC has 68,000 square feet of manufacturing space at its headquarters in Winona Lake. The company also has a 20,000-square-foot manufacturing facility located in Grand Junction, Colorado. ABC currently has 75 employees. Fifty-five work at the Winona Lake headquarters, and the remaining 20 individuals are employed in Colorado.

D. Blaine Mikesell, who was raised on the approximate site of the present Indiana Hall on the Grace College campus, lived for many years at 100 Chestnut Avenue in Winona Lake, overlooking the Winona Hotel. Mikesell was well-known and well-respected in the area as a businessman, civic leader, and philanthropist.

In addition to his leadership at ABC, he owned a management corporation in Palm Bay, Florida. He was the founder of ABC Travel Agency, he served on the board of directors and was part-owner and president of Wagon Wheel Playhouse from 1970-1984, and was part-owner and on the board of directors for the Warsaw Holiday Inn from 1970-1979.

He served two terms on the Winona Lake Town Board, was an elder in the Winona Lake Presbyterian Church, was past-president and lieutenant governor for the Warsaw Kiwanis Club, was former president of Junior Achievement, and served with many organizations including the Chamber of Commerce, United Fund, Community Concert Association, President's Committee for Grace College, and more.

He was honored by his alma mater, Manchester College, with an alumni award in 1987. The Winona Town Council honored him with a ceremony in November of 2003. Grace College and Seminary named the lobby and conference area of the historic Westminster Hall the "D. Blaine Mikesell Conference Center" in July of 2004.

Mikesell had served on the Westminster Campaign Steering Committee in the mid-1990s. At the dedication ceremony Grace's President Ron Manahan said, "Because of Mr. Mikesell's esteemed life, community leadership, business leadership, history with this building, commitment to campus, and generous support, we are privileged today to have this conference center named in honor of D. Blaine Mikesell." A plaque in the lobby of Westminster Hall commemorates the award.

Mikesell died on Christmas Day, 2006, at the age of 92 in Kosciusko Community Hospital in Warsaw, Indiana. Services were held in the Presbyterian Church in Winona Lake. Survivors included his wife, Charlotte (Lawton); daughter, Marcia Neff of San Diego; four grandchildren and six great-grandchildren.

THE GREENWAY

In partnership with the city of Warsaw, Winona Lake has a 1.8 mile segment of an eight-mile linear route for bicycle/pedestrian path called Lake City Greenway. The Heritage Trail begins at Winona Avenue, continues through downtown Winona Lake, along Canal Street and winds through the area of the old Chicago Boys Club, terminating at Roy Street in the Southtown addition.

Several other extensions and trails are in the works, thanks to a very thorough master plan. The next Winona Lake trail project will include expanding the trail from the Chicago Boys Club entrance to Grace College campus and out to Lakeland Christian Academy.

Phase A of this segment will connect the existing trail constructed in 2006-2007 to Grace College athletic fields and campus, and eventually to Lakeland Christian Academy. The trail will route northeasterly through the former Chicago Boys and Girls Club property, cross Pierceton Road at Miller Field, and terminate at Grace College campus. Phase B of this segment will connect Phase A in the vicinity of the Grace College athletic fields and will travel easterly to terminate at Lakeland Christian Academy where a trailhead will be located. Connector spurs to nearby neighborhoods will be placed to increase access to the primary trail network.

The Warsaw newspaper noted that on January 8, 1965, it was learned that all but a few acres of Camp Kosciusko at Winona Lake—former summer conference center of the United Presbyterian Synod of Indiana—has been sold to the president of the board of directors of the Chicago Boys Club Inc.

W. Clement Stone (1902–2002) of Chicago reportedly paid approximately $75,000 for 14.4 acres of the camp grounds and planned to use the land as an expansion to the present Chicago Boys Club facilities which were adjacent to Camp Kosciusko. At the same time it was announced that the United Presbyterian Synod would start developing a new $600,000 conference center near Rochester, Indiana, the following spring to replace the Camp Kosciusko facilities.

It was reported on February 27, 1931, that Chicago Boys Club had bought an additional 11 acres on the northeast side of its existing property at Winona Lake. The land, which was purchased from the estate of Matilda Johnson, included a "fine spring of water," according to the report.

Beginning in 1915 and continuing until the 1970s, thousands of inner-city boys enjoyed weeks of recreation at the large camping site located at the southern end of Winona Lake.

Paula Heckman, writing in the 2001 coffee table book *Winona Lake Summers,* which she co-authored with Jane Gordon Cook, noted that in 1984 her husband, Steve Heckman, along with Joe Prout, former owner of Owen's Supermarkets, purchased the Chicago Boys

Clubs acreage in order to prevent the construction of high-density housing. Heckman said, "The maintenance of Winona Lake's integrity, tranquility, and serenity was their priority. After their decision to purchase, Steve drove to Chicago, met with realtors, and bought the 150 acres."

Noting that Chicago Boys Clubs had been incorporated in 1902 after its founding by John F. Atkinson, Heckman said the corporation at one time operated sixteen clubs, seven camps (including the one on Winona Lake), and two medical/dental clinics. Its national headquarters were in Chicago.

When finances became a problem for Chicago Boys Club in the early 1980s, most of the seven camps had to be sold, and the Winona Lake property was one of the first to be offered.

The plat contained wetlands protected by the federal government. Working with the architectural firm Paul I. Cripe Associates of Indianapolis, the developers took care that wetlands were designated, specified, and approved by the DNR.

The waterfront was divided into 18 lakefront lots and 18 rear lots. A paver stone street and sewers were installed and the subdivision was named Stone Camp in honor of W. Clement Stone, the wealthy Chicago businessman and philanthropist who had been a major financial supporter of the Chicago Boys Club.

The Stone Camp area of Winona Lake had long been known as a haven for rattlesnakes. Leesburg resident Jean Lynch, who grew up in Winona, recalled a day in the late 1940s or early 1950s when her young cousin suddenly began throwing rocks at something while he was playing baseball in a field near the present Stone Camp.

He was killing a rattler, and after the snake was dead, the boy got some string, tied the reptile to the back of his bicycle, and dragged it around the village.

"You always had an eye out for rattlers," Lynch said about playing around the Boys Club property. "They were back there and we knew it."

Lynch also recalled that in the summertime the boys at the Boys Club would catch rattlers, put them in cages, and then collect and sell their venom.

"That's how [the boys at the camp] made some money in the summertime," she recalled. "In the fall, they'd release [the snakes] back into the woods."

Paula Heckman noted that eventually the remainder of the Boys Club land was sold to Dane Miller, "who has provided and continues to provide, assistance for Winona's renovation."

Local news media from September, 2002, said "Known for a long time as the site of the Chicago Boys Club, a section of about 20 acres will become what's expected to be one of the most luxurious residential neighborhoods in Kosciusko County." The report noted that much of the land's natural beauty and Cherry Creek, located on the southeast side of Winona Lake would be retained.

The approximately 110 acres of rolling land on the southeastern banks of Winona Lake house a trail system that has gained tremendous popularity and has become one of the Midwest's most highly touted cycling stops. More than 10 miles of rolling, diverse mountain bike trails on the former Chicago Boys Club property include fast, smooth, weaving single-track sections along with root and log crossings, bridges, jumps, technical drops, descents, lung-busting short climbs, and a number of fun flat sections throughout the wooded landscape. The easy-to-navigate paved path is sprinkled liberally with benches for resting and stimulating pieces of artwork.

Every year a number of events are hosted on the trails including mountain bike races, a Fat and Skinny Tire Fest, monthly time trials, and the endurance race of the year, the 24 Hours of Winona, where participants in either solo or relay teams compete for 6, 12, or 24 hours to accumulate the most laps.

All users are encouraged to know the trail markings and to follow them. Mountain bikers follow the course in a counter-clockwise rotation following the green and black arrows, while walkers, hikers, and trail runners follow the yellow arrows in a clockwise rotation. Maps and more information may be found on the trail website at http://www.winonalake-trails.com

Terrain and route lengths of the well-marked trails vary, and accommodate beginners to seasoned experts. The addition of a paved bikeway, Heritage Trail, linking The Village at Winona to the far southern point of the trail system, allows families and recreational cyclists to enjoy the outstanding scenery of the area. The trails play host to several of the region's largest cycling events, races, and festivals throughout the year. The Trailhouse Village Outdoor Store in the Village at Winona always has updated information on cycling events.

LAKELAND CHRISTIAN ACADEMY

Private secondary and elementary schools provide their communities with educational alternatives for their children. Lakeland Christian Academy, located on Co. Rd. 250E in Winona Lake, has been in operation since 1974.

LCA began classes in the Winona Lake Brethren Church facilities with 42 students in grades 7-9. Rick Brundage served as the first administrator, and taught along with several others.

Dr. and Mrs. Norman Uphouse made available to the school a 13-acre site on Wooster Road east of Grace College. The property was purchased and the school moved there on February 5, 1975, when the first modular building was erected.

Rev. Howard Mayes became the administrator in the fall of 1976. During his administration a multi-purpose building was constructed and the junior and senior years of high school were added. The first graduating class of eight seniors received diplomas on June 2, 1978, in ceremonies held at the Winona Lake Brethren Church.

Ted Franchino, administrator from 1978 through 1981, presided over a period of significant growth and campus improvements. LCA moved to its new campus on County Road 250 East on November 1, 2000. At this writing, the school enrolls about 130 students in grades 7-12 and the current administrator is Joy Lavender.

NOTED PERSONALITIES

JAMES AND RUTH RODEHEAVER THOMAS were named "Man and Woman of 1968" on September 18, 1968, at the 57th annual dinner meeting of the Greater Warsaw Chamber of Commerce. The Thomases were the first husband-wife team selected in the same year since the awards were instituted in 1959. Approximately 250 persons attended the event at Petrie's Wagon Wheel Restaurant.

Thomas for many years managed the Westminster Hotel and the Rodeheaver Hall-Mack company. His wife, Ruth, a half-sister to Homer Rodeheaver, was a musician who had a local radio program on the Warsaw station well into the 1970s.

Local news media noted that Mrs. James E. (Ruth Rodeheaver) Thomas, 81, of Rainbow Point, 1300 Court St., Winona Lake, well-known singer and voice coach, died at 12:45 p.m. Sunday, February 12, 1979, at the Mason Health Care Facility. Death was due to complications following an extended illness.

Many artifacts from Rainbow Point are on display at the Reneker Museum of Winona History, and many more are in the possession of longtime Rodeheaver employee Bruce Howe. A public auction of most of the contents of Rainbow Point was held on Wednesday, June 25, 1980.

Although they did not live in the Town of Winona Lake, the Winona Lake/Warsaw area had several well-known authors who lived for a time in the area.

THEODORE DREISER (1871-1945), author of *An American Tragedy*, lived in Warsaw from 1885 to 1889. His family moved to Warsaw when he was 14, and he attended West Ward and Warsaw High School. Dreiser returned to Warsaw for a visit in the early 1900s, and died in December of 1945, seven years before *A Place in the Sun,* based on his 1925 novel, won an Academy Award.

His older brother, Paul Dresser (Paul changed the spelling of his last name from "Dreiser" to "Dresser" to Americanize it after beginning his entertainment career) was a well-known songwriter. One of his compositions was *On the Banks of the Wabash, Far Away* which was adopted as the official state song by the Indiana General Assembly. A bill containing its lyrics was signed into law by Governor Winfield T. Durbin on March 14, 1913.

Theodore Dreiser referred to the building of the original park on Eagle Lake in his book *A History of Myself: Dawn* (1931). He also told of stopping to cool his feet in the lake while returning home from work on a farm.

In his 1916 book *Hoosier Holiday*, in recounting the story of his trip back to the scenes of his childhood, Dreiser again referred to

Eagle Lake, now named Winona, as an outlying town and park that was a wooded area in his earlier days.

JAMES WHITCOMB RILEY (1849-1916), later named the "Hoosier Poet," spent his youth as an itinerant sign painter, house painter, and Bible salesman, and he lived in Warsaw at several times. His father, an attorney and member of the Indiana State Legislature, named his son for Indiana Governor James Whitcomb. Later in life Riley was a frequent headline speaker at the Winona programs, and he was president of the Midwest Writers Conference, which met in the Winona Hotel. He was a frequent Chautauqua lecturer and program guest in Winona. He is buried in Indianapolis. A sign painted by Riley and containing his signature was on display for many years at the Phillipson Clothing Store in Warsaw, and is now on display in the Indiana Room of the Warsaw Community Public Library.

AMBROSE BIERCE (1842-1913), once described as "America's one genuine wit," grew up in Kosciusko County, attending high school at Warsaw. The tenth of thirteen children, Bierce lived for some time with his brother Gus on a farm southwest of Eagle Lake (later named Winona Lake). At the age of 17, Bierce worked as a "printer's devil" on the old *Northern Indianian,* Warsaw's early newspaper, living with the editor, Reuben Williams and Mrs. Williams.

Falsely accused of theft, Bierce left Warsaw and never returned. He later fought in the Civil War, attaining fame as a journalist and writer of short stories. Author Kurt Vonnegut once stated that he considered Bierce's *Occurrence at Owl Creek Bridge* to be the greatest American short story and a work of flawless American genius. In 1916 Bierce left his post as editor of the *San Francisco Chronicle* and went to Mexico, where he disappeared.

CHICAGO EXPRESSWAY DESIGNER

One Winona Lake native has had a significant impact on the traffic arteries of Chicago. An article in the Warsaw *Times-Union* on October 12, 1955, noted that Roger Nusbaum, son of Mr. and Mrs. Ralph Nusbaum of Winona Lake, was playing a leading role in designing the Congress Street Expressway in Chicago, described as "probably one of the biggest superhighway jobs ever attempted."

Noting that the expressway would be "built right through the skyscraper area of Chicago," the paper noted that "Miles of skyscrapers have been demolished to widen Congress Street from Grant Park on the lakefront for miles west to the Chicago city limits." Other expressway systems included in Nussbaum's department, the article noted, included the Edens Expressway; the Northwest Expressway, extending north from the loop to Chicago's new airport; and the Calumet Expressway, extending south from the Chicago business area.

Nussbaum attended engineering school at Purdue University for three years, and then, during World War II, went to Panama as a civilian engineer with the War Department, where he obtained valuable experience designing airports and roads. Later finishing his education at the University of Illinois school at Navy Pier, Nussbaum eventually became chief expressway design engineer for the state of Illinois.

CURIOSITIES

JERRY, THE WATERSKIING LION

One of the more startling sights in Winona Lake in 1935 or 1936 was a sleek Chris-Craft speedboat towing a water ski board carrying a full-grown lion and its owner, who clasped the tow-rope and straddled the beast's shoulders and back.

Paul Lowman, a Winona Lake man "who had a penchant for doing the unusual," was the owner of the lion, whose name was Jerry. Jerry (named Jerry I because there was a second one named Jerry II) was old when he arrived in Winona Lake, and he died after only a year or so.

Lowman was known for riding a motorcycle—unusual in the 1930s—and for piloting airplanes, including an amphibian plane which he liked to land on Winona Lake in front of the Winona Hotel. He also had a water-skiing troupe that performed stunts on Winona Lake, and he owned the Tippecanoe Gardens dance hall on the south shore of Lake Tippecanoe.

Lowman and Jerry I would zip around the lake on a wide board, pulled by the speedboat, with Lowman straddling the lion's shoulders. Winona Lake resident Bruce Howe claims to have ridden the board with Jerry, as well. Lowman often put Jerry on a leash and took him for long walks around Rainbow Point and the canal.

When Jerry I died, Lowman obtained a second lion in 1938, named Jerry II, but this Jerry wouldn't behave. He never learned to water ski. He several times got loose in the town and terrorized local residents by crawling under their porches, by extending himself to look in their windows, and by prowling about their lawns and gardens.

One time Jerry II got loose and rambled through the Eagle Arcade, which included a souvenir shop, small grocery, and several other establishments. He thoroughly trashed the building and then hid on the second floor, stubbornly refusing to emerge until he was finally coaxed out by his owner. Jerry II attacked Lowman one time, causing several serious injuries. Jerry II ended his career somewhere in the south, allegedly at an animal park near Cypress Gardens in Florida.

The third lion, Congo, was obtained in 1939 when he was a cub. He, too, never learned to water ski, but he was often seen around town with his owner and eventually grew to be about 500 pounds. All three lions were likely acquired from the Clyde Beatty Circus.

The 1939 Winona Schools Reunion newsletter carries this summary: "Paul Lowman's lion got us in the papers this summer. His surf board riding old lion, Jerry I, died of pneumonia in the winter, so Jerry II was bought. But he feared the water, and refused to be trained.

At the first attempt he shook off his chain, scampered along the lakeshore, taking refuge under a house, from which he was lured back into his cage. Next time, he brought his big paw down, severely clawing Paul. When Paul recovered, Jerry was put under an anesthetic and his claws were clipped. But, it was six days before he came out, and meantime he had to be fed.

His final escapade came during Bible Conference, when he broke loose, dragging his rope, ran towards the park, and as a crowd gathered, dashed into the Arcade, jumped thro' the screen to a table loaded with china. Policemen brought guns, the cage was drawn up, and finally Jerry pulled in. Then the order went out. No more surfboard training in the county.

When Lowman wanted to move away from Winona Lake, he couldn't take Congo with him, and he could find no one to whom to sell or give the lion. So he killed Congo in November of 1940 with a shot from a high-powered rifle. Lowman died in the Orlando, Florida, area in 2002 at the age of 88.

MERBRINK AND THE GHOSTS OF WINONA

Every town has its "mystery properties" around which legends have grown up, and where some strange and mysterious activities are alleged to have occurred. Winona Lake is no different.

Premier among the "mystery properties" in Winona is the Merbrink, a lakefront two-story home with a wraparound porch which sits right on the waterfront at the northwest tip of McDonald Island, four doors from Sol Dickey's Killarney Castle.

Shari Benyousky of Winona Lake has investigated and propagated the legends of the Merbrink. She was the recipient of an Indiana Arts Commission Individual Artist Grant to write a manuscript about Merbrink and its famous ghost named Miss Phebe. Benyousky's blog is at http://winonalakehauntedhouse.blogspot.com and her novel's website is www.thelostcloe.com. Much of the following comes from Benyousky's research. The tale of the house and Miss Phebe are also told in *Kosciusko County, an Oral and Pictorial History* by Daniel Coplen.

Billy Sunday once remarked, while speaking to a group of society women at the home of Mrs. Rufus Dawes in Evanston, Illinois, that God does not permit things to happen by chance. "We are put here for a purpose," Sunday said. "I know of a house by the lake, beautifully furnished for a bride. But the girl changed her mind and it still stands there, all boarded up. The furniture is still in that unoccupied house—dust covered." Sunday didn't elaborate, but he was referring to the Merbrink.

According to legend, W. H. Bruning, the wealthy president of the F. J. Bruning and Son Company, wholesale spice and tea merchants of Evansville, Indiana, and New York, built the home in 1903. He called it "Merbrink" because it stood on the brink of the lake. Supposedly, Bruning never spent a night in it, but for at least the first 15 years after its completion, he regularly came back to visit it. On his visits he spent weekends at the Swiss Terrace Hotel, managed by Mrs. John Cooper and her daughter, Miss Nelle Cooper.

As the story goes, locals came to realize that there was "deep and sincere affection" between Bruning and Miss Nelle Cooper. Sunday afternoons, Miss Cooper and her mother were reported to accompany Bruning to the "mystery house" to enter with him via the one key for the door which he carried. Passers-by could hear the piano within, awakening under the young woman's fingers.

Eventually the elder Mrs. Cooper's health failed, so the daughter remained at home while Bruning made his pilgrimages alone to the closed-up lakeside house. Local cottagers believed that Bruning was waiting for Miss Cooper to marry him—they told visitors that the house had been prepared as a bridal house.

But no wedding occurred. The elder Mrs. Cooper neared 90, her daughter was nearing 60, and Bruning, in his 70s, continued to make sizable gifts to the religious organizations in Winona Lake and lent his business expertise to his friend and fellow board member, William Jennings Bryan.

But there was another "back story" that persisted and grew as a legend. Many years earlier John Cooper, an educator from New York, moved to Evansville, Indiana, to become the superintendent of schools. His daughter, Nelle, was a girl of 18.

After several years his health began to fail, and his wife and daughter began taking in boarders to shore up the family finances. One of the first to come was W. H. Bruning, a bachelor of 30, and a partner in his father's tea and spice business. It is said that he loved Nelle Cooper from the first, and she loved him, and they were reported to have become engaged.

Friends believed the girl felt it was her duty to remain with her parents in their difficulties. They moved to Winona Lake in 1901 when her father decided to open a hotel. Named "The Homestead," their cottage, though small, was popular with vacationers. An old-world charm and the Coopers' courtesy brought them local fame.

A year passed and John Cooper died. Bruning, who grieved along with the Coopers, built a magnificent cottage, capable of housing some hundred guests, named it *The Swiss Terrace* and installed the two Cooper women as proprietors.

That same summer Bruning bought a lot on the point of the island. For weeks the dredges and drays worked as he built out and filled in the area, making it "Bruning's Point." When the land was ready, he imported carpenters who began erection of the house which he himself had designed. The house dates from circa 1905.

The house was reported to have been very well done. The best timber was used, and modern conveniences were installed. There was a wraparound veranda and rounded sleeping porch upstairs. An example of Free Classic style of architecture, the Merbrink featured distinctive windows: Palladian leaded and beautiful art-glass. There were wide fireplaces, mirrors, chandeliers, thick Brussels rugs, and many other luxurious furnishings. Twenty-one rocking chairs were scattered throughout, gas lights were ready, fires were laid on the hearths, and a magnificent silver dinner set was placed beside rare china in the cupboards.

But Miss Nelle never came, and no one knows why.

Bruning kept coming. Each year the house was painted anew. The piano was tuned. Water and gas pipes were examined and all loose boards replaced. Several times new draperies were carried in. The stone sundial which Bruning set up on the lawn was kept in perfect alignment. The grass in summer was mown weekly, and in winter snow and sleet were cleared away by workmen who never saw the house's interior.

During the 1920s, many people reported that they saw a ghost in or near the Merbrink. They recognized the figure as that of Miss Phebe, Chloe's old nanny. In the "juicy part" of the tale, William and Nelle were reported to have birthed an illegitimate daughter, Chloe Ellen Cooper, and she is the subject of Benyousky's novel.

Although the house has now been owned for some six decades by another family, many people have reportedly had contact with the apparition. One writer reported that visitors to the house heard eerie, harp-like sounds which they attributed to the ghost.

Don White, a former Purdue basketball All-American who bought the house at a tax auction in 1933, had a habit of fishing before dawn. One morning while he was fishing he thought he saw his wife, Nina, on the sleeping porch. He waved to her and she waved back. Later, at breakfast, when White asked his wife what she was doing awake so early, she said it wasn't her that he saw. They knew, he said, that it was Miss Phebe.

Local photographer Al Disbro also claims to have photographed the apparition, which once appeared in an upstairs window as he was photographing the house. When the photo was developed, however, the figure in the window had disappeared.

Blogger Sheri Krichbaum, who claims to have done significant research on the Merbrink, posted the following on July 14, 2009:[51]

William H. Bruning did finally marry Ellen (Nelle—his pet name for her is Ellen spelled backwards) in Kosciusko County on October 25, 1920. It is recorded in marriage book AA:158. It is said that date was the anniversary of their meeting in Madison, Indiana in 1895. She was 58 and he was 75 at the time of their marriage. Sources state they had been lovers for years. His parents did not approve of actresses and she had been one for a time. The marriage license states she is from Winona Lake, but he is from New York City.

It is rumored that they had a child named Chloe. Chloe's birth date is Sept. 10, 1892 in Indianapolis. Miss Phebe is the nanny of Ellen's cousin. From what I have read the reason that Ellen never wanted anyone to know that she had a child with William was that she feared for Chloe's life. It is said that she feared so much for Chloe's life that she didn't even tell William Bruning that Chloe was their child until many years later.

Ellen Cooper Bruning died on October 2, 1925. She is buried in Springdale Cemetery in Madison, Indiana, alongside his parents John F. and Catherine Adelaide Von Broke Zur Lage Bruning (his mother descended from some royal

---

[51] http://groups.yahoo.com/group/warsaw1974/message/10940?var=1

blood). Ellen Cooper Bruning was born April 6, 1862; she was 63 at the time of her death. According to the marriage record when William died in 1930, he would have been 85.

There are several other ghost stories in and around Kosciusko County, including the ghost of William Hull, whose body was found on the Pennsylvania Railroad tracks in December of 1882.

The train tracks east of Winona Lake are reported to be haunted by the ghost of Mike Fitzgerald, who was killed on New Year's Eve in 1868 when he was struck by a passenger train. Trainmen report seeing his pale white ghost, with a lantern in his hand, near the spot where Fitzgerald was killed.

Other ghost stories from the county were chronicled by David Slone in a Warsaw *Times-Union* article from October, 1998. One was the ghost of Winona Lake resident Johnny Bond, "well-known in the area," who is said to walk the streets of Winona.

THE COAST GUARD CUTTER WINONA

Many are unaware that there was a U.S. Coast Guard Cutter which, according to the U.S. Coast Guard History program,[52] was named for Winona Lake, Indiana.

The USCGC *Winona* (WPG-65), call sign NRUN, was built by the Western Pipe & Steel Company in San Pedro, California. She was commissioned on 19 April, 1946, under the command of Capt. A. F. Werner. From 15 August 1946 to 11 September 1947, the *Winona* was stationed at San Pedro, California, and used for law enforcement, ocean station, and search and rescue operations. She was subsequently home-ported at Port Angeles, Washington, until 31 May 1974.

While in service she was assigned to ocean station patrols, Bering Sea patrols, fisheries patrols and other law enforcement operations as well as search and rescue duties when needed. She typically served on Ocean Station November, mid-way between San Francisco and Hawaii, and Ocean Station Victor, midway between Hawaii and Japan.

---

[52] http://www.uscg.mil/history/webcutters/Winona1946.pdf

In April, 1967, while under the command of Capt. Herbert J. Lynch, she received word that she was scheduled to serve a tour of duty with Coast Guard Squadron Three in Vietnamese waters in support of Operation Market Time. She departed Pearl Harbor for Vietnam on 16 January 1968 and she arrived in theatre on 25 January.

Her service with Squadron Three lasted through 17 October 1968. While in service in Vietnam, she visited Subic Bay, Philippines; Kaohsiung, Taiwan; Yokosuka, Japan, and Hong Kong, where she served as the administration ship for the Senior Officer Present Afloat (SOPA) for 21 days.

While engaged in patrol duties off the coast of Vietnam, her boarding crews boarded suspect craft, resupplied inshore patrol craft and Coast Guard patrol boats, provided medical assistance to villages on the mainland, and conducted naval gunfire support missions to ground units.

On 1 March 1968 she engaged a North Vietnamese trawler, becoming "the first High Endurance Coast Guard Cutter to singly engage and destroy an enemy vessel since World War II." Offshore from the CuBoDe River, a waterway south of Saigon, a 125-foot North Vietnamese trawler was detected infiltrating arms and ammunition to the Viet Cong. The action was described in *Winona's* Vietnam cruise book:

> We shadowed the trawler for six long hours into the night before it finally turned for the beach, our cue to intercept. Closing to 700 yards we illuminated and challenged them to stop when a running gun battle ensued. The effect in the night outfourthed the 4th of July. .50 cal. tracers, fiery red in the black, streaked both ways, punctuated by 5" gun flashes, white with the intensity of burning magnesium. The ricochets whined off into the distance, or metal piercing rounds thwacked through steel. For seven minutes we fought until a 5" round found home at the base of the trawler's deckhouse, and the night was day, and our ship rocked from the explosion that rained debris on our decks. For meritorious achievement that night, Captain Lynch was awarded the Bronze Star. Lt. Commander [J. A.] Atkinson, conning of-

ficer, Lt. [M. J.] Bujarski, gunnery officer, and BM3 "Audie" Slawson, director operator were awarded Navy Accommodation Medals. All four were authorized a Combat "V."

There were no enemy survivors. Enemy fire pierced *Winona's* hull and deckhouse six times and also left a number of dents, but she sustained no personnel casualties. On 29 June 1968, CDR Robert A. Moss relieved Capt. Lynch as Commanding Officer while at Subic Bay. Returning home to Port Angeles on 4 November 1968, she had accumulated a number of impressive statistics while serving in Vietnam.

She steamed 50,727 miles, spent 203 days at sea, treated 437 Vietnamese, sank one enemy trawler, destroyed 50 sampans and damaged 44 more, destroyed 137 structures and damaged 254, destroyed 39 bunkers and damaged 27, destroyed two bridges and damaged another, destroyed three gun positions and killed 128 enemy personnel, expending a total of 3,291 five-inch shells.

On 29 February 1972, due to budget constraints, the Coast Guard decommissioned *Winona* temporarily. Congress restored funding in May of 1972, and she returned to duty primarily as a fisheries patrol vessel. She was recommissioned at Port Angeles on 27 July 1972 under the command of CDR Neal Nelson. She escorted the damaged CGC *Jarvis* after the latter had run aground on a reef near Dutch Harbor, Alaska, in December, 1972.

She was decommissioned on 31 May 1974 and was sold for scrap. *Winona's* awards included: World War II Victory Medal, Korean Service Medal, United Nations Service Medal, National Defense Service Medal, Vietnam Campaign Medal (one battle star), and the Republic of Vietnam Meritorious Unit Citation (Gallantry Cross).[53]

Because of the name Winona, the city of Winona, Minnesota, also took an interest in identifying with the ship. The anchor from the cutter sat for years at the intersection of Main Street and Lake Park Drive in Winona, Minnesota, where it was mounted on blocks of granite from Wausau, Wisconsin. It was obtained for the Minnesota city after the local newspaper editor, Adolph Bremer, urged

---

[53] http://www.uscg.mil/history/webcutters/Winona1946.pdf

the city to secure a piece of the ship and indicated that the Winona County Historical Society had contacted the Coast Guard.[54]

The anchor is included in a monument that honors those who served "above, upon and beneath the waters of the earth" and was permanently mounted in Veterans Park in Winona, Minnesota, by Lake Winona. It was financed through a $5,000 grant from the Winona Community Foundation.

THE 'HOT WATER HEATER' INCIDENT

One incident in the storied folklore of Winona Lake is the "water heater incident" which is repeated in varying forms when long-time residents reminisce. Documentation of the incident was finally found in the 1941 newsletter of the annual Winona Schools Reunion, in the "park news" section:

> The Daguerre Building has more repair work than planned, as one night an overheated 30-gallon water tank at the Dundu Vu, south of Bethany Lodge, exploded and went sailing through the air ending, we hear, with crashing through the roof of the Daguerre. It blew out the entire end of the Dundu Vu, wrecking that house and the one next door, breaking 31 windows in neighboring houses, Roseville, Parkhill, and 13 at Miss Elliot's, the old home of Dr. Scott. Ever since the Daguerre building was bought by the photographers, all changes and repairs have been in the care of Homer Sailor.

---

[54] "Piece of 'Winona' Anchors Monument Honoring Those Who Served at Sea." By Chris Hubbuch. *Winona Daily News.* Thursday, June 28, 2007

CHAPTER 19
Crimes and Tragedies

❦

"No one is exempt from tragedy or disappointment—God himself was not exempt. Jesus offered no immunity, no way out of the unfairness, but rather a way through it to the other side."
Philip Yancey

EVEN IN A SMALL, CLOSE-KNIT COMMUNITY LIKE WINONA LAKE, IT is inevitable that crimes and tragedies occasionally make the news. Through the years there have been a number of murders, drownings, and other tragedies. Several stand out because of their nature and because of the press attention they attracted.

A DOUBLE LOSS

Particularly poignant were the incidents that befell the family of evangelist O. A. Newlin whose newly-purchased home, it was noted earlier, was destroyed in the Great Fire of 1914.

The Newlin family, having lost their newly-purchased cottage in the fire, experienced further tragedy three years later, according to this report from the *Fort Wayne News* on Saturday, September 1, 1917:

Warsaw, Ind. Aug. 31 - Dwight Newlin, aged fourteen years, son of Evangelist and Mrs. O.A. Newlin, of Winona Lake, was almost instantly killed shortly before noon by a large touring car driven by Dr. James A. Gordon, pastor of the Winona Federated church. The Newlin boy was riding his bicycle and crossed the street as Dr. Gordon

301

was backing his car out of his garage. He was caught by the machine and thrown under the wheels which passed over his body twice. Fred King and Charles B. Taylor, who witnessed the accident, assisted the injured lad to his feet and he walked to the sidewalk, saying that he was not hurt, but that he could not get his breath. Shortly after being taken to his home, he passed away. Physicians were unable to find any fractures on the first examination, and internal injuries caused his death. The boy, who was an only child, an older brother having died some time ago, was a favorite at the park. He had a paper route and was making collections when the accident occurred. The parents and Dr. Gordon are prostrated with grief.

JACK RODEHEAVER AEROPLANE ACCIDENT

One of the more graphic aeronautical tragedies of Winona occurred in late August, 1921. On August 26, the headlines of the *Warsaw Daily Times* and the *Northern Indianan* newspapers screamed,

"Two Dead in Aeroplane Accident."

"Homer Rodeheaver Witnesses Tragedy from Porch of His Home."

"First Flying Trip Proves Fatal to Well-Known Winona Lake Youth."

"Jack Rodeheaver and Lieut. L. D. Merrill are victims of crash just east of Warsaw. Machine turns turtle with Winona Lake youth at levers and Auburn, ME, aviator. Plunges 2,000 feet to death east of Dalton Foundry."

Jack Rodeheaver, 19, a half-brother of Homer Rodeheaver, and the 29-year-old Merrill were flying over Winona Lake that day at about 5:15 p.m. With Rodeheaver piloting the plane, they were seen to descend to about 1,000 feet when the engine suddenly stopped.

Golfers below, on the links that were approximately where Argonne Road is now, said the machine turned a little to one side and as it did so, Merrill was seen to arise from his rear seat and attempt to reach forward, apparently trying to help Rodeheaver. Moments later Merrill plunged to his death, landing in a pasture about 350 feet east of the Dalton foundry about 175 feet north of the Pennsylvania railroad tracks.

The airplane continued upside-down, flying southwest, crossing the Pennsylvania right-of-way, finally crashing into a cornfield about a half-mile from where Merrill had landed. Rodeheaver was alive when rescuers reached him, but had multiple injuries and died shortly thereafter.

The airplane was described as an "old-style Curtiss machine," which had been brought to Winona Lake by Merrill from Cincinnati about six weeks earlier. It had been given the name "Rainbow Records" and was used as an advertisement for Homer Rodeheaver's "Rainbow" phonograph records. Since its arrival, scores of people from Warsaw and Winona Lake summer residents had taken air trips, soaring over Warsaw and Winona Lake.

Souvenir hunters quickly converged on the crash site and, according to news reports, "they carried off small pieces of metal, parts of the canvas wings and splinters of wood from the demolished machine."

Billy Sunday, who was engaged in an evangelistic campaign at Hood River, Oregon, was notified of the crash by telegraph. Homer Rodeheaver, who had been seated on his front porch, saw the plane go down and jumped in his automobile and rushed to the scene of the accident.

At the Bible conference that evening, Dr. G. Campbell Morgan offered prayer for the two deceased fliers. News media reported that there was a "spirit of depression" at the announcement, but after the prayer "there was a decided change as the great minister pictured the boys, not as dead, but gone to meet their God face-to-face."[55]

JOHN DILLINGER ROBS POLICE STATION

One of the more storied events in Warsaw's history took place on April 13, 1934, when noted gangster John Dillinger and his gang

---

[55] "Two Dead in Aeroplane Accident" article from *Warsaw Daily Times* and the *Northern Indianian*, Friday, August 26, 1921.

robbed the Warsaw city police station of its guns and bullet-proof vests. The local jail museum has artifacts and accounts of that occurrence on display.

THE BENSON BROTHERS RESCUE

N. Bruce Howe, Jr., chief emeritus of the Winona Lake Fire Department who actively served the Winona Lake Fire Department and the Kosciusko County Firemen's Association for 65 years, was honored in December of 2003 with Indiana's highest civilian award. On behalf of Indiana Governor Joseph Kernan, State Fire Marshall Tracy Boatright presented Howe with the prestigious Sagamore of the Wabash award during the department's annual Christmas banquet held in the Westminster.

On April 30, 1956, while serving as the Winona Lake fire chief, Howe, whose career had been managing the Rodeheaver Hall-Mack Music Company, pulled two brothers, Dale and Jay Benson, out of a burning house. He received a Meritorious Service medal from Gov. Robert Orr for that action in 1988.

The boys, ages 14 and 11, were the sons of John Benson, plant manager of the Free Methodist Publishing House printing operations. The Benson family lived at 203 Seventh Street. Lightning struck the furnace room outside a basement bedroom during the night, trapping the two boys. The door of their room was on fire, and they soon lost consciousness.

Howe, who was then living at the nearby Westminster Hotel, came running to the house and quickly donned an airpack that enabled him to go down into the hot and smoke-filled room and find the boys. That very morning the boys had watched the airpacks being unpacked—their father, John, was a member of the town council which had approved the purchase of the expensive airpacks at the strong urging of Bruce Howe.

The boys had lengthy hospitalizations, but eventually recovered fully. The late Jay Benson went on to be magazine editor at the Free Methodist Publishing House and later became president of World Missionary Press, which prints millions of topical Scripture booklets in 337 languages distributed free to 210 nations.

Dale, the older brother, went on to have a distinguished career as a family practice physician in Indianapolis and executive director of HealthNet—the result of his vision to grow two storefront clinics into a quality healthcare system for the indigent neighborhoods of Indianapolis.

Dale Benson wrote a number of books on quality health care, and upon his retirement was given the Sagamore of the Wabash Award by the governor of Indiana. His passion for the underserved most recently led him to serve the indigent Latino population in east Los Angeles for five years.

In a 2012 e-mail to Jay Benson, Howe said, "I think of you and Dale often . . . you and Dale are the greatest part of my life . . . God has been good to me."

In 2010 Howe was further honored as a recipient of the Bill Reneker Memorial Community Service Award during the annual Winona Lake Community Appreciation Dinner at Westminster Hall in Winona Lake. The award honors Bill Reneker, former Winona Lake town council president, who died in 1993, and is presented each year by his widow, Judy, in honor of her late husband. The award is to recognize individuals who make a contribution to the betterment of Winona Lake.

In the citation, it was noted that Howe had been a member of the Winona Lake Presbyterian Church for more than 80 years. He joined the Winona Lake Volunteer Fire Department in 1938 and served the department for 65 years, 23 as fire chief. He served nearly three years in the U.S. Army in World War II and received five battle stars in actions ranging from Omaha Beach to the Battle of the Bulge.

For more than 50 years he dedicated his life's work to the world of gospel music publishing. His associations with Homer Rodeheaver, Rodeheaver Music Publishing, Word Records, and the American Broadcasting Corp. helped to maintain Winona's prestige as the gospel music capital of America.

Beginning in the 1960s he worked to honor local Salvation Army Brigadier Phillipson through fundraising efforts dedicated to support the Tree of Lights campaign. To the present Howe is active in fund-raising for the local Rotary Club.

Howe took particular pride in helping to maintain the legacy of Homer Rodeheaver. Visitors to the Reneker Museum of Winona History today can enjoy many of the artifacts associated with "Mr. Homer" because of the loving care and preservation done by Howe.

MURDER ON COLLEGE AVENUE

Local media reported on February 6, 1963, that a widowed daughter of a once socially-prominent pioneer Warsaw family was found murdered in her modest Winona Lake home at 1102 E. College Ave. The brutally stabbed and bludgeoned body of Mrs. Louise (White) Bolinger, 56, an employee since 1956 in the bindery department of the Free Methodist Publishing House, was discovered in the single-car garage by a fellow employee, Albert Wilson.

Law enforcement officers immediately began searching for clues. The entire student body of Grace College and Seminary, which was located only several blocks from the murder scene, was interrogated during the investigation to see whether anyone had information that could lead to an arrest.

Seventeen days later, on February 22, it was announced that officers had cracked the case with the confession of Mark Alvin Wilson, 18, of 383 N. Detroit St., Warsaw. The youth broke down and admitted the brutal slaying during questioning at the county jail. He said robbery was his motive.

According to newspaper accounts, the slightly built youth sobbed out to officers how he went to the Bolinger home on the night of February 5 with the express purpose of robbing the widow so that he and his 16-year-old girlfriend could elope. Wilson was indicted by a grand jury on a first-degree murder charge a few weeks later, but the jury did not return an indictment against Wilson's 16-year-old sweetheart, Juell Daisy, of Warsaw. Daisy had admitted being with Wilson when he hid the weapon used to beat Mrs. Bolinger.

Wilson pleaded guilty to a second-degree murder charge on April 20, 1963, and threw himself on the mercy of the court. He was sentenced to life imprisonment by Judge Gene B. Lee in circuit court on April 24, and was immediately sent to the Indiana State Prison at Michigan City. He could be eligible for parole in 15 to 20 years.

The newspaper noted that "he is one of the few from this county ever sentenced to a life term."

News reports on September 2, 1970, announced that Mark Alvin Wilson, 26, who was serving a life sentence for the February 5, 1963, bludgeon murder of a Winona Lake widow had escaped from the Indiana State Prison at Michigan City. Two days later he was to be returned to the prison after having surrendered to officers at Calumet City, Illinois.

A *WINONA QUEEN* TRAGEDY

Over the years, a series of watercraft named *Winona Queen* provided touring and excursion entertainment for visitors and residents of Winona Lake. Over the July Fourth holiday in 1984, divers from area police forces were called out to search for a 23-year-old amateur magician from Strongs, Michigan, who was believed to have fallen handcuffed off the *Winona Queen* pontoon boat at about 9:45 a.m. The man was apparently practicing an act he was to perform later for a conference which was being conducted in Winona Lake. The pontoon boat was approximately 400 feet out from the shore near the Winona Hotel.

At first, it was thought that the man and a companion were in Winona Lake for a meeting of Christian magicians. Later it was discovered, however, that the young magician, who was pulled dead from the lake four hours later, was, in fact, a 23-year-old Christian college student who was working for the summer at the Winona conference grounds and, as an amateur magician, billed himself as "Rayburn the Great."

Jess Rayburn Hopper, who was president of the student council at Grand Rapids Baptist College (now Cornerstone University), had just finished his junior year as a speech major. He had been recruited by Ron Busch, his college speech professor, to work at the Bible conference for the summer along with Jess' roommate, Terry Knauss, 23. Busch was executive director of the Winona Lake Christian Assembly at the time.

Hopper had grown up in Strongs, near Sault Ste. Marie, in the Upper Peninsula of Michigan. He was described as a "slender, sandy-haired youth with a quick, curious mind and a fascination for the mysteries of Houdini." Hopper's fascination with the world of magic began when he was five years old, and by age eight, he was putting on shows for his neighborhood. Later he would perform at small clubs in Sault Ste. Marie, and one summer he performed at the famed long-porch Grand Hotel on Mackinac Island.

Like Houdini, he learned how to escape from a straitjacket, hold his breath for long periods of time, pick handcuffs, and perform other escape tricks.

On that Friday, July 6, 1984, Hopper and his roommate, Knauss, shoved off from shore aboard the *Winona Queen,* a 34-foot pontoon boat with a canvas awning. When they were about 400 feet from shore, with the water at a depth of about six feet, they began to practice his underwater escape trick which he planned to perform the following week during the annual meeting of a thousand or more members of the Fellowship of Christian Magicians. The trick had worked six or seven times previously, but always in a small pond or swimming pool.

Hopper had Knauss wrap the chains around his torso. His hands were handcuffed behind his back. Then, attired only in a tight blue swimsuit, he jumped overboard. Almost immediately, he knew he had problems.

"I'm in trouble," he called out when he surfaced. "Bring the boat over."

But the winds had picked up and Knauss had difficulty maneuvering the boat, according to a coroner's report. Witnesses saw what was happening and one—Steve Frankowski, a land surveyor—jumped from his truck, stripped down, and hurriedly walked/swam to help.

But it was terribly windy, and all efforts failed. Twice the young magician surfaced. Neither time could Frankowski or Knauss reach him. Then the boat passed over Hopper and witnesses said, "We never saw him again."

When divers found the body four hours later, Hopper's hands were still handcuffed behind his back, but he had freed himself from the chains around his torso. According to the coroner, the handcuffs were functioning and were not jammed. More than 300 mourners attended the funeral in Strongs. Jess Rayburn Hopper, "Rayburn the Great," was buried on his 24th birthday.[56]

TRAGEDY ON THE ISLAND

Over the years there have been a number of drownings, boating accidents, and deaths associated with the lake. One of the more poignant events occurred on a balmy Friday evening in September, 2010, when two Grace College students were walking around the island and paused to sit on a hammock facing the lake.

"I was walking with a girl. I sat down on a hammock and when I sat down, the tree uprooted and hit me in the head and landed on her," Jeremy Mohr later recalled.

The head of the college's campus security told the news media that the two students were hanging out by Winona Lake when a dead tree with a poor root system fell on them. He said there was no wind that evening to cause the tree to fall.

Killed immediately was 18-year-old Mallori Kastner from Wabash, Indiana, a Grace College freshman and a well-liked member of the college's volleyball team. Jeremy Mohr, 21, a Grace College senior from Lorain County, Ohio, majoring in sports management, survived, but was paralyzed from the neck down.

---

[56] *St. Petersburg Independent,* July 17, 1984, p. 4-A

CHAPTER 20
The Enduring Values of the Winona Movement

"What are you to do with the Christ when from the north, the south, the east and the west the trumpet of Gabriel sounds and the unsaved dead come out of their graves to the last judgment? Now, our acceptance with God is going to depend on what we do with Jesus. The vilest sinner on earth, if he accepts Jesus Christ, will be accepted; and the very moment you accept Jesus Christ your sins are forgiven. If you reject Jesus, God will spurn and reject you."
Billy Sunday

A HISTORY OF THE TOWN AND OF THE WINONA MOVEMENT AND ALL that it spawned would be incomplete if it focused only on the historical, the physical, and the personalities involved.

To understand Winona fully, one must understand that a consistent spiritual thread drove much of the activity right from the beginning, and it continues today in the many lives associated with Winona organizations present and past.

Historically and theologically, Winona and its theologians and conferences have been major players in advancing personal spiritual commitment based on a belief in the Bible as God's inspired truth and as His word to man.

Many of the speakers and key personalities of Winona have been key figures in the development of the fundamentalist movement which is characterized not by narrow-minded modern caricatures of fundamentalists, but rather by a fundamental belief in the Bible as the source of a proper and theologically sound worldview.

311

Although Winona's roots were in Presbyterianism, through the decades conference leadership skillfully maintained a balanced, non-denominational flavor to the conferences. An analysis of conference sermons throughout its history shows a remarkable consistency in theological tenets, whether the message was being delivered by the flamboyant Billy Sunday or the cerebral J. Gresham Machen. Theologically, the bulk of the speakers were dispensationalist and premillennial in their eschatology, although a careful analysis of the rosters of speakers shows a remarkable variety, including addresses by a Roman Catholic priest.

The theology of the Bible conference speakers—and of the Free Methodists and Grace Brethren who have succeeded them as stalwarts in Winona—has a decidedly Pietist flavor. That is, it has always emphasized the biblical message that an individual needs a personal relationship with the Creator, regular Bible study and prayer, and other spiritual disciplines as a means of spiritual growth. This message emphasizes, also, God's constant accessibility through prayer.

The early Winona programming was established on four cornerstones—the Fatherhood of God, the Deity of Jesus Christ, the Personality of the Holy Spirit, and the Divine Inspiration of the Bible. As advised by Dwight Moody, all controversy on theological questions was rigidly excluded.

Winona directors created several doctrinal platforms to crystallize and direct their activities—one adopted in 1929 and another in 1937. Here, taken from the 1937 doctrinal statement of the Winona Lake Christian Assembly, are the enduring values of the Winona Movement:

1. We believe that the Holy Scriptures in their entirety, both Old and New Testaments, are the inspired Word of God; that this divine inspiration was given in such a way as to furnish us with an absolutely infallible and authoritative Bible as a rule of faith and practice.

2. We believe that there is one God, existing in three persons: Father, Son, and Holy Spirit, equal in power and glory.

3. We believe that Jesus Christ was conceived by the Holy Spirit and born of the Virgin Mary; that while on earth He was possessed of two natures, divine and human, in one person, and that as the Eternal Son of God He has precisely the same nature, attributes, and perfections as God, and is worthy of precisely the same worship, confidence, and obedience.

4. We believe that Jesus Christ voluntarily assumed the sinner's place in substitutionary atonement for the sins of mankind by the shedding of His blood on the cross.

5. We believe that Jesus rose from the dead in the same body, though glorified, as that in which He lived and was crucified; that He ascended into heaven, and is in His present life our High Priest and Advocate, and that from thence He shall visibly return to judge the quick and the dead.

6. We believe that the Holy Spirit is a divine personality co-equal in power and glory with God the Father and with God the Son; and that He is the Executive of the Godhead in all the Kingdom activities.

7. We believe that man was created by God in His own image and after His own likeness, and that man is, therefore, in no sense the descendant of brute ancestry.

8. We believe that no one can enter the Kingdom of God until he is "born again" of the Spirit of God according to the teaching of Jesus Christ, receiving thereby the gift of eternal life.

9. We believe in a coming judgment for all mankind issuing in eternal reward for the righteous and eternal punishment for the wicked.

Through the decades there have been many prayers of dedication and consecration prayed on the grounds and in the buildings that comprise Winona. A prayer that reinforces these longtime values was written by Winona Lake resident Carol Forbes, a longtime employee and volunteer of the Reneker Museum of Winona History, for the dedication of that facility on May 12, 2000.

Our Heavenly Father,

It is with thanksgiving and excitement in our hearts that we have arrived at this day.

We thank you for Winona:

> For the many ways You have blessed in this town through the years;
>
> > For the many people who have served You here;
> >
> > > And for the many who have come to this place
> > >
> > > > To find rest
> > > >
> > > > > And to learn of You . . . and Your goodness.

We thank You

> For all those who have helped make it possible for us to have now
>
> > This special place
> >
> > > To remember
> > >
> > > > And to learn
> > > >
> > > > > From the past.

And now in prayer,

> We dedicate
>
> > The Reneker Museum of Winona History
> >
> > > To You
> > >
> > > > For Your glory.

May Your name be honored here,

> And may our hearts be blessed
>
> > As we take time to reflect on the work of Your hands.

We pray these things in Jesus' name.

Amen

Appendix A
Winona Lake Town Leadership
(as of Spring, 2013) – www.winonalake.net

Town Council Members

Craig Allebach – Town Coordinator
Philip Hood – Ward 1 (council vice-president)
Terry Howie – Ward 2
Bruce Shaffner – Ward 3 (council president)
Greg Winn – Ward 4
Randy Swanson – Ward 5
Larry Long – Town Engineer
James Walmer – Town Attorney
Kent Adams – Clerk-Treasurer
Mitch Titus – Fire Chief
Paul Schmitt – Police Chief/Town Marshal
Pete O'Connell – Street Superintendent
Gene Seiman – Building Commissioner
Holly Hummitch – Director of Parks Department and Senior Center
Ryan Burgher – Managing Director, Village at Winona

APPENDIX B
Winona Walking Tour

ONE PLEASANT WAY TO GAIN A STREET-LEVEL ACQUAINTANCE WITH the history of Winona Lake is to take a walking tour. Here is a suggested route, with three alternate loops if you have more time, coupled with more information from the book about various sites along the way. Enjoy!

Begin your tour in the parking lot of the BakeCafé, just behind the row of businesses that include the Cerulean Restaurant and the Trailhouse. Leave your vehicle here—you are now approximately on the site of the 230-room former Miniwanan Inn (pg. 21) and this area also included horse barns that housed horses used in races and military exercises on the island during the Spring Fountain Park period (pg. 25). Immediately across the street is the white dormered building that was built as the Billy Sunday museum (pg. 213) and now houses the Remnant Trust (pg. 216).

To its left is the Rodeheaver Auditorium, built in 1958 (pg. 158) which stands on the approximate site of the first large wooden auditorium that housed large gatherings from the Spring Fountain Park days through the Winona Bible Conference years. Immediately across Auditorium Boulevard from the BakeCafé (same side of the street), note the rounded porches of the building on the corner—the Brookside (pg. 280).

Walk north (toward the BoatHouse). If you want the shorter route, continue down the block to the next street corner. If you wish to take

ALTERNATE LOOP #1, go left (west) on Auditorium Boulevard, cross the bridge over the canal, which was created in 1902, (pg. 44) and take the loop out around McDonald Island (pg. 43).

As you approach the lake and round the point on Esplanade, look to your left to see Rainbow Point (pg. 272) the former home of Homer Rodeheaver. Right on the tip of the island you will see Killarney Castle (pg. 273), built by Sol Dickey and containing the guest room where William Jennings Bryan always stayed on trips to Winona. As you scan the lakeshore from left to right, note the town park (formerly Bethany Camp, pg. 54 and the Winona School of Theology, pg. 110), then the Stone Camp subdivision (pg. 285) and various residences and points of interest on the other side of the lake, including the county fairgrounds to the right (northwest). Downtown Warsaw is to your right.

As you round the point on Esplanade and walk back toward Park Ave., the Merbrink (pg. 292) is on your left, with its rounded porches and oval second-story window. Look carefully, and you may see the ghost of Miss Phebe in an upstairs window!

Recrossing the canal on Administration Boulevard, try to envision the nighttime parade of decorated boats and floats during the Venetian Nights celebrations (pg. 48).

When Administration Boulevard dead ends into Park Ave., immediately across the street is the imposing frame building (with columns) that since earliest days was the Administration Building for the Winona Bible Conference. Turn left (north), and note that the Post Office is the only building on this block that once housed the Eskimo Inn (pg. 251), the Lakeside Apartments, and a number of commercial establishments, including a Zondervan book store. The bust of Solomon Dickey, the "founder of Winona" (pg. 35, 108) faces the post office, on the other side of Park Avenue.

Behind the post office, on the lakeshore at the mouth of the canal, is the current BoatHouse Restaurant, which is built on the site of the original boat house (pg. 265). Earlier establishments on this foundation included the original boat house, a roller skating rink and a cafeteria.

Walking north down the lakeshore toward the Winona Hotel, note the curving bay where Paul Lowman used to land his amphibian plane and waterski with his pet lion, Jerry (pg. 290) and this is also the site of the tragic Houdini-trick drowning over the Fourth of July weekend in 1984 (pg. 307).

Pause at the far west end of the parking lot to note the entrance to Winona Lake, including the site immediately to the right of the stoplight where the Texaco station used to be (pg. 280) and the Eagle Arcade Building (pg. 281) which was the main entrance to Winona by railroad passengers. The area now housing the shrub "Winona" and the mound is where the entrance building and gate once stood, through which all visitors and residents had to enter (pg. 26).

The Winona Hotel (pg. 261) is the oldest commercial building in Winona, dating to 1888, and it has now been beautifully restored to contain 24 luxury condominium private living units.

Cross over Park Avenue and take the sidewalk up along the right side of the hotel, along the ridge that is parallel to Chestnut Street. This is the area where the Great Fire of 1914 (pg. 70) destroyed 23 residences. The fire department that was formed after the fire was housed in the square building on Park Ave. (pg. 72) beside the Lakeside Prayer Chapel (pg. 267).

As you walk along the trail halfway up the ridge, you will see a circular walk below that is on the approximate site of the Cyclorama (pg. 32). You will pass the Faerholm (pg. 277) and will come to the Hillside Amphitheatre (pg. 211). To your left is the imposing Beyer Home (pg. 265) which was built by two of the three Beyer brothers who founded the town in 1881 and developed Spring Fountain Park.

The grassy meadow below is the site of the Billy Sunday Tabernacle (pg. 263) which was built in 1920 and seated 7,500. Drop down to the crossing sidewalk and continue southward (left). Up and to your left is a row of houses, beginning with The Hillside (pg. 279), which was once owned by Homer Rodeheaver and then by Blanche and Virgil Brock, who wrote the hymn *Beyond the Sunset*. It is the second-oldest residence in Winona. Further along this row of houses you will see the ornate Swiss Terrace residences Geneva and Interlaken, (pg. 278) which Nelle Cooper and her mother rented out to thousands of summer Winona visitors.

The picnic pavilion on your right is adjacent to the concrete block and plaque commemorating the founding of the Brethren Foreign Mission Society in 1900 on this spot (pg. 239).

You are now at the foot of Ninth Street, alongside the Rodeheaver Auditorium. If you wish to take ALTERNATE LOOP #2, climb the steps, cross Chestnut Street, and enter Westminster Hall/Hotel on your left (pg. 268). It houses the Reneker Museum of Winona History, which contains much more explanatory information about the places and people in the rich history of Winona Lake. Immediately behind the Westminster, at the corner of Chestnut and Seventh Streets, is the historic Federated/Presbyterian/Church of the Good Shepherd (pg. 227), which was the first organized church in Winona Lake.

As you exit the Westminster, looking left, you will see Mount Memorial, one of the oldest and most venerable buildings in Winona Lake (pg. 262). It once housed some of the colleges of Winona, then became headquarters for the Free Methodist Church, and is now used by Grace College and Seminary for classes and administration. As you look south (left) en route back to College Avenue, the large building in the next block is the Gordon Recreation Center (pg. 255) which once housed the Word/ABC music publishing shipping and inventory.

As you come down the hill you will pass the Winona Lake Free Methodist Church (pg. 229) on your left, immediately across from the Westminster. The current church building was built around the former Otterbein Hall (pg. 206), which once housed students for Winona's colleges.

At the foot of the hill, go left and walk past the front door of the Rodeheaver Auditorium, and you will be on a gently curving sloped sidewalk that passes the Studebaker Fountain (pg. 268). Look up on the hill to your left, and you will see the Franconia (pg. 275) and the Baldwin (twin rounded porches, pg. 279) , which are now both private residences but date to the earliest days of Winona Lake. Five residences south of the Studebaker Spring, the long set of concrete steps to your left leads to Mount Hood (pg. 94), the home Billy Sunday and his family occupied after 1911. Shortly you will come to the stone grotto which sheltered some of Mrs. Sunday's favorite koi ponds. This entire area beneath the Sunday home was once Garfield Park (pg. 268) As you descend Evangel Hill (a favorite sledding hill), you will return to the parking lot where you left your vehicle.

As a THIRD ALTERNATE LOOP, you may want to venture further south on Park Avenue, past the town park and tennis courts. This was Bethany Camp (pg. 54) and later the site of the Winona School of Theology (pg. 110), but it now houses the town offices and police department. Follow Park Avenue even further south, crossing Cherry Creek and veering left on Boys City Drive, and you will come to the Chicago Boys Club property (pg. 56) which now includes the bicycle trails and greenway (pg. 273) and the Stone Camp subdivision.

Thank you for visiting Winona Lake! If you care to explore further to the east (up on the hill behind Mount Memorial), you will find the campus of Grace College and Seminary, the Tree of Life bookstore and café, Winona Lake Grace Brethren Church, Grace College's Miller Athletic Field, and most of the offices of Grace Brethren organizations. Even further, out the Pierceton Road and CR250E, you will find Christ's Covenant Church, Celebration Church, Lakeland Christian Academy and, on Wooster Road East, Grace Village Retirement Community.

References

Becker, C. M. "Brighten the Corner Where You Are: Homer Rodeheaver." *Timeline: A Publication of the Ohio Historical Society*, May/June 2000, Vol. 17, No. 1, pp. 38-56

Bormet, M. J. (2001). *A History of the City of Warsaw, Indiana.* Bourbon, IN: Harmony Marketing Group

Cook, J. G. & Heckman, P. (2001). *Winona Lake Summers.* North Manchester, IN: ICanPublish

Coplen, D. (n.d.) *Moments in Time: Events in the History of Kosciusko County*, Warsaw, IN: Kosciusko County Historical Society

Coplen, D. L. (1995) *Kosciusko County: A Pictorial History.* Warsaw, IN: Kosciusko County Historical Society

Disbro, A. (2012). *Images of America: Winona Lake.* Charleston, SC: Acadia Publishing

Dorsett, L. W. (1991). *Billy Sunday and the Redemption of Urban America.* Grand Rapids, MI: Wm. B. Eerdmans Publishing Company

Firstenberger, W.A. (2005). *In Rare Form: A Pictorial History of Baseball Evangelist Billy Sunday.* Iowa City: U. of Iowa Press

Gaddis, V. H. & Huffman, J. A. (1960). *The Story of Winona Lake.* Winona Lake, IN: The Rodeheaver Co.

Graham, B. (1997). *Just As I Am: The Autobiography of Billy Graham.* New York: Harper Collins

Heaton, Mrs. James. *Winona Lake's Mr. Chautauqua.* Winona Lake, IN: Self-published

Heroes Who Live On, Vol. 1. (2002). Winona Lake, IN: CE National, Inc.

Jones, Bob, Jr. (1985). *Cornbread and Caviar.* Greenville, SC: BJU Press

Kavanaugh, P. (2008). *The Maverick CEO: Dane Miller and the Story of Biomet.* Self-published.

Kazin, M. (2006). *A Godly Hero: The Life of William Jennings Bryan.* New York: Alfred A. Knopf

Ma Sunday Still Speaks. (1957). Winona Lake, IN: Winona Lake Christian Assembly

McGloughlin, Jr., W. G. (2005). *Billy Sunday Was His Real Name.* Chicago: University of Chicago Press

Nye, G. 37 Bound Volumes of Local History, Warsaw (IN) Public Library

Osbeck, K. W. (1982). *101 Hymn Stories.* Grand Rapids, MI, Kregel Publications

Plaster, D. (2003). *Finding Our Focus: A History of the Grace Brethren Church.* Winona Lake, IN: BMH Books

Rizk, H. S. (1964). *Stories of the Christian Hymns.* Nashville: Abingdon

Rodeheaver, H. A. (1936). *Twenty Years With Billy Sunday.* Winona Lake: Rodeheaver Hall-Mack Co.

Royse, L. W. (1919). *A Standard History of Kosciusko County, Vol. 2.* Chicago: The Lewis Publishing Co.

Scoles, T. (2009). *Restoring the Household: The Quest of the Grace Brethren Church.* Winona Lake, IN: BMH Books

Sidwell, M. E. (1988). *The History of the Winona Lake Bible Conference.* Ph.D. Dissertation, Bob Jones University.

Taylor, M. W. (2000). *The Way I Remember It.* Carol Stream, IL: Taylor Press

Wiersbe, W. "His Typewriter Belongs to Teens." *Youth for Christ* magazine, July, 1961

Wilhoit, B. H. (2000). *Rody: Memories of Homer Rodeheaver.* Greenville, SC: BJU Press

ACKNOWLEDGMENTS

A PROJECT OF THIS SIZE IS NEVER A SINGLE-SOURCE PRODUCT. Dozens and dozens of people have fact-checked, proofread, tweaked wording, suggested changes, and generally improved the early drafts of the manuscript.

That said, the author still bears the final responsibility for any errors in fact, emphasis, or of omission. We have worked hard to make this a quality product that will endure and will be helpful to the curious and to the serious researcher alike.

Of greatest help were those who read the drafts and suggested additions, omissions, or changes in content. Among these were Carol Forbes, Bill Darr, Sharon White, and Brent Wilcoxson. Jesse Deloe was the immensely helpful general editor. Al Disbro contributed many of the photographs, including the front-cover image.

We owe a great debt of thanks to the Kosciusko County Historical Society, to their quarterly magazine *Thaddeus*, and in particular to the writing and research of county historian Dan Coplen. Thanks to Jim Nesbitt for the use of his lakeside writer's retreat. A special thank-you to Dr. Mark Sidwell, whose doctoral dissertation on the history of the Winona Lake Bible Conference was of inestimable value to this project.

It was a delight to see how willing people were to help. Many have gone out of their way to check their diaries, to hunt for old newspaper and magazine articles, and to track down information that only insiders to their organizations or circles of acquaintance could provide.

Thank you to all who helped. We hope you like the final product.

Terry White and Steve Grill

ABOUT THE AUTHORS

TERRY D. WHITE, ED.D., is a native of Pennsylvania who entered Grace College as a freshman the fall of 1960. He was educated at Grace College, Indiana University, the University of Iowa, and Indiana Wesleyan University. Living and working in Winona Lake for 17 years, he served in town government, held multiple positions at Grace College and Seminary, was board chair of his local church, owned a number of local businesses, was a realtor and real estate broker, wrote a weekly column for the *Warsaw Times-Union,* programmed 24 hours a week on local cable television, and acted in more than a dozen Ken Anderson films.

Employment took White and his family away to Minneapolis in 1977 and later to Washington, D.C. He returned to Winona Lake in 2003 to take on the task of re-vitalizing and directing the Brethren Missionary Herald Co. and BMH Books. He is married to the former Sharon Auxt, and they are the parents of two adult children (one deceased).

STEPHEN A. GRILL, ED.D., is currently Dean, The School of Adult and Community Education at Grace College. He is a 1970 graduate (magna cum laude) of Grace College and received his M.A. and Ed.D. degrees from Ball State University. He taught at Grace College for 17 years, then served as the Director of Ivy Tech State Community College/Warsaw for 12 years before returning to Grace in 1999.

Dr. Grill has provided leadership in numerous local education programs such as the Kosciusko Leadership Academy which he moderated for 25 years. He continues to serve as an Executive Committee member of KLA. He was a founding member of The Winona Lake Historical Society, and he launched The Reneker Museum of

Winona History in 2000, serving as its only Director. Dr. Grill was named Warsaw/Kosciusko County Chamber of Commerce "Man of the Year" in 1999 and Winona Lake Bill Reneker Community Service Award winner in 2003. His wife, Susan, is an interior designer and a long-time Winona shop owner.

Index